BEYOND RHETORIC AND REALISM IN ECONOMICS

Recent years have seen a resurgence of interest in the philosophy of economics, with an array of different methodological perspectives each attempting to establish the primacy of their intellectual positions. Two of these in particular have undermined the hegemony once enjoyed by positivism and later the philosophies of Kuhn and Popper. The first is represented by 'rhetoric' as expounded in the works of McCloskey, Klamer and others. Attacking what they claim to be imperiously prescriptive methodologies emanating from philosophy of science they have sought to widen the economic conversation, frequently by introducing work from other disciplines. In contrast, the realists such as Lawson and Mäki take issue with the relativizing tendencies of the rhetoric school and argue that scientific realism is the most compelling framework for economics.

Beyond Rhetoric and Realism in Economics provides a clear introduction to both of these positions but also shows why neither is a satisfactory resolution of the methodological issues facing economics. In direct opposition to these positions, the authors construct and develop an alternative framework, which they call 'causal holism'. With its origins in the work of Quine and van Fraassen, this shifts the focus of attention onto the role of economic models, especially their descriptive adequacy, and provides a challenging analysis of economic theory, causality and explanation.

Thomas A. Boylan is currently Head of the Department of Economics at University College Galway. He is the author of *Political Economy and Colonial Ireland* (with T.P. Foley, 1992). **Paschal F. O'Gorman** is Associate Professor of Philosophy at University College Galway. He is the author of *Rationality and Relativity* (1989).

ECONOMICS AS SOCIAL THEORY
Series edited by Tony Lawson
University of Cambridge

Social theory is experiencing something of a revival within economics. Critical analyses of the particular nature of the subject matter of social studies and of the types of methods, categories and modes of explanation that can legitimately be endorsed for the scientific study of social objects, are re-emerging. Economists are again addressing such issues as the relationship between agency and structure, between the economy and the rest of society, and between inquirer and the object of inquiry. There is renewed interest in elaborating basic categories such as causation, competition, culture, discrimination, evolution, money, need, order, organization, power, probability, process, rationality, technology, time, truth, uncertainty and value, etc.

The objective for this series is to facilitate this revival further. In contemporary economics the label 'theory' has been appropriated by a group that confines itself to largely a-social, a-historical, mathematical 'modelling'. *Economics as Social Theory* thus reclaims the 'theory' label, offering a platform for alternative, rigorous, but broader and more critical conceptions of theorizing.

Other titles in the series:

ECONOMICS AND LANGUAGE
Edited by *Willie Henderson*

RATIONALITY, INSTITUTIONS AND ECONOMIC
METHODOLOGY
Edited by *Uskali Mäki, Bo Gustafsson and Christian Knudsen*

NEW DIRECTIONS IN ECONOMIC METHODOLOGY
Edited by *Roger Backhouse*

WHO PAYS FOR THE KIDS?
Nancy Folbre

RULES AND CHOICE IN ECONOMICS
Viktor Vanberg

BEYOND RHETORIC AND REALISM IN ECONOMICS

Towards a reformulation of economic methodology

*Thomas A. Boylan and
Paschal F. O'Gorman*

London and New York

First published 1995
by Routledge
11 New Fetter Lane, London EC4P 4EE

Simultaneously published in the USA and Canada
by Routledge
29 West 35th Street, New York, NY 10001

© 1995 Thomas A. Boylan and Paschal F. O'Gorman

Typeset in Garamond by
Ponting–Green Publishing Services, Chesham, Bucks
Printed and bound in Great Britain by
T.J. Press (Padstow) Ltd, Padstow, Cornwall.

British Library Cataloguing in Publication Data
A catalogue record for this book is available from
the British Library.

Library of Congress Cataloging in Publication Data
Boylan, Thomas A.
Beyond rhetoric and realism in economics: a reconstruction
of economic methodology / Thomas A. Boylan and
Paschal F. O'Gorman.
p.   cm. – (Economics as social theory)
Includes bibliographical references and index.
ISBN 0–415–08220–X. – ISBN 0–415–12513–8 (pbk.)
1. Economics–Methodology.   2. Rhetoric.
I. O'Gorman, Paschal F. (Paschal Francis), 1946–
II. Title.   III. Series.
HB131.B68   1995
330'.01–dc20   95–39813
CIP

ISBN 0–415–08220–X (hbk)
ISBN 0–415–12513–8 (pbk)

To the memory of our parents,
John and Mai Boylan and
Frank and Delia O'Gorman respectively

CONTENTS

PREFACE

This study engages two of the most significant developments to emerge in the literature on economic methodology during the course of the 1980s. These developments represent, in their respective positions, polar extremes on the methodological spectrum. At one end of this spectrum realism, and more specifically scientific realism, as expounded in the works of Lawson and Mäki, is deeply embedded in philosophy of science as the source of methodological insight. Their objective is to argue the validity of scientific realism as the preferred and most plausible methodology for economics. At the other end, rhetoric, as presented by McCloskey and others, represents a frontal assault on all prescriptive methodologies emanating from philosophy of science and, in particular, on Modernism, with its positivist tendencies. This book examines both of these positions in detail and ultimately rejects them, arguing instead in favour of an alternative methodological position which we term causal holism.

Our causal holist approach to economic methodology is predicated on a number of general principles which we wish to make explicit at the outset. We subscribe to the general tenet that philosophy in general and philosophy of science in particular represent the proper domains for central analytical insights into any epistemological reflection on the methodological problems facing a subject such as economics. This is neither to dismiss, much less to denigrate, the expanding and challenging array of alternative methodological positions which has characterized the demise of positivism within the literature on economic methodology. Commitment to this general tenet has led us to consider the work of major figures in twentieth-century philosophy, especially that of Quine, who becomes a pivotal figure in our narrative. Within the philosophy of science, the work of van Fraassen, especially his constructive empiricism which attempts to forge an intriguing position between scientific realism and classical positivism, has been a major source of origin for causal holism. Since the implications of Quine's and van Fraassen's works have not been to-date systematically examined within economic methodology, this work provides an extended exposé of the sophistication and subtlety of their respective positions. Clearly, our analysis is predicated on the belief that these major twentieth-century developments within philosophy in general and philosophy of science in particular have not received the attention they deserve from economic methodologists.

Our presentational strategy is to critically engage the wide range of philosophico-methodological issues raised by McCloskey, Lawson and Mäki in their respective approaches to the philosophy of economics. This range extends from rather general issues, such as whether or not philosophy of science is methodologically relevant to the discipline of economics, through more specific topics, such as the ontological and unificatory implications of realism, mathematical models and metaphors, causality, explanation and theory, to the very specific applications of the latter in the philosophy of economics. Our critique of this wide range is executed through our interpretation of Quine and van Fraassen, thereby demonstrating that causal holism is a more challenging framework than either rhetoric or realism for the philosophy of economics. This strategic emphasis on methodological frameworks, rather than on detailed methodological analyses of specific issues in economics, was influenced and indeed legitimated by the agendas set by Lawson, Mäki and McCloskey whose work is the central focus of this study. None the less, like the latter authors, we are ultimately concerned with economic methodology and how it should be practised. In addition to showing the advantages of causal holism over both rhetoric and realism for the practice of economic methodology, we further articulate this framework by examining the contributions of Friedman and Kaldor, two major figures who contributed, albeit from different perspectives, explicitly and influentially to economic methodology. In this we maintain a direct symmetry of presentation in that the economic realists with whom we are centrally concerned, Lawson and Mäki, have also engaged the methodological contributions of these two major figures of economics.

Finally, we wish to make explicit our understanding of economics, which we take to be primarily and quintessentially an empirical science which ultimately must address a bewildering array of complex substantive issues concerned with the working of 'real' economies in historical time and space. This understanding has greatly influenced our approach to the search for an adequate methodological framework, which at once recognizes the complexities of a highly complicated and interactive world and, at the same time, keeps faith with what we consider to be among the most important philosophical insights of the twentieth century. To facilitate the reader we provide, in the Introduction, an adumbrated overview of the central tenets of causal holism, focusing particularly on the issues of description, causality, explanation and economic theory. The book itself contains the elaborated arguments for causal holism and is structured as follows. In Chapter 1 we examine the major developments in economic methodology since the 1930s, especially the array of alternative methodological positions which have accompanied the demise of positivism in what has come to be termed the 'post-positivist era'. In Chapter 2 we outline the case for rhetoric, display its paradoxical nature and resolve this paradox by distinguishing between global and local economic rhetoric. Chapter 3 takes the debate in the methodology of economics beyond the standard Popperian–Kuhnian–Lakatosian debate by focusing on Hempel's reinstatement of scientific explanation, Black's analysis of scientific models and Quine's holism. The road to scientific realism is mapped in Chapter 4 and Lawson's challenging application of this philosophy of science to the methodology of economics, especially his particular realist reading of Kaldor, is articulated. Chapter 5 continues down this realist road by engaging Mäki's realist analysis of economic methodology and his realist critique of Friedman. In Chapter 6 van Fraassen's constructive empiricist critique of scientific realism is outlined, with special reference to his analysis of scientific explanation, empirical adequacy and causality and its implications for economic methodology. Chapter 7, by extending the debate between constructive empiricism and scientific realism, reconstructs economic methodology from the perspective of causal holism. This reconstruction puts the focus on the descriptive adequacy of economic models, especially the identification of the observable economic causes operating in real historical time. In Chapter 8 the causal holist reconstruction of economic methodology is further articulated by re-engaging the methodological contributions of Friedman and Kaldor. Finally, in the concluding chapter we demonstrate how causal holism takes the methodological debate beyond the confines of both scientific realism and rhetoric.

ACKNOWLEDGEMENTS

In writing a book there are many debts of gratitude incurred and this one is no exception. We would like to thank the staff of the James Hardiman Library, University College Galway for their assistance, which was efficiently and generously provided. Likewise we would like to acknowledge our gratitude to the Library of Trinity College Dublin, the Bodleian Library, Oxford, and the Marshall Library, Cambridge. We would also like to thank the participants at a number of scholarly meetings with whom we were able to discuss certain aspects of the work contained in this book as it developed. In particular the participants at the 9th International Congress of Logic, Methodology and Philosophy of Science at the University of Uppsala in Sweden, including Uskali Mäki, Andrea Salanti, Wade Hands, Philippe Mongin, Maurice Lagueux, Robert Nadeau and especially Clive Granger. To the participants at the Royal Irish Academy Seminar on 'The Methodology of Economics: Critical Perspectives on Recent Developments', especially Dr. Rory O'Donnell of the Economic and Social Research Institute, Dublin. A special word of thanks is due to Tony Lawson, University of Cambridge, for his generous support, constructive criticism and sustained encouragement as editor of this series; for inviting us to address his seminar on 'Realism and Economics' in Cambridge, and to the members of that seminar for their contributions and warm hospitality.

We would like to thank the Departments of Economics and Philosophy at University College Galway for their sustained interest and encouragement and especially Dr. Tom Duddy of the Department of Philosophy, who painstakingly read the entire manuscript, and contributed extremely helpful comments and constructive suggestions. Alan Jarvis and Alison Kirk of Routledge displayed heroic patience, in addition to their unstinting encouragement and assistance at every juncture and for this we are most grateful. Finally, we would like to thank Ann O'Higgins, Imelda Howley and Claire Noone for their customary efficiency and cheerfulness in typing various drafts of a difficult manuscript.

INTRODUCTION

The central thesis of this work is that a novel philosophical framework is required to successfully negotiate the contested terrain between rhetoric and scientific realism in the contemporary debate in the philosophy of economics. We call this framework causal holism. Historically, causal holism emerges from the shadows of Quine's holism and van Fraassen's constructive empiricism.

Causal holism shifts the central focus of attention onto the role of models in economics, especially their capacity to furnish empirically adequate descriptions of actual economic events and their observable causes. In the process of shifting this central focus of attention, it simultaneously provides a challenging re-examination of numerous tacit presuppositions in orthodox philosophy of economics, ranging from the concept of economic description to that of the empirical adequacy of economic theory. Moreover, it effects this re-examination without embracing the inflationary claims of either rhetoric or scientific realism. Thus causal holism constitutes a middle ground between rhetoric and scientific realism in which both philosophers of economics and economists can enrich their understanding of the science of economics.

In particular, causal holism explicitly challenges an influential and deeply ingrained picture of economic explanation and economic theory. This influential picture is as follows. The science of economics has a twofold aim, namely, to accurately describe the economic events and happenings in both our social world and past social orders and, second, to furnish scientific explanations of these events. The latter naturally takes one into the domain of economic theory. This is clearly analogous to the situation which obtains in the physical sciences. Just as Newtonian theory furnished physics with the approximately correct explanation of the motion of terrestrial and celestial bodies, economic theory furnishes us with the correct explanatory framework for economic events and happenings. In this appealing picture economic explanation and economic theory are inextricably linked: a basic, if not the basic, function of economic theory is to explain.

Although we certainly do not accept that this picture forms an indispensable part of the tacit conceptual framework of the economic mind,

1

there is little doubt that it is quite influential in that numerous economists think from, rather than about, it. Such economists feel uneasy at any suggestion of a possible divorce of theory from explanation. They intuitively think that any such suggestion must be based on a misleading analysis of the situation. Economic theory and explanation are inseparable. One simply cannot have one without the other. The rhetorical question 'what is the function of economic theory if it does not explain?' sums up this very plausible attitude.

Indeed, when these economists look at the history of twentieth-century philosophy of science, they can reasonably read it as a philosophical vindication of their specific picture. The inseparable relationship between theory and explanation is not peculiar to economics. Philosophy of science teaches us that it also holds in the paradigmatic exemplars of the physical sciences, such as atomic physics or chemistry. Despite the fact that in the early decades of this century logical positivism attempted to marginalize scientific explanation, Hempel, in the 1950s, firmly re-established its indispensability. Through the Deductive-Nomological pattern of explanation, or the covering law model as it is sometimes called, Hempel forged an intimate connection between explanation, theory and deduction.

In forging this inseparable union, Hempel also distinguished between the pragmatic usefulness of science, exemplified in its technological exploitation, and its use in satisfying our intellectual curiosity. We call the latter the epistemic dimension of science. It concerns the relationship between a scientific theory and the world in terms of warranted assertability, belief or truth. In the Hempelian approach explanation and theory are centrally located along with description in the epistemic dimension of any science. All other human interests served by science we call non-epistemic or pragmatic. Applied science, such as its technological contribution, falls within this non-epistemic dimension. This distinction between the epistemic and non-epistemic is central to causal holism.

With Hempel's influential contribution, the union of explanation and theory, centrally grounded in the epistemic dimension, has flourished in contemporary philosophy of science. In particular, since the late 1960s, this union has matured and developed in a unique manner within the dominant framework of contemporary philosophy of science, namely, scientific realism. Scientific realism, as the adjective 'scientific' suggests, is a specific philosophy of science. Historically speaking it developed since the 1960s in direct opposition to the logical positivist account of science on the one hand, and relativist theories, associated with Kuhn and Feyerabend, on the other. While in Chapter 3 a brief account of this development is furnished in order to give the reader an appreciation of its historical context, for our introductory purposes we focus on the standard scientific realist picture of the union between any economic theory and the scientific quest for explanation. In this realist picture the observable economic world is like the face of a clock

2

which has hidden mechanisms generating or causing the observable events on its face. Thus behind the observable economic world there are real but unobservable mechanisms which generatively cause the observable economic events. The aim of economics is to discover these generative unobservable causes. The economic scientific realist now adds an argument from precedence to this clockwork analogy. The precedent is established by Newtonian theory. Gravitational theory reveals the real unobservable mechanisms behind the observable motions of terrestrial and celestial bodies. Thus the theoretical term 'gravity' refers to the real, but unobservable, cause of the observable motions of these bodies. Economics, by modelling itself on Newtonian physics, can, through well-confirmed theory, reveal the real generative causes hidden from economic observation. In this fashion, the union of economic theory and explanation is inextricably linked to the notion of real, unobservable causes. To explain is to reveal by means of economic theory the real economic causes which generate the observable economic phenomena. The nexus of economic explanation, theory and cause is given a unique interpretation by scientific realism. Moreover, this challenging interpretation leaves this nexus firmly located within the epistemic dimension of economics.

One of our aims in this book is to introduce the reader to the engaging manner in which scientific realism has been articulated in the recent philosophy of economics, with special focus on the intriguing, divergent accounts of Lawson and Mäki. While scientific realism is the dominant philosophy of science at the present time, minority dissenting voices have emerged. Two of these dissenting voices have been largely ignored in the philosophy of economics. The first is that of Quine. His position is certainly counterintuitive to any economist who thinks from the inseparable union of economic theory and explanation. Quine unequivocally challenges us to reconsider this relationship. According to Quine, theory is indispensable to science. We cannot do science without theory. None of us will disagree with him on that score. However, theory is indispensable at the descriptive level. Quine is maintaining that the proper analysis of scientific description shows that theory is necessary for this epistemic activity. Theory is inextricably linked to scientific description. The truism of contemporary philosophy of science, namely, all description is theory-laden, is creatively pioneered by Quine.

The theory-ladenness of description, which clearly depicts the indispensability of theory for description, is plainly visible in elementary scientific identifications. For instance, chemists identify the contents of a specific test tube as oxygen. The factual or observational statement, 'that gas is oxygen' – and it certainly is factual – is theory-laden in that chemists could not make this factual claim without presupposing atomic theory. The observational term 'oxygen' was not constructed independently of atomic theory and its sense is located in that theoretical framework. Atomic theory is presupposed in the background to the above chemical fact. In general, past or contemporary theories are indispensable backgrounds to our scientific descriptions. Moreover, in this Quinean approach theory is still central to the epistemic dimension of science. However, it is separated from explanation and inextricably linked to the basic element in the epistemic dimension, i.e. description.

In this work we endeavour to take this Quinean marriage between description and theory seriously and we spell out its implications for the philosophy of economics. Quine, however, did not systematically address the issue of scientific explanation. One could maintain that theory serves two distinct masters, namely, description and explanation, and thereby keep faith with the deeply-ingrained realist picture of the inextricable link between theory and explanation. In this approach, theory would be inextricably linked to both description and explanation. This brings us to the second neglected voice in the philosophy of economics, namely, that of van Fraassen. In the 1980s van Fraassen developed constructive empiricism in explicit opposition to scientific realism. Van Fraassen is also challenging us to think about, rather than from, the influential picture which draws an inseparable connection between theory and explanation. We must, to use Hüsserl's expression, bracket judgement on that picture and, with an open mind, reconsider the nexus of theory, explanation and cause, especially its location in the epistemic dimension of science.

The constructive empiricist puts an alternative picture before us. Like Quine, theory is indispensable to science and its indispensability resides in its descriptive, not its explanatory, role. Theory is integral to science in that it furnishes us with the required resources for accurately describing the observable world. Thus, through description, theory remains firmly rooted in the epistemic dimension of science. At this basic epistemic level the aim of any empirical science, including economics, is to construct theoretical models which furnish true theory-laden descriptions of the observable world. Like Quine, van Fraassen divorces theory from explanation and remarries it to description.

Constructive empiricists commence their reflection on scientific explanation with the truism that any explanation is an answer to a 'why-question'. We normally offer explanations when asked why did such-and-such happen. This is an unproblematical starting point. Next, constructive empiricists correctly point out that why-questions occur in specific contexts. Indeed, the same why-question has different meanings in different contexts. For instance, the question 'why did Adam eat the apple?' could, depending on the context of the question, mean 'why did Adam, rather than Eve, eat the apple?' or 'why did Adam eat the apple, rather than cut it and plant its seeds?' and so on. Moreover, different explanations, all equally satisfactory, are given to the same why-question, depending on the specific context in which it is posed. The context-ladenness of why-questions implies that there are different explanations, all equally satisfactory in context, with no one having precedence over the others. There is no such thing as *the* explanation of an event.

4

The concept of explanation is rich and subtle and this richness and subtlety is fully acknowledged by constructive empiricists. In this connection they maintain that the context-ladenness of explanation extends beyond the domain of science to a variety of other domains, such as literary criticism, common sense, theology, superstition and so on. What makes an explanation scientific, rather than, say, theological is that the relevant explanatory factors are chosen from the scientific, rather than the theological, domain. Moreover, within the domain of science itself, we can, depending on the context, have different satisfactory explanations of the same event. Successful explanation in science is also context-laden in that specific human contexts invariably influence the choice of relevant explanatory factors. In view of the variety and depth of penetration of these contextual influences, according to van Fraassen, scientific explanation does *not* pertain to the epistemic dimension of science. Rather, he relocates scientific explanation in the non-epistemic dimension. In this radical innovation scientific explanation is the subsequent or derivative usage of an empirical science. Like technological exploitation, scientific explanation pertains to applied science. In giving a scientific explanation one is applying an empirical theory in a specific context permeated by non-epistemic human interests. In short, scientific explanation is contextually linked to rich and sophisticated human narratives and these links demand its relocation to the non-epistemic dimension of science.

This constructive empiricist picture is counterintuitive to any economist who thinks from the orthodox picture in which explanation is firmly rooted in the epistemic dimension of science. In this constructive empiricist picture the link between theory and explanation is unequivocally severed. On the one hand, theory is inextricably linked to scientific description which remains located in the epistemic dimension of science and, on the other, the richness and subtlety of scientific explanation is fully acknowledged thereby necessitating its relocation to the non-epistemic dimension. In the course of this book we spell out the details of this challenging relocation and introduce the reader to the manner in which this provocative picture impinges on the philosophy of economics. In this connection we openly admit that we are impressed by Quine's arguments for marrying theory and description and by van Fraassen's arguments for relocating scientific explanation in the non-epistemic dimension of science.

We are not, however, constructive empiricists. Rather, from our critical analysis of Quine and van Fraassen, we develop an alternative framework which we term causal holism. This methodological framework represents a novel synthesis of scientific realism on the one hand and constructive empiricism on the other, a synthesis which is accomplished in the context of Quine's holism. The causal holist picture of the science of economics is as follows. The epistemic aim of economics is the construction of theoretical models which furnish accurate theory-laden descriptions of the observable economic world. Thus the causal holist endorses the Quinean marriage of theory and description and the housing of this couple in the epistemic domain. The term 'holism' in the name of this methodological framework symbolizes our indebtedness to Quine who is universally recognized for a holistic, rather than an atomistic, approach to any science. The adjective 'causal' symbolizes a distinctive feature of our methodological framework which is neither that of scientific realism nor that of constructive empiricism.

The concept of causality is both indispensable and central to scientific realism. Contrary to the traditional empiricist's analysis of causality which reduces causal connections to Humean regularities, scientific realism contends that causes are ontological or real and that they are irreducible to Humean regularities. Moreover, not only are causes real, these causes are frequently unobservable. For instance, the hidden generative cause of the fall of an apple to earth is gravitational attraction which is unobservable. In this scientific realist perspective the epistemic function of a scientific theory is to enable the scientific community to discover hidden unobservable mechanisms which generatively cause the observable phenomena. Clearly, the scientific realist's concept of causality is firmly located in the epistemic dimension of science.

This location of causality, however, is rejected by constructive empiricism. In relocating scientific explanation into the non-epistemic or pragmatic domain, van Fraassen also relocates causality. Causal discourse is inextricably related to our explanatory endeavours and, since the latter can be shown by rational argument to belong to the non-epistemic dimension of science, the former must also be relocated into that same non-epistemic dimension. In this constructive empiricist approach, causes, as distinct from Humean regularities, are neither real nor observable. Rather, causal discourse belongs to the rich narrative context of explanation which is inseparably linked to anthropomorphic considerations and interests and consequently does not correspond to anything in the real observable world. Like traditional empiricism, Humean regularities are both real and observable, and the epistemic dimension of science is confined to knowledge of these regularities. In short, causality is a non-epistemic pragmatic concept.

In direct opposition to constructive empiricism, the causal holist argues that the concept of causality is epistemic. To this extent there is some convergence between causal holism and scientific realism. Causal holists maintain that the epistemic dimension of any science, including economics, incorporates the accurate (theory-laden) description of the real observable causes in operation in the actual world. Thus, contrary to constructive empiricism, causes are real and some are observable. The epistemic focus is on observable causes. Some actual causes are among the observable events of the world and the epistemic aim includes the identification and accurate description of these observable causes.

Contrary to scientific realism, causal holism severs the various realist links between explanation, theory and causality. The epistemic aim of a scientific theory does not include the discovery of unobservable causes which explain the observable world. Realist generative non-empirical mechanisms play no epistemic role in causal holism. Rather, an indispensable epistemic aim of a scientific theory is the construction of models which furnish accurate descriptions of the real observable causes. In causal holism the epistemic focus is on generative, empirical causes. Discovering actual observable causes in any science, including economics, is a demanding epistemic task which requires the construction of theoretical models. These theoretical models, however, do not reveal any mechanism which is non-empirical or unobservable. Moreover, this epistemic task of discovering and describing the observable causes is independent of the various anthropomorphic factors which invariably penetrate our explanatory endeavours. Hence this epistemic task has nothing to do with scientific explanation. Like constructive empiricism, scientific explanation is relocated in the non-epistemic dimension of science. Thus the scientific realist's tacit epistemic links between theory and explanation on the one hand and causality and non-empirical generative mechanisms on the other are irrevocably broken. Description, theory and observable causal webs are domiciled in the epistemic domain of science, and explanation is housed in the non-epistemic domain, while the realist non-empirical generative mechanisms are located in the realm of the epistemically inaccessible.

By contrasting causal holism with the scientific realism of Mäki and Lawson on the one hand and the constructive empiricism of van Fraassen on the other, we articulate the significance of this novel methodological framework for the philosophy of economics. Moreover, this articulation is further extended by engaging the methodological approaches of two eminent twentieth century economists with divergent economic commitments, namely, Friedman and Kaldor. Finally, causal holists, in emphasizing the centrality of economic models to the epistemic aim of economics, also maintain that the general philosophy of science is relevant to the philosophy of economics and that the Popperian question of demarcating science from other disciplines is significant. McCloskey's economic rhetoric, however, challenges these latter two claims. Like the causal holist, McCloskey advocates the centrality of economic models to the discipline of economics but, contrary to causal holism, he maintains that economic models are really nonornamental metaphors. Thus in McCloskey's rhetoric, all economic models must be evaluated in light of the criteria of literary criticism, rather than in light of the spurious criteria of enlightenment philosophies of science. In our opinion, economic rhetoric is a challenging and sophisticated philosophical thesis. We address this challenge by presenting a nexus of considerations which explains why causal holists, despite their sympathy, reject economic rhetoric. In short, causal holism takes the debate in the contemporary methodology of economics beyond both economic rhetoric and scientific realism.

1
PHILOSOPHY OF SCIENCE AND ECONOMICS
Methodological perspectives

The past two decades have witnessed an explosive growth in the literature on economic methodology. This has taken the form of specialized monographs, general introductory surveys, anthologies and the emergence of new journals devoted to the field. Over the same period there has also been a preoccupation with the general state of economics as a scientific discipline and profession. As noted by Coats (1986a) these two issues, economic methodology and the general state of economics, are strictly speaking distinct. Economic methodology represents a sub-set of general methodology, which is an integral part of philosophy. The agenda of economic methodology may appear far removed from the concerns of the practising economist. This distance from the practising economist is well captured in the following quotation:

> Methodology is like medicine. We tolerate it because it is supposed to be good for us, but secretly despise it. We would rather prescribe it for others than use it ourselves. The study of methodology takes place in a shadowy other-world, and its few participants are accepted as eccentrics. Only occasionally do our philosophical norms and our day-to-day practice clash head-on. For the most part we are too busy pushing out the frontiers of knowledge to question whether those frontiers are of any significance.
>
> (Jones 1977: 350)

Allowing for developments that have occurred in the interim and a certain element of hyperbole, the author of the above quotation may well reflect the general attitude of the economics profession towards methodology as something that is indeed reluctantly tolerated but secretly despised, or that it is only on rare occasions that 'our philosophical norms and our day-to-day practice clash head-on'.

In contrast with the writings on economic methodology, preoccupation with the general state of economics addresses a much broader agenda. This includes the public standing of the subject, particularly with respect to its performance in the policy domain; the methods of recruitment and training of new entrants to the profession; the allocation of resources within the discipline which in turn reflects the reward and control system in the profession. This agenda, much of which is integrally connected with the professionalization of the discipline, is more properly addressed within a sociology of knowledge framework. Direct links can be forged between these ostensibly disparate issues based on the fact that for many economists there exists a prima facie connection between the general standing of the discipline and its methodological base. The relationship is, however, both complex and subtle.

The current resurgence in economic methodology is linked to a complex set of interacting influences, both internal and external to the discipline. This has arguably been the general historical pattern of concern with methodo- logical issues within economics since the emergence of modern economics and the current revival of interest in methodology is no exception. The development of the current 'crisis' in contemporary economics stems from the breakdown of the postwar Keynesian paradigm during the course of the 1970s (Coats 1977; Bell and Kristol 1981). This has resulted in a protracted period of theoretical reassessment with its correlate in an intensive methodo- logical interrogation of the discipline. Reflecting on the current crises Coats has noted that:

> whenever efforts to resolve basic disagreements over theoretical, empir- ical, and policy issues prove unavailing there is a natural urge to return to fundamentals in an effort both to expose the roots of current controversies and in the hope of establishing more solid and reliable foundations for subsequent work.

> (Coats 1982: 311)

This hypothesis provides a plausible 'endogenous' explanation for the growth in methodological research in economics as a response to the unsettled state of the discipline. A second contributing factor, exogenous to economics, but which has arguably exerted very considerable influence has been the 'crisis' in the philosophy of science. This crisis, which pre-dated the current upheaval in economics, arose from the sustained critique of logical positivism and its more muted variant of logical empiricism which was launched in the 1950s. The ensuing decades have been characterized by the elaboration of an expanding array of alternative paradigms preoccupied with the role, status and evolution of scientific knowledge in general and specifically the contribu- tion of scientific theories. This has been a period of uniquely intense activity in the philosophy of science with implications for all the sciences, including economics.

Economic methodology has been influenced by all the major developments in the philosophy of science and it is in the evolution and interaction between these two areas of discourse that provides the context within which any contribution, including this study, must be located. In this chapter we provide, albeit briefly, an outline of the changing context by tracing the major

developments in economic methodology and its interaction with the philosophy of science since the 1930s. Of necessity a brief survey such as this
chapter must be selective as any attempt to achieve a comprehensive coverage
would require a full-length study, a number of which exist, such as Blaug
(1980a), Caldwell (1982, 1984a), Hausman (1984), Redman (1991). In this
chapter we will first trace the major methodological developments since
the 1930s with particular attention to the dominance of the positivist
paradigm. Second, we will examine the breakdown of this paradigm and the
consequent proliferation of alternative approaches within the philosophy of
science and economic methodology in the post-positivist era (Caldwell
1984a), which in turn was a response to the demise of what Suppe (1979)
called the 'received view'.

FROM DEDUCTIVISM TO LOGICAL POSITIVISM

Up to the 1930s economic methodology was dominated by what Caldwell
(1982: 99) described as 'subjectivism, methodological individualism and the
self-evident nature of the basic postulates of economic theory', or what
Hausman (1989: 116) has described more succinctly as 'deductivism'. This
methodological perspective was articulated in Lionel Robbins's monograph,
An Essay on the Nature and Significance of Economic Science, first published
in 1932. Described as a 'potential masterpiece that generated a veritable
furore' (Blaug 1980a: 87), it was essentially a continuation of a line of
methodological thought contained in the work of Senior, Mill and Cairnes,
with Mill as the principal figure to whom Robbins acknowledges his
intellectual debts (Robbins 1935: 121).

In Mill's view the complexity of political economy demands that its
scientific study can only be achieved by means of the deductive method. Since
economic phenomena are influenced by so many causal factors and experimentation is in general not feasible, the methods of induction cannot be
directly applied. Induction can, however, be used and, for Mill, must be used
as a first step in establishing the basic laws of economics, be they technical or
psychological. From these basic laws the economic implications can be
deduced within specified parameters which define the context or relevant
circumstances. For Mill, empirical verification or confirmation has a role in
establishing the correctness of the deductions and in determining whether
important causal factors have been omitted. But such empirical verification
or confirmation does not determine one's epistemic commitment to the basic
laws; they have already been established by introspection or experimentation.
On this reading, political economy relied heavily on the application of
independently established laws. As Blaug notes:

> Over and over again, in Senior, in Mill, in Cairnes ... we have found
> the notion that 'verification' is not a testing of economic theory to see

whether they are true or false, but only a method of establishing the boundaries of application of theories deemed to be obviously true: one verifies in order to discover whether 'disturbing causes' can account for the discrepancies between stubborn facts and theoretically valid reasons; if they do, the theory has been wrongly applied, but the theory itself is still true. The question of whether there is any way of showing a theory to be false is never even contemplated.

(Blaug 1980a: 81)

Mill believed that these established laws provided an accurate account of how specific causal factors operated, but they were not universal laws. Rather, they represented statements of tendencies. But since these tendencies were subject to numerous 'disturbances' or 'interfering causes', which cannot all be specified in advance, then *ceteris paribus* clauses that allow for these disturbances will play a crucial role in the formulation of these tendency 'laws'. Economics explores the implications of these established laws, but given the influences of the disturbing causes, these implications will not always be realized. In his recent work Hausman has cogently defended Mill's methodology of deductivism for the 'inexact sciences' such as economics (Hausman 1989, 1992). For Hausman, a close reading of Robbins's 1932 essay represents in essence a twentieth-century restatement of Mill's position, albeit overstated and lacking in the balanced qualification of Mill's treatment. Whatever the relative merits of Hausman's defence of Mill's methodology, he is correct in arguing that the transition from classical to neoclassical economics brought changes in economic theory and its methodology. Neoclassical theory emphasized the centrality of individual decision-making and the role of preferences in that activity along with concern with the short-run allocative functions arising from the interaction of individuals within markets. Classical economics, in contrast, focused primarily on the role of social classes and the implications of their activity for long-run growth and the distribution of wealth within society. Notwithstanding this shift in the emphasis of theory there was fundamental methodological continuity. Despite the differences in the theoretical agenda between the classical and neoclassical writers, economists such as Knight (1935, 1940), von Mises (1949, 1978, 1981), and Robbins (1935) all agreed with Mill that the basic premises of economics were justifiable and that empirical failures did not call them into question. Hausman, in fact, generalizes this position and argues that historically not only writers on methodology such as J.E. Cairnes (1857) and John Neville Keynes (1891) adopt Mill's methodology, but that 'if one updates the language and the economic theory, one has the view to which most economists (regardless of what they may say in methodological discussion) still apparently subscribe' (Hausman 1992: 124).

This entrenched view of deductivist methodology was challenged in the 1930s with the publication of Hutchison's *The Significance and Basic*

11

Postulates of Economic Theory in 1938. This was not in fact the first attack on deductivism. In the nineteenth century the Historical School had launched a sustained attack on the abstract deductive methodology of political economy (Schumpeter 1954). During the 1930s a number of writers had alluded to the weakness of the deductive method from a similar perspective to that of Hutchison (Hausman 1992: 153). It was Hutchison's work, however, which caught the attention of the economics profession. Hutchison's work is generally credited with the attempt to introduce into economics some of the central ideas of the logical positivists, with which he was acquainted having held a lecturing post at the University of Bonn between 1935 and 1938 (Caldwell 1982).

In introducing logical positivist ideas into economics, Hutchison, apart from counteracting Robbins's restatement of deductivism, was exposing the economics profession to what had become by the beginning of the twentieth century, the modern scientific worldview. It was this scientific worldview that Suppe termed the 'received view' in his account of twentieth century philosophy of science (Suppe 1979). Positivism, which has a long and complex history, had exerted immense influence on epistemology long before the logical positivist's variant emerged at the turn of the century. By the nineteenth century positivism was the dominant epistemological theory of knowledge, having impinged on such diverse areas as biology, ethics, sociology and medicine. In Kolakowski's words, 'positivism dominated the spirit of the age' (Kolakowski 1972: 122).

While historians of philosophy generally view positivism as a response to the metaphysical system builders in general, which by the nineteenth century were represented by the Hegelian and neo-Hegelian systems, Suppe has argued that logical positivism was primarily a Germanic movement and must be understood within this context (Suppe 1979; Passmore 1967, 1968). By the turn of the twentieth century, in Suppe's reading, three alternative philosophic schools of thought prevailed within the German academic community: mechanistic materialism represented by the work of Ludwig Buchner; neo-Kantian philosophy of science associated with the Marburg School; neo-positivism based on the work of Ernst Mach. Of the three positions, neo-Kantianism was the most commonly adhered to, but it was developments in theoretical physics and the emergence of relativity and quantum theory which presented particular problems for the prevailing philosophies of science. The efforts at a solution were based on an attempt to reconcile Mach's neo-positivism with Poincaré's conventionalism and, influenced by developments in the philosophy of mathematics, a remodified version of the synthesis of Mach and Poincaré emerged as the original version of logical positivism (Suppe 1979: 12).

Excavating the central tenets of positivism is a difficult task given its intricate history and the continual modifications that it has undergone. Accepting that Hutchison's aim was to introduce some of the central ideas of positivism into economics, and that many practising economists today may still adhere to some variant of positivism, what were the central tenets of positivism that Hutchison argued for in 1938? Beed (1991) has identified the following characteristics of positivism based on the historical systematization of the central tenets of positivism by contemporary historians of philosophy:

(a) scientific knowledge, including logic and mathematics, is the only valid form of knowledge;
(b) metaphysical claims, normative statements, value judgements, and opinions are not valid knowledge;
(c) empirical data, based on sense experience, is the only source of valid knowledge, with the exception of logic and mathematics;
(d) valid knowledge can only be obtained by the methods of the natural sciences, particularly physics, using logic and mathematics;
(e) generalizations, principles, and theories in science can only be derived from empirical data through induction, with the exception of logic and mathematics;
(f) generalizations, principles, and theories in science can only be verified from empirical data, again with the exception of theories in logic and mathematics;
(g) generalizations, principles, and theories should be formulated and expressed in mathematical logical form;
(h) normative views, value judgements, beliefs and opinions should not enter into empirical data collection, theory formulation, or verification;
(i) the methods of obtaining valid scientific knowledge are the same for all fields of experience (the unity of the scientific method).

While the above represent the central tenets of positivism, which along with Popper's early work, informed Hutchison's contribution of 1938 (Caldwell 1982: 112–17), his critique of economic methodology focused on a number of specific aspects of economics which he clearly saw as fundamentally defective. His central criticism of theoretical economics, or the 'propositions of pure theory' as he termed them, was that they do not have testable implications. These propositions are for Hutchison either pure tautologies or if asserted to be fundamental 'laws' are so circumscribed by *ceteris paribus* clauses that their interpretation and testing are rendered impossible. Hutchison does not, however, eliminate all uses of *ceteris paribus* clauses. He is prepared to admit their use in conjunction with empirical generalization, which have been verified in a large number of cases, but which may not be realized in exceptional cases which can be clearly specified and described (Hutchison 1938: 46). Hutchison advocated legitimizing conditions on the admissible use of *ceteris paribus* clauses. The practice in economics was precisely the opposite; *ceteris paribus* clauses were appended to economic generalizations which were not universally true. Consequently, since economists had done little to specify and classify the circumstances in which their generalizations fail, they cannot identify what interferences are ruled out by the *ceteris paribus* clauses. For Hutchison the standard use of *ceteris paribus* clauses in economics is inadmissible. Another area which Hutchison singled out for criticism was what he termed the 'hypothetical' or 'isolating' method, by which he meant the method of reducing complex situations to simplified cases with a view to providing an understanding of actual situations through 'successive approximations' (Hutchison 1938: 43, 119–20). Related to this line of criticism is his critique of economic laws as statements of tendencies. Hutchison's repeated insistence was that 'economists should start behaving like responsible empirical scientists' (Hausman 1989: 118). This could only begin to happen when economic theorists were liberated from the abstract, tautologous and empirically vacuous mode of theorizing and began to develop empirical laws that would permit real 'progress'.

Hutchison's attack was disconcerting to many in the profession. The central issue of Hutchison's critique was: could conventional economic theory, more specifically neoclassical microeconomic theory, measure up to the standards of contemporary philosophy of science, or alternatively stated, could the profession's high regard for microeconomic theory be made compatible with the demand that good science be well confirmed by empirical data? The initial response to Hutchison's challenge was swift and hostile. Frank Knight (1940), in what Blaug has described as 'a wild and confusing essay-length review' (Blaug 1980a: 97), attacked the positivist basis of Hutchison's critique. Knight argued that the positivist or empiricist under-estimated the complexity of testing scientific theories in general, but that their philosophy of science was singularly inapplicable to the social or human sciences, which of necessity had to engage issues of motives, values and goal directed reasoning and behaviour. In restating his adherence to the doctrine of *Verstehen*, Knight was repudiating the unity of scientific method, one of the central tenets of logical positivism (Gonce 1972). What ensued was a short but unresolved interchange between Hutchison and Knight, which anticipated very well a paradigmatic example of Kuhnian incommensurability (Hutchison 1941, Knight 1941). It is interesting, however, to note Hutchison's considered position written almost forty years after that interchange:

> Regarding the view expressed in that earlier essay (*The Significance and Basic Postulates of Economic Theory, 1938 and 1960*), I would still support for economics the criteria of testability and falsifiability. However, though this early essay could be claimed to have been, in many ways, a sceptical work by the standards of 1938, its optimistic 'naturalism' seems now indefensible: that is, its suggestions that the 'social sciences' could and would develop in the same manner as physics and the natural sciences. This is certainly not now to assert that economists and 'social scientists' *should not try* to follow natural scientific methods, and the 'mature' sciences, *as far as they can, while*

14

respecting the nature of their material. . . . Whether these differences between economics and physics are regarded as a matter of degree or a matter of principle does not seem to be very important as long as their full significance is understood. However, it seems highly misleading to insist on certain general similarities between the natural and social sciences (although such general similarities certainly exist), *without* making it clear how important in practice these differences are.

(Hutchison 1977: 151)

Hutchison's reconsidered position represents a finely modulated balance between a continued insistence on the correctness of the positivist and Popperian criteria of testability and falsifiability while highlighting the practical differences between the sciences.

Independent of Hutchison's work in the 1930s, another development, which was intellectually compatible with, even if not directly informed by, a positivist philosophy of science, was Samuelson's operationalism as contained in his early contributions to economics. More specifically, these early contributions consisted of his doctoral thesis, begun in 1937 and published in 1948 (Samuelson 1948a), along with his early work on revealed preference theory (Samuelson 1938, 1948b). His published dissertation had as one of its central objectives the derivation of 'operationally meaningful theorems' in economics. By a meaningful theorem Samuelson meant, 'simply a hypothesis about empirical data which could conceivably be refuted if only under ideal conditions' (Samuelson 1948a: 4). Samuelson's conception of operationalism is not to be equated with that of Bridgman (1927, 1938). Operationalism, as expounded by Bridgman, argued for the construction of correspondence rules that would connect the abstract concepts of a scientific theory to the experimental methods of physical measurement. Blaug has interpreted Samuelson's definition of operationally meaningful theorems and by implication his operationalism as amounting to 'Popperian falsificationism expressed in the language of the Vienna Circle' (Blaug 1980a: 100). More recently, Hausman (1992) has offered a more searching critique of Samuelson's operationalism. Hausman correctly argues that Samuelson was proposing a radically behaviourist basis for economic theory as reflected in his revealed preference theory, but that 'few economists (and certainly not Samuelson himself) do such behaviourist theorizing' (Hausman 1992: 157). Hausman goes further and argues that the general methodological view which Samuelson propounds, that of replacing theories in so far as possible with correct representations of their empirical implications, is 'incoherent and unhelpful, and to attempt to implement it would mean abandoning the whole enterprise of economic theory' (ibid.: 157). Drawing on Mirowski's (1989b) analysis of Samuelson's methodology, Hausman finds a striking contradiction, in fact 'a vivid example of the methodological schizophrenia of contemporary economics' (ibid: 158), between Samuelson's methodological prescriptions to reduce theories down to their empirical consequences and his 'use of theoretical idealizations and simplifications that have many false empirical implications' (ibid.). When Machlup (1964) confronted Samuelson with this inconsistency between his methodological prescriptions and his practice, Samuelson replied that 'scientists constantly utilize parables, paradigms, strong polar models to help understand more complicated reality. The degree to which these do more good than harm is always an open question, more like an art than a science' (Samuelson 1964: 739). This may appear an unsatisfactory response and, in attempting to provide an explanation, Hausman conjectures that Samuelson's inconsistency is partly due to his belief that equating a theory with its empirical consequences is prescribed by 'up-to-date philosophy of science'. Given his refusal to 'reject this authority' and his failure to contain his 'economic theorizing within behaviourist boundaries', Samuelson sustained the contradiction (Hausman 1992: 158).

The profession's response to Hutchison's critique and Samuelson's operationalist programme emerged during the 1940s, which was characterized by intense empirical research that attempted to test fundamental propositions of neoclassical economics, particularly the neoclassical theory of the firm, such as that of Hall and Hitch (1939) in the United Kingdom or Lester (1946, 1947) in the United States. Their results, which questioned the acceptability of key propositions of neoclassical theory, attracted attention and provoked an immediate response which is well represented in the work of Machlup (1946, 1947), who developed a sophisticated methodological response more compatible with the later work of the logical positivists or logical empiricists as they had now become. Machlup's response to the emerging critique was to charge it with propounding an erroneous methodological thesis which insisted on testing directly the basic assumptions of economic theory, rather than focusing on their empirical consequences. For Machlup there is no direct way to test the assumptions of economics; one can only test them indirectly by testing the empirical implications that can be derived by their use. In defence of this position Machlup appeals to contemporary philosophy of science to defend his view that theory should only be assessed by reference to its capacity to generate correct empirical implications. The parallel for Machlup is reflected in the writings of the later logical positivists who accepted the role of theories in physics, which contained unobservable entities, yet generated correct empirical implications. Similarly, economics should recognize the acceptability of theories, though not directly capable of testing their basic assumptions, that deliver correct empirical observations. Machlup's methodological writings contain many ambiguities and subtle shifts of position which are difficult to reconcile with the thrust of his overall position, but by judicious use of the work of logical empiricist's philosophy of science he deflected what he considered to be the most damaging dimension of the ultraempiricist attack on economics.

In any event, it wasn't Machlup's writings that came to dominate methodo-

16

logical thinking in economics in the postwar period, but rather Friedman's essay, 'The Methodology of Positive Economics', published in 1953 (Friedman 1953). It has been described variously as, 'the centrepiece of postwar economic methodology' (Blaug 1980a: 103), and 'probably the best known piece of methodological writing in economics ... a marketing masterpiece' (Caldwell 1982: 173), while Hausman has described it as, 'by far the most influential methodological statement of this century' (Hausman 1992: 162). Its influence is easily understood, arising from the general agreement among commentators that it is the one essay on methodology, perhaps the only one, that has been read by virtually every economist at some stage in their career. The rapid assimilation of the central message of Friedman's essay by the majority of practising economists amounted to providing the profession with a methodological manifesto. Its reception poses a curious conundrum: among practising economists it was greeted with a sense of liberation (Hausman 1992: 164). This sense of methodological liberation can no doubt be accounted for from a profession that was still smarting from Hutchison's philosophical critique which in turn was re-inforced by the problems emerging from the empirical research of Hall and Hitch in the United Kingdom and Lester in the United States. Among writers on economic methodology however, Friedman's essay has won few, if any, enthusiastic admirers. A remarkable feature of the essay is that over a forty year period since its publication it has generated a sustained flow of critical assessments and interpretations (Hausman 1992: 163). This reaction to Friedman's essay is hardly surprising given its style and content. As an essay it remains one of the more perplexing pieces of writing in the field of economic methodology; at times prescriptively dogmatic in insisting on the criteria for correct theory testing in economics, combined with subtle qualifications, ambiguities and lacking any reference to work in the con-temporary philosophy of science literature which would shed any light on the informing influence on his thinking.

Predictive capacity rather than explanatory power was Friedman's declared aim for a positive science such as economics and integral to the adoption of Friedman's instrumentalist position was the redundancy of the realism of assumptions debate (Boland 1979). Friedman could then argue that the whole thrust of the empirical critique that emerged during the 1940s was mistaken as it attempted to assess the 'assumptions' of neoclassical theory rather than its predictions. By dismissing the arguments for testing theories through an assessment of their assumptions, Friedman was not only responding to contemporary critics of neoclassical economics, but was also undermining a critical tradition within economics which extended back to the German Historical School and, in the United States, the American Institutionalists (Schumpeter 1954; Backhouse 1985). This critical tradition had questioned the value of abstract theorizing and opposed what it argued to be the unreasonable and unrealistic assumptions of neoclassical theory. Friedman's 'instrumentalist' defence of neoclassical theory facilitated the rejection of all such criticism as fundamentally misguided and confused. When Blaug cast a retrospective eye back at the entire debate surrounding Friedman's essay he was struck 'by the lack of methodological sophistication that it displayed', and argued that the unsophisticated position adopted can 'only be understood as a reaction to a century of critical bombardment of orthodox theory' (Blaug 1980a: 120). But the unsophisticated state of the methodological basis of orthodox theory is dramatically highlighted when we reflect on Koopman's perceptive diagnosis of the contradiction prevailing when he wrote with reference to Robbins's and Friedman's methodological contributions:

> After more than a century of intensive activity in scientific economics, two economists who have made outstanding contributions to our science, and whose positions on questions of economic policy are moreover not far apart, seek the ultimate basis of economic knowledge in considerations which (a) contradict each other and (b) are each subject to strong objections. One is lead to conclude that economics as a scientific discipline is somewhat hanging in the air. . . . The positions which our two authors so strongly (but contradictorily) embrace have in common that, in so far as either is adopted, its effect is a conservative one . . . in either case the argument surrounds and shields received economic theory with an appearance of invulnerability which is neither fully justified nor at all needed.
>
> (Koopmans 1957: 141–2)

Here Koopmans was drawing attention to the fact that the methodological foundations of orthodox neoclassical theory were perceived to rest quite happily on the co-existence of two mutually incompatible philosophies of science: the aprioristic and deductivist perspective of Robbins with its ontological commitment to the correctness of the fundamental postulates of economic theory, and Friedman's instrumentalist opposition to the role of realism of assumptions. As Salanti (1989) has perceptively pointed out, apart from the impossibility of reconciling the fundamental differences between the conflicting perspectives of Robbins and Friedman, both methodological positions were at variance with the prevailing philosophy of science: the mature version of logical empiricism or the portion of Popper's work which was available at that time.

THE POPPERIAN INTERLUDE:
THE DEMISE OF POSITIVISM

Popper has acknowledged his role in killing off logical positivism, at least to the extent that he can claim to have sown the seeds of its destruction (Popper 1976a). While disavowing that his intention was the destruction of logical positivism, his sole intention was rather 'to point out what seemed to me

18

a number of fundamental mistakes' (Popper 1976a: 88). This endorses Passmore's view that the dissolution of logical positivism was due to insuperable internal difficulties (Passmore 1967, 1968). The emergence of what followed, generally referred to as the 'growth of knowledge' tradition, proved very attractive to economists, economic methodologists and historians of economic thought. De Marchi has described the potential appeal that Popper's philosophy of science held for economists:

> Quite apart from what he had to say viewed as matters of logical relations and of the properties of statements, he represented an *attitude* – to be critical. Neither fact nor theory is more than an element in the process of identifying error. This was liberating for economists in a special way. Popper's balanced insistence on empirical content *and* on the epistemological priority of theorizing might have been tailored to appeal to practitioners in a discipline where experimentation is difficult and inconclusive and theory seems more solid, yet where numbers are seen to be essential to adapting theory to yield advice for policy making. His stress on methodological conventions – rules of the game – was helpful to a group of social scientists anxious to be useful and to explain themselves to a somewhat reluctant public, yet conscious of the fallibility of their pronouncements. In short, in contrast to much writing in the philosophy of science, Popper's work was not only accessible to economists but seemed relevant.
>
> (de Marchi 1988: 4)

While Popper's work may have been accessible and deemed relevant by economists, was it implemented in practice?

The economic methodologists and historians of economics took to Popper with some enthusiasm. Among the economic methodologists one of the earliest and consistent proponents of Popperian falsificationism was Hutchison, who in his seminal work, *The Significance and Basic Postulates of Economic Theory* of 1938, had introduced testability as a criterion for distinguishing science and non-science. Throughout his later work Hutchison has maintained his commitment to the Popperian programme (Hutchison 1964, 1968, 1977, 1978, 1981). It was this aspect of Popper's work, demarcation and falsification, that was the main focus of interest in the writings of economic methodologists. Hutchison was joined later by Blaug (1975, 1980a), Klant (1984) and Boland (1982, 1985b), who adopted the Popperian methodological framework to critically evaluate the practice of economists.

All of the major schools of economics were subjected to a stringent Popperian critique based on the criterion of falsifiability. The Austrian school, as represented by von Mises, and the Marxist position were accused of infallibilism. In the case of von Mises, his infallibilism resided in the claim that the axioms of economics, though untestable, were deemed to be true a priori. Hence the claim to certain infallibilist knowledge was dogmatic and if

19

the axioms were in turn unfalsifiable, then the Misesian system could not be admitted into the domain of science (Blaug 1980a: 91–3). Marxism also stood accused of infallibilism, though with the difference that the system of ideas has been falsified rather than being in principle unfalsifiable (Blaug 1980b, Hutchison 1981). American institutionalists were also criticized for formulating theories which are too easy 'to verify and virtually impossible to falsify' (Blaug 1980a: 127). Equilibrium theorizing is severely criticized by Hutchison as the empirical content is rendered vacuous by the use of assumptions such as perfect foresight (Hutchison 1938, 1977). Mainstream economics of the Marshallian partial equilibrium variety is admitted as scientific, but the use of immunizing stratagems seriously undermines the enterprise. The result is 'innocuous falsificationism' (Coddington 1975: 542), which is metaphorically characterized as 'playing tennis with the net down' (Blaug 1980a: 256). Blaug concluded his survey on economic methodology by arguing that for 'the most part, the battle for falsificationism has been won in modern economics', but that the problem 'now is to persuade economists to take falsificationism seriously' (Blaug 1980a: 260).

For those who took falsificationism seriously, problems quickly emerged which called into question the viability of the Popperian programme of falsificationism in economics. Even the most resolute advocates of falsificationism have acknowledged the difficulties associated with pursuing this prescriptionist methodology (Blaug 1980a; Hutchison 1981). Others have offered more stringent critical evaluations of the falsificationist programme in economics. These have included objections to the principle of testability of economic theories based, it is argued, on the impossibility of testing all the models that could conceivably be formulated to represent any particular theory (Papandreou 1958; Boland 1977). Additional objections have been raised against the testability of assumptions in economics, including the problem of large numbers of initial conditions that are liable to change and in many cases are not independently observable, or the absence of truly general laws to be falsified (Machlup 1955; Melitz 1965, Robbins 1979). Further criticisms of the falsificationist programme arise from the problems of attempting to falsify single hypothesis due to the implications of the Duhem–Quine thesis (Cross 1982, 1984), while Salanti (1987) has argued against the adoption of either Popperian fallibilism or falsificationism as providing a proper epistemological or methodological basis for economics.

More recently, Caldwell (1991) has re-examined the critique of falsificationism and its application to economics. Caldwell himself has been a persistent critic of falsificationism (Caldwell 1981, 1984b, 1985, 1986). However, in his most recent assessment Caldwell concedes that one of his major arguments against falsificationism was seriously incomplete. His error was to argue that falsificationism was an inappropriate methodology for economics because most economic theories could not be conclusively falsified, and proceeded to buttress this line of criticism with the various obstacles to achieving clear cut tests of theories in economics. But Popper anticipated the central thrust of this objection, as noted by Blaug (1984) and Hausman (1985). The Popperian response is essentially that every science, because of the Duhem–Quine thesis and related problems, and not just economics has difficulties with delivering unambiguous refutations. Notwithstanding these difficulties for Popperians, the principle of testing should be retained and when a refutation occurs, the response should not be recourse to the use of immunizing stratagems in any subsequent theory modification. This explains for Caldwell the centrality of the analysis of *ad hoc* theory changes and immunizing stratagems in Popper's methodology. If unambiguous tests of hypotheses cannot be achieved, the critical requirement must be to ensure that our hypotheses are not further protected by adjustments designed to immunize them from falsification. Given this Popperian response, Caldwell argues that it is not an effective argument against falsificationism to argue solely that unambiguous tests of hypotheses are difficult to achieve or that decisive refutations are rare. This is the norm rather than the exception. The argument must now be redirected against 'Popper's insistence that *nevertheless* refutations should be taken seriously, and that when one occurs, certain theory adjustments are forbidden' (Caldwell 1991: 7). On this interpretation the focus of attention for critics of falsificationism is Popper's position on the role of immunizing stratagems.

With the focus of analysis now directed to Popper's analysis of immunizing strategems, Caldwell adduces an extensive array of objections, which for purposes of schematic presentation, he organizes around three topic areas distinguished by their different source of origin. The first he terms the 'philosopher's objection', which contains a number of different strands of criticism. These include an argument which notes that 'Popper never makes clear *why*, if tests results are always so ambiguous, scientists should adopt his prescriptions to avoid *ad hoc* theory adjustments' (Caldwell 1991: 8). Popper's strident anti-inductivism is also seen as a problem. It implies that even in the case of recurring confirmations, these will not be allowed to carry any 'evidential weight'. The empirical data cannot be used to support theories, only to refute. For Caldwell the criticisms emerging under the rubric of the 'philosopher's objection' implies that the Popperian programme is inadequate as both an epistemological and methodological basis for a satisfactory philosophy of science. At the epistemological level, Popper's anti-inductivism rules out any analysis of how evidence might support theories, which represents one of the central questions of any philosophy of science. At the methodological level, pursuit of Popper's prescriptions could lead to very unsatisfactory results, including the rejection of true theories.

The second source of Caldwell's critique is termed the 'historian's objection', which challenges the proponents of the Popperian position to provide examples of its successful application within a particular science. Popper's response to this challenge is contained in his later writings where he argues against the need to test his falsificationist methodology against the history of science, precisely because it is a prescriptivist doctrine. Notwithstanding this position he provides an extended list of examples of refutations from the history of science, albeit exclusively from the realm of natural science, and argues for the superiority of refutability as a theory of science in explaining the historical evolution of science (Popper 1983a). With respect to the social sciences Popper offers no examples of historical refutability. Within economics, advocates of falsification have not observed Popper's dictum against the need to test falsificationism against the history of economics. This is hardly surprising, as noted by Caldwell (1991), since two of the leading proponents of falsificationism, Hutchison and Blaug, are distinguished historians of economic thought. But Caldwell is not impressed with the specific examples produced by either Hutchison or Blaug. His critical conclusion of Hutchison's examples is that they 'do not accord well with the falsificationist image of a theory being subjected to a decisive refuting test', while Blaug in developing his examples is charged with moving away 'from Popper and into the camp of the erstwhile Popperian, Imre Lakatos' (Caldwell 1991: 9). The substantive issue here is the capacity of prescriptive methodologies to provide a descriptively adequate framework to intellectual historians to help them decode coherently the historical development of their respective disciplines. For the critics of falsificationism in economics the issues identified within the ambit of the 'historian's objection' remain a formidable source of unresolved issues.

The final source of critique for Caldwell is what he labels the 'economic methodologist's objection' (Caldwell 1991). The central idea here, which is developed at length by Caldwell, is that within economics there are 'good reasons' for rejecting Popper's arguments against immunizing stratagems. Drawing on the earlier work of Popper (1945, 1957, 1963), along with two more recent statements (1976b, 1983b), which together constitute the corpus of Popper's writings on what he considered to be the most appropriate method for the social sciences, namely, the method of situational logic or situational analysis. The fundamental tenet of this method is that explanations of social behaviour must be sought in the 'situation' in which individuals find themselves. Given the objective situation there will be a unique response which follows from the 'logic' of the situation. The resulting observed action is then explained as a 'rational' or 'logical' response to the objective situational environment in which the individuals found themselves. This type of explanation is underlain by the rationality principle which simply states that people act in a way appropriate to their situation (Koertge 1974). With the exception of Latsis (1972) and more recently Hands (1985a), this aspect of Popper's work has not received the attention it deserved within economics. What Caldwell argues as his central thesis against Popper's prohibitions on immunizing stratagems is that 'the actual methodology followed in much of economics may best be described as one in which a particular immunizing strategem is elevated, and for good reasons, to the status of an inviolable methodological principle' (Caldwell 1991: 13). This immunizing strategem is none other than Popper's own analysis of situational logic. Caldwell goes on to identify the tensions that exist between the requirements of falsification and the logic of situational logic, but finds a solution to these tensions in another area of Popper's writings, namely that of critical rationalism (Caldwell 1991: 13–31).

The comprehensive review of the arguments against Popperian falsificationism documented in Caldwell (1991) provide intriguing insights into the Popperian contribution to economic methodology. Historically, the fundamental source of criticism of Popper's methodology was originally provided by Kuhn (1962). The details of the Kuhnian thesis are well known and need not be rehearsed here. In developing his theory of the growth of science, Kuhn called into question the legitimacy of prescriptivist models of the growth of scientific knowledge when they clashed with the historical record. As a historian of science, Kuhn found that these prescriptivist models, including Popper's, were inappropriate in providing an explanatory framework for the historical evolution of particular sciences. Kuhn clearly favoured a more balanced approach, which incorporated the descriptive tools of the sociologist of knowledge to counteract the ahistorical dominance of the prescriptivist models favoured by philosophers of science. The ensuing debate between the leading proponents was to exert considerable influence on the historiography of many disciplines. Economics was no exception and historians of economic thought were quickly off in search of paradigm shifts, scientific revolutions and periods of normal science (Coats 1969; Bronfenbrenner 1971; Kunin and Weaver 1971).

The arrival of Lakatos was to provide a compromise between the normative prescriptions of the philosophers of science and the descriptive historians of science. The Lakatosian Methodology of Scientific Research Programmes (MSRP) provided a theory of science which claimed to be both prescriptively coherent and descriptively adequate (Lakatos 1970). Lakatos introduced the central concepts of 'hard core' and 'protective belts' to describe the structure of scientific disciplines. Each scientific discipline contains one of a number of research programmes, which in turn are comprised of a sequence of theories which are subject to change over time. The hard core of a research programme contains its most fundamental assumptions, which are usually deemed to be irrefutable and are therefore not the object of interrogation by those working within the programme. The encounter with empirical data takes place in the protective belt, where the empirical implications of the programme are scrutinized and are eventually modified if deemed necessary. This may be a protracted process and is reflected in a series of 'problem shifts'. The prescriptivist foundation of the Lakatosian methodology is contained in the criteria for evaluating the progressive or degenerative nature of the problem shifts. A research programme is deemed to be progressive if every new theory, or problem shift, identifies some previously unanticipated or novel facts, which are then corroborated. Failure to deliver on these novel facts and their collaboration is sufficient grounds to judge a research programme to be degenerative. However, the process of selecting between research programmes as to their progressive or degenerative capacity is rendered extremely difficult as Lakatos provides no satisfactory decision rule as to when it is rational to abandon a degenerating programme. This is based on the problem of the acceptable time horizon within which to judge the status of a research programme. It is possible for a programme to be initially progressive, then stagnate or even degenerate and then become progressive again. Lakatos does not offer a satisfactory solution to the problem of the time horizon nor an explicit rule for identifying when a degenerating research programme should be abandoned.

The Lakatosian methodology was quickly engaged within economics, initially by historians of economic thought, who were quick to exploit the more subtle compromise provided by Lakatos. As historians of thought they could hardly be satisfied with the ahistorical thrust of Popper's position. Similarly, a retreat to the relativism of the Kuhnian paradigm was an unattractive alternative. Lakatos provided an alluring compromise which provided both a prescriptivist methodology that simultaneously provided methodological criteria of evaluation, while allowing for the testing of the methodology against the history of the discipline.

The application of the Lakatosian framework to economics was initially launched at the Nafhlion Colloquium in 1974 and the proceedings published in Latsis (1976). One of the leading exponents of the Lakatosian programme was Blaug, who in the course of his contribution to the Latsis volume, identified the precise nature of compromise along with his preference for the superiority of this framework over that of the Kuhnian or Popperian:

> As I read him, Lakatos is as much appalled by Kuhn's lapses into relativism as he is by Popper's ahistorical if not antihistorical standpoint. The result is a compromise between the 'aggressive methodology' of Popper and the 'defensive methodology' of Kuhn, which however stays within the Popperian camp. Lakatos is 'softer' on science than Popper but a great deal 'harder' than Kuhn and he is more inclined to criticise bad science with the aid of good methodology than to temper methodological speculations by an appeal to scientific practice.
>
> (Blaug 1976: 155)

Though identified as a proponent of Popperian falsificationism, albeit of the sophisticated variety, Blaug has become increasingly one of the leading advocates of the Lakatosian programme (Caldwell 1991: 12). This advocacy of Lakatos by Blaug is understandable in his capacity as a historian of economic thought, given his misgivings about Popper's ahistorical disposition and Kuhn's relativism. Blaug's commitment to Popperian falsificationism maybe more difficult to reconcile with his adoption of a Lakatosian perspective considering the differences between Popper and Lakatos. The latter's philosophy of science differs from Popper's in a number of respects. One such area is their respective positions on the metaphysical content of science. While Popper allows for a metaphysical component in science, he does not accord it the central position that Lakatos does through the medium of the 'hard core'. A second area is the difference in emphasis on refutation. In contrast to the pivotal role of refutation in the Popperian scheme, the Lakatosian emphasis of testing within the protective belt is as much on the confirmation of theory as it is on their falsification. The central concern is the capacity of theories to predict novel facts. The third area, which is the basis of the attractiveness of the Lakatosian framework to historians of economics, is the claim that Lakatos's MRSP provides a testable and potentially adequate description of the historical trajectory of scientific activity within an academic discipline.

The process of critical evaluation of this phase of post-positivist developments, or what we may term the Popperian interlude, has recently become the focus of intensive interrogation among economic methodologists. De Marchi has captured the perceived distance between the high hopes anticipated in the 1970s and the more modest legacy actually bequeathed:

> It seems fair to conclude that for most, and for a variety of good reasons, there is no very substantial Popperian legacy in economics. That comment does not apply to the critical attitude of mind that Popper sought to inculcate, but refers to his rules for the practice of 'good' science. The rules, of course, are meant to give expression to what is involved in being critical; but if they cannot be used in economics as more than ideals, or to identify examples of good past practice, then we are left with the attitude itself, and not much more. Karl Popper's philosophy of science proved highly instructive to a generation of economic thinkers. But its main lesson was to disabuse economists of the idea that they could establish truth and could test content with criteria for theory acceptance such as plausibility based on introspection, or logical consistency. Quantification, rigor in formulation, explicitness in establishing conditions for rejection – these things were given a fillip in economics by Popper. Those prescriptions having become widely accepted, however, it is entirely appropriate that a new generation of students of the evolution of economics occupy itself with detailed efforts to find out *how* economists use theory, view their models, discuss causation, advance arguments, go about testing, and so on, as necessary first steps towards constructing a methodology of economics that is more than a borrowed philosophy of physics.
>
> (de Marchi 1988: 12–13)

The sustained interrogation of falsifiability has exposed its vulnerability and for many its inappropriateness, if not for science in general, then certainly for the social sciences including economics. Falsifiability has increasingly been replaced by an appeal to 'criticizability' as the prevailing Popperian legacy in economics, which is consistent with de Marchi's perceptive assessment. Criticizability was canvassed earlier within the economics literature by Klappholz and Agassi (1959) and Boland (1982), and is the basis for Caldwell's (1991) clarification of the dilemma he finds in Popper's methodology as applied to economics. This dilemma arises for Caldwell in the tension between the requirement of falsificationism and situational analysis, which Popper views as the generalization of the methodology of economics. Rather than choose between falsificationism and situational analysis, Caldwell finds a solution to this dilemma in Popper's writings on critical rationalism which is persuasively argued. Whatever the relative merits of Caldwell's position, the shift from falsifiability to criticizability as the predominant Popperian influence in economics represents the evolution of more subtle interactions between developments in the philosophy of science and the specificity of the problems encountered in a subject such as economics, which, as de Marchi argued may well require more 'than a borrowed philosophy of physics' (de Marchi 1988: 13).

Similarly, the Lakatosian contribution to economic methodology has recently been subjected to critical reassessment. Following its initial reception (Latsis 1976), it generated extensive research and application within economics (Jalladeau 1978, Robbins 1979; Cross 1982; Rizzo 1982; Schmidt 1982; Fulton 1984; Maddock 1984; Dagum 1986; Fisher 1986; Ahonen 1989, 1990). Historians of economic thought were particularly partial to the Lakatosian framework but Hands (1985b) has summarized a set of reasons which attracted economists in general to Lakatos's MSRP. There were from the outset sceptical voices which doubted whether the Lakatosian framework was appropriate for economics (Hicks 1976; Hutchison 1976; Leijonhufvud 1976). More recently, Hands has offered a more sustained critique of the application of Lakatos's MSRP to economics (Hands 1985b, 1990b, 1991) and in an interesting exchange with Blaug (1990, 1991) the relative merits of the Lakatosian framework have been critically evaluated.

The most extensive re-evaluation of the Lakatosian framework and its application to economics to-date was the second Latsis Foundation symposium at Capri in 1989 (de Marchi and Blaug 1991). The organizers of the symposium took as their starting point that the methodology of scientific research programmes, 'must be considered Lakatos's main legacy to economics', and the purpose of the symposium was:

> to reflect on the question whether MSRP, in the light of 20 years' experience, had proved useful ... whether MSRP, in the hands of methodologists and especially historians of economics, had shown itself

to be an appropriate framework for analysing what economics is and is not like.

(de Marchi and Blaug 1991: 1)

In his Introduction de Marchi provides a perceptive and balanced account of the Lakatosian contribution to economics. He argues for an extraordinarily close correspondence between mainstream economists' self-image and the prescriptive ideals contained in the MSRP. However, he is prepared to concede that there is the possibility of a 'reality gap' between the requirements of the Lakatosian methodology and mainstream economists' preferred self-image and consequently 'whether MSRP truly applies to economics remains open' (de Marchi and Blaug 1991: 6).

Blaug in an Afterword to the conference proceedings, 'was personally taken aback by what can only be described as a generally dismissive, if not hostile, reaction to Lakatos's MSRP' (de Marchi and Blaug 1991: 500). Blaug identified two major criticisms of Lakatos's MSRP. The first concerned the difficulties of specifying the precise content of the hard core of any scientific research programme that would command the universal assent of all the participants in that programme; the second, and more significant criticism, was the problems associated with measuring scientific 'progress' by an empirical yardstick. Blaug was more concerned with the second criticism, dismissing the first criticism as 'at bottom a purely logical one'. His contribution is an attempt to defend the Lakatosian position on this issue by drawing on a subtle distinction, contained in Lakatos, between MSRP, the methodology of scientific research programmes, and MHRP, the methodology of historiographical research programmes. For Blaug there is 'no inherent connection between MSRP and MHRP and it may well be that the former is true and the latter is false' (de Marchi and Blaug 1991: 503). Notwithstanding what Blaug described as 'the jaundiced reaction to Lakatos of many of the Capri participants', he remains a committed Lakatosian, convinced 'that Lakatos is still capable of inspiring fruitful work in methodology' (de Marchi and Blaug 1991: 510–11).

The Popperian interlude, including its Lakatosian extension, has occupied a central position in economic methodology for a considerable period of time (Hands 1992). Caldwell (1991: 11) would even cite the publication of Latsis (1976) as inaugurating 'the modern period in economic methodology'. The Popperian interlude represented a major watershed in methodological work within economics by facilitating the demise of logical positivism and thereby providing the entrée into the more uncharted waters of the post-positivist era, to which we now turn, albeit briefly.

POST-POSITIVISM: EMERGENCE OF METHODOLOGICAL PLURALISM

Evaluations of the work in economic methodology during the Popperian interlude and charting the emergence of the expanding array of alternative methodological positions has become something of a challenging task in its own right. Salanti (1989) has argued that what we have come to term methodological pluralism in the post-positivist era represents the attempts by economic methodologists to overcome what he regards as 'quite exclusively negative' conclusions arising from the work in economic methodology during the 1970s and early 1980s (Salanti 1989: 25). His main conclusions, in summary form, include the following:

(a) despite the efforts of economic methodologists such as Hutchison and Blaug to persuade economists that they should adopt falsificationism as the norm to be pursued, and notwithstanding possible difficulties in its practical application, there has in fact been a critical response which has questioned the feasibility, or even the desirability, of such a prescription,

(b) after several attempts to apply a Lakatosian framework to economics, a number of economic methodologists have pointed to the absence of progressive research programmes, in Lakatos's sense, and the imposs-ibility of reconstructing the most important episodes in the history of economic thought along Lakatosian lines,

(c) the hope of solving problems of theory choice by means of econometric techniques is frustrated, if not totally undermined, by either the Duhem–Quine thesis or specific methodological difficulties within econometrics,

(d) when the structuralist (Sneed 1971, Stegmüller 1976, 1979, Hands 1985c) approach to theory is applied to the most formalized part of mainstream economics (i.e. general equilibrium theory), it turns out that the set of 'intended applications' is empty, which means that what is generally regarded as the 'hard core' of modern neoclassical economics may only have heuristic content,

(e) the methodological foundations of other research programmes within neoclassical economics, such as disequilibrium economics, rational ex-pectations and the microfoundations of macroeconomics, are open to question because of their reliance on the assumed possibility of solving the Humean problem of induction and consequently on an unsatisfactory solution of the problem of agents' belief in economic theory,

(f) a number of theoretical approaches, which represent alternatives to mainstream economics, involve methodological difficulties no less serious than those affecting neoclassical economics and this may explain why these alternative approaches have not succeeded in establishing a 'revolu-tion' in the Kuhnian sense.

(Salanti 1989: 25–6)

As Salanti acknowledges, this is not an exhaustive list of possible conclusions, nor does he attempt to provide either an extended assessment of, or a substantive vindication for, these claims. He poses what he considers to be a potentially very embarrassing question: 'this being the state of the art, why should we continue to bother about (economic) methodology?' (Salanti

1989: 27). Hands (1990a) in contrast, responding to the criticism that work in economic methodology is sterile, unprogressive and lacking the capacity to reach a consensus, argued that considerable progress has been made and that a number of theses, thirteen as enumerated by Hands, are 'now generally accepted by those writing on economic methodology' (ibid.: 72). A number of Hand's theses were encapsulated in Salanti's conclusions, so what were 'exclusively negative' conclusions for Salanti constitute, at least in the consensual sense, considerable progress for Hands.

Nobody could accuse the current generation of economic methodologists of not attempting to construct new approaches to economic methodology. This is the salient feature of the post-positivist era, which is largely a phenomenon of the 1980s. It represents, as Salanti argued, a reaction to the disappointments of the failures of what we termed the Popperian interlude or the 'growth of knowledge' episode to deliver a workable prescriptive framework to economists grappling with the unique methodological problems facing their discipline. These current developments have propelled us into what Caldwell has called 'a more pluralistic age' (Caldwell 1989: 14). This is for him very good news, but as he also perceptively notes the bad news is that a pluralistic environment is very unsettling. As he succinctly states 'Everyone agrees that we are better off without the Puritanical rigidity of positivism, but is a methodology of free love much better?' (ibid.: 14). The central question on the economic methodologist's agenda is: what lies beyond positivism, more particularly where are current developments of the post-positivist era taking us?

The task of decoding these developments is not an easy task and Caldwell has provided a number of informed and perceptive surveys of recent trends in methodological research (Caldwell 1988a, 1989). Others who have also contributed comprehensive and useful surveys include Gerrard (1990), Beed (1991) and de Marchi (1992). Notwithstanding the burgeoning array of new developments emerging within the economic methodological literature, Caldwell (1989) argues that a discernible trend is emerging. This trend has both a negative and positive heuristic. The negative heuristic concerns the general consensus that certain topics should not receive too much time or attention, more specifically that economic methodologists should abandon the search for some ultimate set of criteria of theory choice. This stated, Caldwell is at pains to emphasize that the negative heuristic is very easily misunderstood and he is anxious to establish what it does not imply. It does not imply that philosophy or more specifically the philosophy of science has nothing to offer economic methodologists. On the contrary, Caldwell is emphatic that we 'have learned a tremendous amount from the philosophy of science' (Caldwell 1989: 15). The issue for Caldwell is that in the past too little attention was directed to the actual practice of scientists within the various disciplines, including economics. Too much attention was devoted to adopting, very often uncritically, various prescriptive methodologies which were based on an idealized version of practice within physics. This sentiment is now shared by an increasing number of both philosophers of science and economic methodologists. Consequently, what is required is a balanced approach which is sensitive to what philosophy of science has to offer in relation to the specificity of the problems encountered within a particular discipline, including economics. Even more significant for Caldwell is a second dimension of the negative heuristic which states that when 'advocates of the new methodology say that a concern with questions of theory choice should no longer be at the top of the methodologist's agenda, it does not mean that all standards disappear' (ibid: 15). Criticism is a central and integral part of the new agenda, an issue which has been emphasized by Caldwell throughout his own work (Caldwell 1982, 1986, 1988b). Other economic methodologists, such as Boland (1985b), have also emphasized the importance of criticism and he argues that criticism should be viewed as a means of understanding rather than a criterion of demarcation.

The latter issue is in fact the basis of Caldwell's positive heuristic, whose objective he states as follows; 'The purpose of the new methodology is to help us to understand better what the practice of economics is all about' (Caldwell 1989: 15). Within the ambit of the positive heuristic a number of different major approaches may be discerned, the emergence of which have dominated developments in the post-positivist period. One approach which has come from the ranks of the philosophers themselves, has emphasized the importance of studying in detail the specific methodological problems of particular disciplines rather than using physics as the paradigmatic case for all the sciences. A small but growing group of philosophers have turned their attention to economics. Alexander Rosenberg represents one of the earlier and most prolific of this group of professional philosophers who have addressed various aspects of the methodological agenda of economics. Since publishing his major study, *Microeconomic Laws: A Philosophical Analysis* (1976) to his more recent *Economics–Mathematical Politics or Science of Diminishing Returns* (1992), Rosenberg's views have shifted significantly. Initially, Rosenberg held that 'there was no conceptual obstacle to microeconomic theory's status as a body of contingent laws about choice behaviour, its causes and consequences' (Rosenberg 1992: xiii). This is a view still held by Rosenberg, but he has conceded that 'this conclusion takes us only a very little way toward understanding the nature of economic theory' (ibid.: xiii). Now he would want to argue that economics is not a science, as reflected in its incapacity to enhance its predictive power which in turn is based on the intractability of the measurement problems of preferences and expectations independent of the choices that are actually made by economic agents. For Rosenberg, the intellectual achievements of economics make it more a branch of political philosophy, while at the same time given its commitment to equilibrium theorizing can live happily, if somewhat unproductively for Rosenberg, as a branch of applied mathematics. Rosenberg's work has evoked a growing literature on economic methodology by philosophers of science and, as noted by Hausman, 'this literature is distinctive in its attention to the details of methodological practice and in its cautious use of philosophical models of science' (Hausman 1989: 123). Hausman is himself another major representative of the professional philosopher who has specialized in economic methodology. Other philosophers have specialized in specific topics within economic methodology and a representative sample of this work would include, among others, MacKay's (1980) work on Arrow's impossibility theorem, Elster's (1983a, b) works on rationality and theories of technical change, Nelson's (1986) examination of the relationship between the philosophy of psychology and linguistics and its implications for an empirical explanation of individual behaviour, and Cartright's (1989) analysis of capacities and its relationship to econometrics.

A second approach that emerged in response to the vacuum created by the demise of positivism has been the application of certain philosophical frameworks to the methodological agenda of economics. A number of examples can be identified to illustrate this development. One is the attempt to apply the ideas derived from the structuralist approach of Sneed (1971) and Stegmüller (1976, 1979). Apart, however, from Hands's (1985c) analysis of this approach it has received little attention from economic methodologists in general. Of much greater significance has been the work of Mäki (1988a, 1988b, 1989, 1990a, 1990b, 1992) and Lawson (1989a, 1989b, 1994a), who are the leading advocates of the reconstruction of economic methodology within the framework of scientific realism. Mäki's earlier work was concerned with the reinterpretation of one of the founders of the marginalist revolution, Carl Menger, but in his more recent writings he has addressed the more ambitious task of establishing scientific realism as the most appropriate model to explain the theorizing of economists. Similarly, Lawson has argued, in a series of lucidly written and cogently argued papers, for the correctness of the realist approach to economic methodology. Other developments that can be mentioned under this rubric of applying different philosophical frameworks to economics include the efforts of Lavoie (1990) to develop a hermeneutic approach to economics, and the work of Boylan and O'Gorman (1991a, 1991b, 1991c, 1992) in applying van Fraassen's constructive empiricism to the methodology of economics.

A related and interesting area that has been investigated by A.W. Coats is informed by a sociological approach and has as a central theme the examination of the professionalization of economics from the turn of this century. Coats (1967, 1980, 1981, 1984) has produced a number of sociological studies on such topics as British economic thought from the 1880s to the 1930s, differences in Anglo-American culture and economists, and the role of economists in government. More recently, the work of Richard Whitley (1984), who has provided a valuable analysis of the social organization of the sciences, has been examined by Coats (1986b). In general, however, this has not been an area that has greatly attracted the attention of economists and has consequently not received the attention it merits due arguably to the superiority syndrome that characterizes economics, particularly in relation to the other social sciences.

A third approach, which has arguably received most of the attention during the 1980s, represents a radically different strategy by addressing issues of economic methodology. The response of this approach is to eschew philosophy in general and the philosophy of science in particular and to approach economic methodology from a different direction. This is illustrated in the work of McCloskey (1983, 1985), Mirowski (1989a) and Weintraub (1991). This has certainly been the stated aim of McCloskey's work since the early 1980s, a pivotal figure in the development of this response, in which he has castigated official methodology when interpreted as the search for some ultimate set of criteria of theory choice (McCloskey 1983, 1985, 1987, 1990). The ironic dimension here is that McCloskey's hostility to traditional philosophy is in fact inspired by the works of yet another philosopher, Richard Rorty. Rorty's influence is reflected in the 'rhetoric approach' and has been brought to economics by McCloskey and Klamer (Klamer 1984a, 1987, 1988). Their hostility to the 'official methodology' is based on the argument that it provides few insights into the ways that economists actually argue and persuade. Their objective, as identified by Caldwell (1988a), is to sensitize the profession to the fact that economics, like any profession, has its own set of metaphors, its own highly developed terminology for in-group communication and for the important task of impressing those outside economics. Their preference is for the analyses of the nuances of language, of identifying the varieties of discourse that have emerged over time, and of exploring the anthropology of the profession. Research within the 'rhetoric approach' would examine how economists change their rhetorical devices to suit the audiences before them, how economists read, and how economists use the narrative form. The emphasis throughout this programme is to demonstrate to economists that in everyday practice rhetoric is the pervasive means of communication. Rhetoric as propounded by McCloskey, its chief protagonist within the economic community, represented a frontal assault on the official methodology of economics and consequently has evoked a voluminous literature by way of response. Illustrations of this literature would include such work as Caldwell and Coats (1984), Mäki (1986, 1988a, 1988b, 1993), Rappaport (1988a, 1988b), Rosenberg (1988a, 1988b), McCloskey (1988), Klamer, McCloskey, Solow (1988), Mirowski (1992).

The developments identified above have been undertaken by scholars who share a particular research interest in the philosophy and methodology of economics and whose objective is to fill the vacuum created by the demise of positivism. Running parallel with this expanding diversity of methodological perspectives have been a number of developments within economics, which Caldwell has argued 'may ultimately have more impact on the practice of economics than will the writings of the philosophical authorities' (Caldwell 1988a: 46). There is first the re-emergence of the neo-Austrian school and their attempts to provide a new methodological foundation for their position. Their objective is to provide economics with a thoroughly subjectivist foundation, in which economic phenomena are to be explained by reference to the subjective interpretations of individual economic agents who face specific institutional constraints. The neo-Austrian school has enjoyed something of a resurgence not primarily due to its general acceptance within economics, though that constituency has undoubtedly expanded, but arguably by virtue of its association with libertarianism (Dolan 1976; Kirzner 1986; O'Driscoll and Rizzo 1985).

A second development has congealed around the emergence of 'behavioural economics'. The assumption of rational maximizing behaviour is fundamental to mainstream economics. Rationality is conventionally defined as transitivity in choice over a well ordered preference function. Empirical studies of choice behaviour reveal that the transitivity condition may be frequently violated. These findings have prompted investigations into the effects of deviations from purely rational behaviour, both theoretically and empirically. The result is a growing literature in the area of 'behavioural economics', which may have profound implications for theorizing in this domain of economics (Gilad and Kaish 1986; Hogarth and Reder 1987; Earl 1988).

A third development is centred on the work of the 'new institutional economics'. Economics has traditionally adopted a rather stand-off position with respect to the institutional setting of economic activity. The conventional wisdom insisted that it was not the economists' task to explain how institutions emerged, how they could be changed, and what the effects of such changes would be. This is precisely the agenda of the new institutional economics and an extraordinarily diverse range of topics is being addressed within this agenda. Game theoretical analysis of the evolution of rules, analysis of the interaction between the economy and the legal system and studies of governance structures in a wide range of different organizations are just a few of the subjects currently under investigation (Langlois 1986; Hodgson 1988).

The final development that should be noted comes from econometrics. In particular, the work of Hendry (1980), Sims (1980), and Leamer (1983) have seriously questioned the basis of econometric analysis and its mode of presentation. The basic claim is that much empirical work in economics is highly unsatisfactory but presents itself as rigorous analysis. One of the major areas they have highlighted is the presence of 'priors' in the construction of econometric models. If an econometrician has prior expectations about the results of a study, these will be reflected in the way that he specifies his model (Granger 1990; Darnell and Evans 1990; Charemza and Deadman 1992). The implications of these writings remain to be fully explored and adoption of the recommended changes could have dramatic effects on the conduct of empirical work in economics.

Of the various developments and alternative perspectives emerging in the post-positivist period of which the aforementioned list is meant to be illustrative rather than exhaustive, a fundamental division can be clearly discerned between those attempting to formulate a methodological framework within the tradition of philosophy of science and those who are radically opposed to the more traditional methodological concerns. The latter position includes the work on rhetoric by McCloskey and others and more recently what Backhouse (1992), drawing on the work of Knorr-Cetina (1981, 1982), has termed 'constructivism', but which Weintraub would argue would 'be better thought of as the set theoretic union of philosophical pragmatism, post-modernist literary theory, post-modern historiography and rhetoric' (Weintraub 1992: 53). While Backhouse's title of constructivism has the merit of economy of title, Weintraub's articulation conveys the wider post-modernist framework within which this work must be more correctly viewed. Weintraub, having relinquished a commitment to a Lakatosian framework in his earlier work (Weintraub 1985, 1988), has emerged within economics as the most cogent advocate of constructivism (Weintraub 1989, 1991, 1992). This work is now giving rise to a new and exciting agenda within economics, which involves philosophy, literary criticism, discourse analysis and linguistics (Samuels 1990; Lavoie 1990; Henderson, Dudley-Evans and Backhouse 1992; Rossetti 1992).

This study, which attempts to keep faith with the major developments in the last decade, is clearly, however, within the tradition of the philosophy of science approach. We would want to acknowledge at the outset our sympathy with many of the issues being raised within the larger post-modernist agenda and we would be less sanguine than Backhouse (1992) in defence of the traditional methodological approach. Notwithstanding this we believe that a judicious and creative fusion of key developments in twentieth-century philosophy, centred for us on the work of Quine, along with recent work in the philosophy of science, particularly that of van Fraassen, has facilitated the forging of an alternative methodological framework, which we have termed causal holism. In articulating this position we are responding to what we consider to be the two most significant and influential developments in the last decade. First, there is rhetoric about which we remain unconvinced but feel obligated to critically and constructively engage, even if ultimately to reject it, and, second, scientific realism as articulated by Lawson and Mäki. Scientific realism in our estimation presents a much more formidable and challenging position, with which we agree with respect to a number of its propositions, but have serious misgivings about others. Consequently, a considerable part of the book is concerned with the analysis of scientific realism, both in its own right and as a prelude to the articulation of causal holism. In this more 'pluralistic age', with we hope its corollary of being a more tolerant one, at least methodologically speaking, we offer our work as a constructive contribution to the difficult but intriguing discourse on the cognitive status of our subject. In the next chapter we address the area of rhetoric as it has been articulated, primarily by McCloskey, within economics.

2

RHETORIC
The abandonment of methodology?

During the course of the 1980s, the emergence of rhetoric represented one of the major developments within the literature on economic methodology. At the hands of McCloskey, a principal advocate and protagonist of rhetoric, conventional economic methodology was radically challenged to reconsider its fundamental status and relevance to economics. More generally, McCloskey challenged the larger intellectual enterprise of modernism and its attendant methodological prescriptions. For McCloskey, economic methodology is entrapped within a dictatorially prescriptive methodological framework, essentially based on positivism, which is both redundant and irrelevant to a subject such as economics. Rhetoric, as envisaged by McCloskey, has the capacity to subvert the 'official' methodology of economics by demonstrating the extent to which the actual practice of economists fails to conform to their proclaimed methodological position. The corollary is the extent to which rhetoric represents a more insightful and plausible framework to account for the actual methodological practice of economists. The agenda arising from McCloskey's insistence on the superiority of the rhetorical approach is both challenging and of fundamental significance. In this chapter we examine McCloskey's case in some detail and challenge various central aspects of his rhetorical thesis.

MCCLOSKEY ON RHETORIC: THE CASE OUTLINED

According to McCloskey, 'economics does not very well understand itself' (McCloskey 1985: xix). Any observer of this so-called dismal science can see that economists extensively use mathematical models, statistical tests and market arguments. Today, however, this economic practice is frequently couched in economics' 'official' methodology, namely, positivism. The latter methodological approach conveys a specific philosophical and, in McCloskey's eyes, a totally misguided understanding of the discipline of economics. In order to obtain a correct understanding a new approach is required. The key to this novel approach is shaped by 'the non-positivist ways' economists use among themselves in discussing, defending or legitimating their own specific economic positions or theses. By focusing on economists' dialogues, especially their attempts to persuade each other of their respective hypotheses, models and so forth, which include, for instance, their discussions on 'the aptness of economic metaphors, the relevance of historical precedents, the persuasiveness of introspection, the power of authority, the charm of symmetry, the claims of morality' (McCloskey 1983: 482), we can obtain a deeper understanding of that science. Thus we are presented with a threefold distinction, i.e. first, economics itself, second, its official philosophy, namely, positivism which is totally misleading and, finally, 'the conversation economists have among themselves for the purposes of persuading each other' of some specific thesis or approach or model (McCloskey 1985: xviii). This third category unlocks a richer and more comprehensive understanding which is currently lacking to the profession itself and to its philosophical observers.

In this connection McCloskey draws our attention to the indisputable fact that economists, like other scientists, use language and to the philosophical thesis that language is social. In particular, the use of language is a social act which serves many purposes other than making statements. Philosophers sometimes refer to this as the performative aspect of language or its illocutionary force and it is frequently studied under the rubric of pragmatics, as opposed to syntax or semantics. In this pragmatic context, obviously economists are not working in a positivistic vacuum: rather they, like all other scientists, are addressing audiences in historically situated contexts. Their sentences have illocutionary force. In particular, economists have specific ways of conversing which transcend their official positivism and the question is how are we to unlock these economic conversations in a way which will furnish us with the correct understanding of this specific human science? McCloskey looks to other domains, such as poetry and literature, in which the quest for understanding is also central. Contemporary literary criticism enables readers 'to see how poets and novelists accomplish their results without passing judgement on how good or bad their works are' and his suggestion is that we use literary criticism 'as a model for self-understanding' in the domain of economics (McCloskey 1985: xix). For instance, the application of 'the devices of literary criticism to the literature of economics shows', without passing judgement on economics itself, 'how it accomplishes its results' (ibid.). More generally, this model will enable us to attain a clear understanding of the success of economics while simultaneously helping the field to mature. This literary criticism model is central to McCloskey's rhetoric of economics.

The initial rationale for the literary criticism model of economic literature and its discursive practices may be outlined as follows. A central aim is to achieve a clearer and correct understanding of the science of economics and this model, rather than the Methodology of Positivism, fulfils this basic aim. Its success in this respect is due in a large measure to the fact that economic discourse is, in crucial respects, no different from other persuasive discourses and hence rhetoric can illuminate both. In this connection it is necessary to distinguish between 'the conversational habits' of economists on the one hand and their 'arcane' terms on the other (McCloskey 1985: xvii). The former are extensively shared by disciplines which have been rendered clear and comprehensible by literary criticism. At first sight this may not be at all obvious. For instance, as we already noted, economists use mathematical models and prima facie these have nothing to do with the devices of literary criticism. McCloskey, however, maintains that, on closer scrutiny, this prima facie difference must be rejected. As we shall see later, mathematical models are literary figures of speech. More precisely, mathematical models are 'non-ornamental metaphors'. Indeed, this intimate relationship between mathematical models and metaphors is one of the central themes of McCloskey's economic rhetoric. In the next chapter we shall briefly illustrate how this theme emerged in the general philosophy of science and in Chapter 7 we will develop an alternative account of this relationship. Be that as it may, in McCloskey's opinion, closer scrutiny reveals extensive similarities between the persuasive discourses of economics and other such discourses and these similarities justify the use of the literary criticism model for the self-understanding of the field of economics.

The upshot of this approach to understanding economics, which for short we call economic rhetoric, is not an attack on economics itself. Economics as practised by the professionals in the field remains largely unchanged. What changes is economists' understanding of their discipline. This new rhetorical understanding, moreover, will help the field to mature in numerous ways, not least by displaying for all to see the true success of economics itself. This success lies in the fact that economics is a historical, rather than a predictive science. 'It is unsuccessful as social weather forecasting . . . it is successful as social history' (McCloskey 1985: xix). The rhetorical approach reveals or exhibits that economics is a specific historical science focused on 'social self-understanding . . . more remarkable even than anthropology or history' (ibid.). We will now proceed to expand on this preliminary account.

McCloskey is, without doubt, skilled in the art of rhetoric. Like many persuasive legal cases, he structures his approach in a pincer movement. First, the case of the opponent is subjected to critical scrutiny and, second, the positive evidence for his own thesis is organized and presented. In connection with the former he draws our attention to the mathematical development of economics since the 1930s. This development, however, was achieved at a cost which is frequently ignored, namely,

> economists adopted a crusading faith, a set of philosophical doctrines, that makes them prone now to fanaticism and intolerance. The faith consists of scientism, behaviourism, operationalism, positive economics and other quantifying enthusiasms of the 1930s. In the way of crusading

faiths, these doctrines have hardened into ceremony, and now support many nuns, bishops, and cathedrals.

(McCloskey 1985: 4)

Despite appearances, McCloskey is not maintaining that this mathematical development is counter productive. He has no objection in principle to the use of mathematical models in economics. Rather, his objection is to the crusading faith which, he perceptively notes, may have been necessary to accomplish the mathematical transformation of the discipline but which is now proving to be an inhibiting liability. This crusading faith was butressed by what McCloskey calls modernism, which is intimately related to the age of Enlightenment, and especially by its positivistic methodology. In other words, economists, in living their faith, *ipso facto* adopted a positivist methodology which is modernist in nature. Modernism is a broad cultural movement which philosophically was dominated by either Cartesian or Humean scepticism and which is antihistorical in its preoccupation with foundations or certainty. Aside from Descartes and Hume, McCloskey includes Comte, Russell, Hempel and Popper in the modernist family of philosophers. The modernist attitude is one of scientism, i.e. it holds that the boundaries of genuine knowledge coincide with those of science. Moreover, it models the latter 'on the early twentieth century's understanding of certain pieces of nineteenth-century and especially seventeenth-century physics' (McCloskey 1985: 5). In particular, science is understood in axiomatic terms with the focus on prediction, control and the observable world.

The influence of modernism on British–American economics is evident since the 1930s. Indeed, McCloskey outlines 'Ten Commandments' of modernist economic methodology which, in summary, celebrate the following constellation: prediction, control, observation, experimentation, measurement, explanation in terms of covering laws and a clear distinction between ends and means with economic silence on ends or values, especially those of morality. Today these modernist rules in economics are pervasive but they are seldom critically scrutinized. For instance he notes that, despite the fact that the Chicago School has provoked much opposition, its official modernist methodology, symbolized by Friedman's famous 1953 essay, remains largely unchallenged among practising economists. Friedman, however, is not the only modernist with extensive influence in the domain of economics. Popperian falsificationism, as articulated by Blaug and others, is another cornerstone.

Like any expert legal counsel, McCloskey exposes the deficiencies of modernism and thereby undermines the official methodology of economics. By recourse to Duhem and Quine, whom we shall be discussing in more detail in the next chapter, he argues that Popperian falsificationism is not cogent. Indeed, even economists who are unaware of the Duhem–Quine thesis are very well aware of its lesson. In their non-official conversations the vast majority of economists recognize that ancillary hypotheses prevail in the testing of economic explanations and these render the Popperian approach obsolete. Moreover, as von Mises, for instance, has amply exhibited, the kinds of predictions made in physics do not obtain in economics. McCloskey asks the obvious rhetorical question 'if it does (make predictions), then it must answer the American Question: If you're so smart why ain't you rich?' (McCloskey 1985: 16). Furthermore, if the modernist methodology as literally enunciated were actually applied, it would prohibit or abort the birth of new economic traditions or research programmes. For instance, modernist methodology would have been too stringent to allow the actual Keynesian revolution to take place. Finally, modernism is now obsolete among philosophers. It has been completely undermined in the British–American tradition by Feyerabend, Kuhn, Rorty, Toulmin, Quine and others.

According to McCloskey, 'the greater objection to modernism in economics, though, is that modernism supports a rule-bound methodology' and 'any rule bound methodology is objectionable' (McCloskey 1985: 20). Earlier he tells us that 'Nothing is gained from clinging to the Scientific Method, or to any methodology except honesty, clarity and tolerance' (McCloskey 1983: 482). The latter is a very strong claim. This claim, when read literally, is not just objecting to modernist, foundational approaches. Rather, McCloskey is objecting to '*any* methodology except honesty . . .' (italics ours). Moreover, he also rejects the claim 'the philosopher of science can tell what makes for good, useful, fruitful progressive science' (McCloskey 1983: 490). This suggests that he is sceptical about any methodology of economics coming from any philosophy of science. One reason for this scepticism is that 'physics and mathematics are not good models for economics' (ibid.: 482) and philosophy of science is centrally focused on the former. Moreover, in McCloskey's eyes, Rorty and Feyerabend in particular have shown that any rule bound methodology is not feasible for science. We have now reached the transitional phase in that McCloskey is about to move away from his negative critique of modernism which underpins Scientific Methodology as articulated in philosophy of science and is moving towards the introduction of his rhetorical approach.

It is perhaps at this transitional phase we see McCloskey at his sophisticated, rhetorical best. In this context he draws our attention to two domains which he views as central. First, he puts the spotlight on the actual practices of economists which he calls 'method with a small *m*' to distinguish it from Methodology as articulated by modernist and other philosophers of science. Economic method with a small *m* is the box of tools actually used by economists in doing their economics. The contents of this box are not summarized for us. The practising economist, however, is clearly familiar with them. Second, and 'at the peak of the scholarly enterprise', McCloskey draws our attention to 'the conversational norms of civilisation' (McCloskey 1985: 24). In this connection he immediately refers to Habermas, especially his theme of *Sprachethik* which McCloskey interprets as 'the meta rules that we implicitly adopt by the mere act of joining what our culture thinks of as conversation' (McCloskey 1984: 580). These Habermasian conditions of ideal communication are, in McCloskey's eyes, unobjectionable and he tells us that 'only rhetorically sophisticated people recognize that they exist' (ibid.: 580). McCloskey, however, does not elaborate on this fundamental Habermasian theme. Indeed, he does not present the reader with a detailed summary of Habermas' position. None the less he uses this Habermasian theme to introduce us to the centrality of conversation to both civilization and philosophy. In his opinion, 'the worst academic sin is . . . to exhibit cynical disregard for the norms of scholarly conversation' (McCloskey 1985: 25) and again, in a footnote, he refers to Habermas and Rorty.

McCloskey is certainly correct in noting the centrality of the theme of conversation/communication in its full richness to the works of Habermas and Rorty. The issue here, however, is the manner in which McCloskey relates this theme to the philosophy of economics. In this transitional phase it serves at least three purposes. First, McCloskey maintains that any legitimation or attempt to understand economics other than in terms of such civilized conversation and the economist's box of tools is either 'comical' or 'amusing'. In particular, Scientific Methodology fails to recognize that civilized conversation is the ultimate philosophical framework for comprehending our economic and scientific endeavours. Civilized conversation constitutes the 'humanist tradition' which 'is to be used to understand the scientific tradition' (McCloskey 1985: 28). Moreover, the legitimating claims of civilized conversation simply do not function in the manner of rule-governed methodologies as articulated by philosophers of science. Second, civilized conversation imposes 'powerful limitations' which save those rejecting Methodology, rather than economic method with a small *m*, from the pitfalls of relativism or the anarchism of 'anything goes'. In other words, it 'gives an answer to the demand for standards of persuasiveness' (ibid.: 27). These standards, however, are not those of rigid methodologies. Finally, civilized conversation is used to show that the issue of demarcation, namely, the question whether or not economics is a science, is insignificant since 'nothing important depends on the outcome' (ibid.: 55). Ultimately, the claim is that 'all science is humanism (and no "mere" about it) because that is all there is for humans' (ibid.: 57). In short, 'what distinguishes good from bad in learned discourse, then, is not the adoption of a particular methodology, but the earnest and intelligent attempt to contribute to a conversation' (ibid.: 27).

The recognition of the central importance of open civilized conversation, which cannot be analysed in terms of rule-bound methodologies, leads McCloskey to focus on the non-official, non-modernist discursive practices or persuasive discussions of economists. The latter extended economic conversation participates in the full richness of any open dialogue which aspires to realize Habermas' conditions of ideal communication. In particular, we are told that this economic conversation 'often takes the form of legal reasoning' (McCloskey 1983: 501). McCloskey initially toys with focusing on legal rhetoric as the model for understanding the persuasive, non-modernist conversation of economics and clearly the long tradition of legal practice cannot be accused of lacking standards, though its standards are not those of Scientific Methodology. However, under the influence of the literary critic Wayne Booth, he views legal rhetoric as 'codifications of reasonable processes that we follow in every part of our lives' (ibid.: 501). Thus, with an eye to the latter, more general, perspective, and especially by focusing on 'the many useful definitions' of rhetoric furnished by Booth (McCloskey 1985: 29), he opts for the broader, 'literary criticism' model of economic rhetoric. Most generally and crudely put, rhetoric is a literary way of examining a conversation be it that of a novelist, poet, mathematician or economist. Alternatively, it is the study of how people persuade or the art of discovering good reasons and of weighing up more-or-less good reasons, thereby arriving at plausible or probable conclusions. It also embraces the improvement of beliefs in shared discourse. He invokes the early Greek rhetorical tradition, especially that articulated by Aristotle, and he sees some significance in the fact that this classical tradition became neglected in the seventeenth century with the birth of modernism. In McCloskey's apt phrase, 'to reinstate rhetoric properly understood is to reinstate wider and wiser reasoning' (McCloskey 1985: 30).

The transition is accomplished. If we wish to obtain a rich and accurate understanding of economics, we should adopt the literary criticism model and thereby develop the rhetoric of economics. In this rhetorical approach, economics is not legitimated as rational by recourse to the modernist's Scientific Methodology or any rule-bound methodology emanating from philosophy of science. Rather, economics, like any other discursive discipline, is shown to be rational to the extent to which it participates in an open, ongoing dialogue or conversation, where all contributors are treated with basic respect in light of Habermas' ideal communicative context. In this conversational context, economists are in the business of persuading their audiences, including fellow economists and others, of their positions. McCloskey's rhetorical approach, based on the literary criticism model, exposes for all to see the nature of this economic persuasion which is a wider and wiser reasoning than conceived by either Modernists or other philo-sophers of science blinded by some rule-bound methodology or other.

The way is now open for McCloskey to practise economic rhetoric. He adroitly uses this model to engage aspects of the works of Muth, Samuelson, Solow and others. During the course of this engagement he claims that the most important example of economic rhetoric lies in its metaphors. In this connection he makes at least three distinct claims. First, 'mathematical theorizing in economics is metaphorical and literary' (McCloskey 1985: 79).

Second, 'each step in economic reasoning . . . is metaphoric' (ibid.: 79). Third, 'even the reasoning of the official rhetoric is metaphoric' (ibid.: 75). Once again McCloskey draws on central philosophical figures. On this occassion he refers to the work of Max Black on metaphors, especially Black's interactive theory. However, as with, Feyerabend, Habermas and Rorty, he assumes the reader is familiar with this work. As we shall see in the next chapter, Black discusses various kinds of scientific models and argues that, if theoretical models are to be understood in a non-instrumental fashion, they must be understood as nonornamental metaphors. Thus, as McCloskey correctly notes (ibid.: 83), Black bridges the gap between the sciences and the humanities in a very specific way. The epistemic priority is given to the humanities over the sciences, especially to a central figure of speech of literary criticism, namely, metaphor.

If Black has demonstrated in a general way that scientific theoretical models are fundamentally based on interactive metaphors, McCloskey spells this out for the specific case of economics. The representation of markets by supply and demand curves, the use of game theory in economics, the notions of elasticity, equilibrium, aggregate capital, human capital, aggregate production functions, etc. are all metaphors. This metaphorical content of economics was appreciated by its nineteenth-century inventors. Today, however, this is forgotten – a fact which of course does not eliminate the metaphorical element. Despite the fact that McCloskey now proceeds to exploit the performative aspect of language by using such phrases as 'a poetics of economics', one must appreciate that his central point coincides with that of Black, namely, metaphors are genuine cognitive tools and not props for feeble minds. They are indispensable to the progress of human knowledge, scientific and literary. The recognition of the fact that metaphor 'is essential to economic thinking, even to economic thinking of the most formal kind' (McCloskey 1983: 507), does not mean the abandonment of rationality. Rather, it 'reinstates' a new and more liberal form of rationality than that prescribed by modernist methodologists. In the case of economics this rationality is displayed by economic rhetoric which acknowledges metaphor as an essential ingredient.

A REINTERPRETATION OF ECONOMIC RHETORIC: A CRITICAL FRAMEWORK

In the preceding section we presented a summary account of economic rhetoric as articulated by McCloskey. Clearly, it constitutes a significant challenge to the more orthodox approaches to the philosophy of economics which function under the shadow of the philosophy of science. More specifically, McCloskey is correct in noting the failure of modernism in general and positivism in particular. Moreover, his central thesis that a Habermasian conversational approach is the ultimate philosophical framework in which our reflections on any science, including economics, should be located is both plausible and liberating. When the rhetoric of economics is thus located, McCloskey is surely correct in pointing out that it does not lack standards: it is just that the standards are not those specified by philosophy of science. In particular, his emphasis on powerful metaphors and their indispensable cognitive role is to be welcomed in any post-modernist account of our human rational processes. This emphasis serves as a clear exemplar of the abysmal failure of the colonial expansionist policy of outdated positivism.

Our objection to economic rhetoric is not on these grounds. What we object to is the manner in which McCloskey exploits these grounds in his discussion of economic methodology. Aside from the vagueness or looseness of the terms modernism and rhetoric, noted by Coats, Caldwell and others, we wish to focus on a different issue, namely, whether or not economic rhetoric entails the total abandonment of *scientific* method? If it does then we cannot accept it. McCloskey, however, is ambivalent on this issue. On the one hand he points out that the concept of economic methodology as articulated by Modernist philosophy is redundant. As Klamer correctly notes, this may merely imply the abandonment of the philosophical search for absolute foundations. If this is so then we have no disagreement with McCloskey. But McCloskey goes much further. He explicitly holds that any rule bound methodology is objectionable and 'that any methodology other than honesty, clarity and tolerance has nothing to offer' (McCloskey 1983: 482). These claims clearly imply the total abandonment of scientific method. Moreover, he tells us that economics is not a predictive science and that neither physics nor mathematics are good models for economics (McCloskey 1983: 482 and 1985: xix). This in turn forces him to throw a sceptical eye on any philosophy of science, since these in turn are usually modelled on the methodology of physics (McCloskey 1983: 490). On the other hand, McCloskey has no objection to mathematical models in economics. This lack of objection is paradoxical, since mathematical models are noted for their predictive capacity, but economics, according to McCloskey, is not a predictive science. Also, mathematical models flourish in Modernist philosophies of science but McCloskey is sceptical about the latter. McCloskey resolves this paradox by arguing that mathematical models are basically nonornamental metaphors and are thus specific literary devices. Consequently, their evaluation is not in terms of scientific methodology. Rather, their evaluation is in terms of the criteria used in literary criticism. He thereby abandons scientific method for the tools of literary criticism.

In this connection it is useful to distinguish between global and local economic rhetoric. Global economic rhetoric asserts that any philosophy of science which accommodates any method other than the standards of literature has no relevance to the philosophy of economics. Clearly, global economic rhetoricians are not without standards: their standards are those of good literature. Their thesis is that philosophy of economics has to liberate itself from the shackles of any and every methodology emanating from any philosophy of science which models itself on physics and, simultaneously, has to adopt the perspectives of good literature. The intellectual history of the human race is an unending dialogue or rich conversation. From physics to economics we are, in McCloskey's words, involved in 'the earnest and intelligent attempt to contribute to a conversation' (McCloskey 1985: 27) and rhetoric, which is 'a literary way of examining conversation', is the only evaluative approach available. In short, global economic rhetoricians, by assimilating rhetoric to literary criticism and to it alone, advocate the total abandonment of scientific methodology and advocate as it were a poetics of economics. As we have just noted, various passages from McCloskey suggest that he is advocating global economic rhetoric, and thereby the total abandonment of scientific methodology.

Local, like global, economic rhetoricians fully acknowledge numerous limitations in Enlightenment empiricism and in its novel articulation in twentieth-century logical positivism. None the less they do not accept the subsumption of economics under the umbrella of rhetoric understood as a literary means of examining conversations. Rather, they maintain that economics is a science in some post-modernist sense as yet to be articulated. In this connection local economic rhetoricians would concur with Max Black and others that the concept of science, like many other of our viable significant conceptions, is a family resemblance one, lacking necessary and sufficient conditions. Such a concept is conveyed by a network of characteristics, in which no specific one is essential for its correct predication. If an activity exemplifies a sufficient number of this network of characteristics to an appropriate extent, the family resemblance concept 'science' may be predicated of it. According to local economic rhetoricians, economics shares a sufficient number of characteristics in the multiple criteria network defining the concept of science and hence it is correctly categorized as a science. In other words, the local economic rhetorician maintains that economics shares to the appropriate degree a sufficient number of characteristics with disciplines like physics, chemistry, biology, geology, oceanography and consequently belongs to the scientific family of disciplines. In this fashion, economics is in a position to attain scientific objectivity, though clearly not as characterized by modernist conceptions. Hence contrary to McCloskey, the issue of demarcation, i.e. the question of whether or not economics is a science, is significant (McCloskey 1985: 55). Within the framework of a Habermasian ideal communicative context, one can distinguish between varieties of conversations. The scientific range is among these and economics pertains to that range.

Nevertheless, local economic rhetoric has no difficulty in acknowledging a limited role for rhetoric. Economics is concerned with the contingent world of human affairs and in our contemporary world economists play many roles:

their work ranges over the construction of economic models to contributions to policy decision making. In many of these contexts economists are involved in instructing varieties of audiences and clearly rhetorical skills are called for. They must merge a communicative expository style appropriate to their audiences with correct deliberation on the audiences' concerns or problematics. However, contrary to global economic rhetoric, prior to their rhetorical efforts, some scientific investigations into the appropriate truths or probabilities of their specialized domains occur. In these prior investigations economists are investigating economies in a scientific fashion and they draw on this scientific knowledge when presenting their case in a rhetorical way to non-economic audiences. In this fashion, there is no incompatibility between the status of pure economics as a science and the acknowledgement of a limited role for rhetoric in its numerous applications. Post-modernist philosophy, contrary to the assumption of global rhetoricians, can legitimately recognize a plurality of conversations or language-games each with its own specific range of evaluative criteria and, contrary to McCloskey, the local economic rhetorician holds that economics belongs to the scientific range of conversations or language-games rather than those of poetry, drama or literature.

In order to further articulate this distinction between global and local rhetoric we will briefly consider Feyerabend's epistemological anarchism. As we already indicated, McCloskey places Feyerabend among the post-modernist philosophers with whom he closely empathizes. Indeed, there are notable parallels between the McCloskey–Klamer presentation of economic rhetoric and Feyerabend's epistemological anarchism. In the first place, each have a flair for a similar rhetorical style in presenting their positions. According to Feyerabend, the epistemological anarchist is an undercover agent who plays the game of reason in order to undermine that very same game! Similarly, economic rhetoricians use their rhetoric to undermine our confidence in economics as a science. Thus Klamer maintains in a recent interview with Choi:

> Economists like to think of themselves as the physicists of the social sciences and they are. Like physicists they are political animals, in love with conferences and competition. They are hedgehogs not foxes. . . . They like to colonize other fields, the way biology was colonized after the War by physicists ashamed of making bombs. And economists are approximately as arrogant about their neighbouring fields as physicists.
> (Choi 1991: 6–7)

Moreover, according to McCloskey, economics has a neurosis, the neurosis of modernism. This neurosis is exposed by the rhetoric of economic inquiry, and rhetorical criticism, like psychoanalysis, makes economics more self-aware, modest and tolerant (McCloskey 1985: 175). Similarly, Feyerabend tells us that contemporary epistemology, especially its philosophy of science, is sick and requires a dose of medicine. The medicine is epistemological anarchism (Feyerabend 1978: 127). Feyerabend's presentation of epistemo-logical anarchism, however, is open to two readings which we shall call respectively the strong and the weak. Strong epistemological anarchism holds that the illness is so serious there is no hope for the patient. Epistemological anarchism replaces the dead patient and operates under the catch-phrase of 'anything goes'. The weak epistemological anarchist holds that the illness, though serious, is not fatal. When the patient receives the appropriate dose of the medicine of epistemological anarchism she recovers and the medicine is withdrawn. The outcome of this severe but necessary intervention is 'a more enlightened and more liberal form of rationality' (Feyerabend 1978: 127).

Aside from such intriguing parallels between economic rhetoric and epistemological anarchism, the latter furnishes us with a series of questions which the engaged reader may wish to put to the economic rhetorician. These questions, needless to say, are not rhetorical. On the contrary, they help to further articulate the distinction between global and local economic rhetoric. The epistemological anarchist holds that 'all rules have their limits' (Feyerabend 1978: 32). As it stands this is trivially true. For instance, the rules of logic are limited in the sense that knowledge of those rules will not tell us anything about, say, market forces. Epistemological anarchists are, pre-sumably, not referring to this trivial truth. Rather, they are asserting that each methodological principle, enunciated by philosophy of science, is limited in the sense that one can always envisage circumstances in which it is rational, i.e. it contributes to the progress of science, to violate that principle. Let us assume that well documented historical case studies can be presented in support of this conclusion. What response will economic rhetoricians make? Global economic rhetoricians will celebrate such case studies and see in them the vindication of their abandonment of scientific methodology. Presumably they would cite creative imagination and other literary virtues in accounting for the progress of economics. On the other hand, the local economic rhetorician, while fully acknowledging the accuracy of the case studies, will see these as part of our scientific rational development, akin to the well known discoveries of the limitations of the applicability of scientific laws. Part of the progress of optics, for instance, is the discovery that Snell's law has limited application. Similarly, our methodological principles have limited application and part of the progress of scientific methodology lies in discovering these boundaries of application. There is no question, however, of abandoning scientific methodology *tout court* for the tools of literary criticism. In light of this retention of bounded methodological principles, local economic rhetoricians would examine the specific ways in which methodological principles are limited in economics. Our simple question is the following: where does McCloskey stand on this issue? If he is a local rhetoricist, we have no objection. His writings, however, do not provide an unambiguous answer to this question.

Let us now turn to the vexed issue of the proliferation of theories.

According to the epistemological anarchist, proliferation is beneficial for science, whereas methodological uniformity impairs its critical powers. Indeed, Feyerabend goes so far as to say 'there is no idea, however ancient and absurd that is not capable of improving our knowledge' (Feyerabend 1980: 47). Before we dismiss this latter claim as yet another piece of rhetorical hyperbole, one should pause to consider some examples. The notion of non-Euclidean geometry is absurd to anyone raised in the Kantian tradition as is the denial of the principle of the excluded middle to anyone committed to classical logic. Clearly, open-minded consideration of some ideas which are reasonably deemed to be absurd is integral to the development of our fallible knowledge. This, however, does not mean that we must proliferate any and every absurd idea. For instance, should one devote scarce funding resources to a proposal that the operations of our economic structures are remotely controlled by beings in a distant galaxy? Although it is possible that the investigation of this proposal may lead to some new discoveries, if one had to make a rational choice between financing it or a research project into the relationships between political and economic structures, most people, we suspect, would agree on what to do. In short, while proliferation must be accommodated, it is limited by many factors. Clearly, there is a close parallel between this open methodological approach acceptable to the local economic rhetorician and Caldwell's critical pluralism. The global economic rhetorician, however, rejects all methodology, including critical pluralism. In this connection it is, perhaps, worth noting that McCloskey, in the final analysis, is not sympathetic to this pluralist approach. He speculates whether pluralists 'can in fact keep their toleration and balance for long in a conversation about my Truth and thine. As Rorty might say, they haven't yet' (McCloskey 1985: 26). This speculation is clearly in the spirit of global rhetoric.

Finally, we come to the epistemological anarchist's rejection of the standard distinction in contemporary methodology between the context of discovery and the context of confirmation. According to the received view, especially that of Popper, there is no 'logic' of discovery, i.e. there is no rational method for making discoveries. Discoveries depend on factors ranging from sheer luck to hard work. Scientific method comes into its own at the level of confirmation: our theories are subjected to critical scrutiny and in light of this objective method we choose the most rational one. The epistemological anarchist readily concedes that, given the popular accounts of discovery in science, such as Newton sitting under an apple tree, one cannot exclude the possibility that these two contexts are distinct. In the history of science, however, they are not, i.e. this possibility is not realized in actual science. Rather, the activities which are conventionally included within the context of discovery conflict with those located in the context of confirmation. For instance, in the so-called context of discovery, scientists use *ad hoc* devices, ignore or refuse to take some experimental evidence seriously, adjust data to fit their theories and clearly such moves are deemed inadmissible in the so-called context of confirmation. Thus, 'science as we know it today could not exist without a frequent overruling of the context of justification' (Feyerabend 1980: 62). In short, both

are equally important to science and (that) they must be given equal weight. Hence, we are not dealing with an alternative either, we are dealing with a single uniform domain of procedures all of which are equally important for the growth of science. This disposes of the distinction.

(Feyerabend 1980: 167)

Does a McCloskeyan economic rhetorician concur with this rejection? Second, does this rejection necessarily imply the abandonment of methodology? Prima facie it does, for the abandonment of this distinction results in the history of science being the 'single uniform domain of procedures' in use. In other words, when this distinction is obliterated, the only real thing left is the history of science and we all know that the historical development of, say, physics is very complex, containing accidents, mistakes, errors, magic, rhetoric, ideology, propaganda, persecution and so on. In short, the abandonment of the distinction between the context of discovery and the context of confirmation leaves us with 'anything goes' and a persuasive rhetoric explaining the historical dominance of certain paradigms over others. The global economic rhetorician is merely documenting this general theme in the particular instance of economic thought.

Local economic rhetoricians, however, retain the distinction, but in a modified form, in the context of a dynamic scientific rationality. They readily concede the data furnished by historians and sociologists of science which clearly document how magic, astrology, anthropomorphism, religion, persecution, propaganda and socio-political intervention influenced the actual development of physics and other sciences. Their basic question is whether or not we should continue to cultivate these on equal par with, say, coherence and the bar of experience? In other words, they feel confident that they can abstract a fallible dynamic methodology from the history of science, a scientific methodology which, though clearly post-modern, is none the less evaluative.

We have used some of the themes of epistemological anarchism to further articulate what is entailed by both global and local economic rhetoric. Of course we can be accused of creating 'straw men', in that no contemporary economic rhetorician fits neatly into either category. These categories, however, serve a different purpose. Economic rhetoricians should not use their rhetoric to avoid facing the fairly blunt questions posed by the above adumbration of global and local economic rhetoric. McCloskey's writings do not enable us to clearly ascertain whether or not his position consistently implies global rhetoric. On the one hand, McCloskey is very committed to systematic inquiry using theoretical, empirical and, when useful, mathematical techniques and concepts. On the other hand, as we already noted, he maintains that any rule bound methodology is objectionable and that any methodology except honesty, clarity and tolerance has nothing to offer. The latter utterances imply global economic rhetoric. Moreover, if the concept of global economic rhetoric does not apply to McCloskey, then the onus is on McCloskey to spell out his post-modernist account of economic methodology in terms other than those of literary criticism. This, however, he fails to do. In short, McCloskey is ambivalent in his presentation of economic rhetoric, with many of his claims implying global rhetoric while others imply local rhetoric.

ARISTOTELIAN RHETORIC: THE RETRIEVAL OF METHOD?

According to McCloskey, economic rhetoric can legitimately claim Aristotelian rhetoric as a significant historical source. In this section we shall claim that Aristotelian rhetoric presupposes method and, second, Aristotle, contrary to McCloskey, does not assimilate rhetoric to literary criticism. In the Western tradition, rhetoric is as old as philosophy itself. According to Aristotle, Empedocles was the first to discover it. Originally its principal aim was persuasion in the domains of political assemblies, judgements by tribunals and public orations where praise or blame was allocated (Aristotle 1954). Indeed, it could be argued that rhetoric was among philosophy's oldest enemies. Plato, for instance, condemned it as the art of deception and illusion. As Ricoeur so aptly puts it, 'it is always possible for "the art of saying it well" to lay aside all concern for "speaking the truth"'(Ricoeur 1986: 10). This Platonic conception of rhetoric as the art of persuasion which is centrally concerned with convincing one's audience of the advocated position, irrespective of its truth or legitimation, we call the pure oratorial theory of rhetoric. Clearly, pure oratorial rhetoric serves those whose interests are deception and illusion and, according to Plato, there is little else to this rhetorical technique.

Aristotle, however, was much more subtle in this regard than Plato. He attempted to create an intellectual space for what one might call authentic persuasion. According to Aristotle, public assemblies or legal tribunals deliberate on human affairs. In such deliberations one cannot attain the same kind of proof or establish the rationality of one's position as a mathematician can establish a theorem in geometry. Public deliberations in such settings are concerned with the contingent world of human affairs where the standards of proof of geometry simply do not apply. Rather, in this world of human affairs the deliberator is concerned with focusing on a range of beliefs which 'for the most part' are true. Thus, for Aristotle, rhetoric oscillates between two poles, namely the degree to which the matter under discussion is true and the persuasive effectiveness of the case being made. On the one hand, if the oscillation becomes jammed at the pole of persuasion, rhetoric is reduced to its pure oratorial form. On the other hand, the oscillation may become jammed at the other pole: if this happens rhetoric is reduced to the domain of logic or philosophy called dialectical argumentation. While Aristotle is justifiably recognized for his investigation of demonstrative or deductive argumentation in terms of syllogistic reasoning, our elementary text books on logic frequently fail to note that he also pioneered the investigation of dialectic argumentation in terms of enthymemes. Aristotelian dialectic refers to the general theory of argumentation in the domain of beliefs which for the most part are true, a central piece of which is the enthymeme. A common form of enthymeme is an incompletely stated syllogistic inference where one of the premises is not explicitly stated because the speaker assumes that the audience knows it. As Aristotle himself noted, such enthymemes can be more persuasive or powerful than when enunciated in complete syllogistic form. Be that as it may, the principal point we wish to make is that Aristotelian rhetoric is not devoid of method: enthymemes are to rhetorical argumentation what syllogistic reasoning is to demonstrative argumentation.

According to Aristotle, rhetoric comes into its own in specific concrete situations (e.g. political or legal decision making) and as such is directed at specific audiences. Its central aim is to persuade an audience of a probable truth in the contingent world of human affairs. While the effectiveness of a rhetorical argument depends on many factors, ranging from the orator's character to the mood of the audience, what we previously called 'authentic persuasion' merges an elegant style, which is appropriate to the occasion, with correct deliberation. The latter deliberative process, however, entails a method other than that of literary criticism. In order to highlight the indispensability of both style and deliberation to the Aristotelian notion of rhetoric, it is helpful to look at rhetoric in the context of the instruction of an audience. Most are inclined to agree that there is a sharp distinction between what Ricoeur calls the *how* and the *what* of any piece of discourse: the way in which something is said is clearly distinct from what is said. It is a short step from the acknowledgement of this distinction to the reduction of rhetoric to what we called its pure oratorial format, i.e. to Plato's limitation of rhetoric to the how, rather than the what, of a persuasive discourse. However, once we focus on the context of instruction we see that this dichotomy between the how and the what of a discourse is not absolute. In the context of instruction the way in which something is said can and does affect its intelligibility. The 'how' is cognitively relevant to the 'what'. For instance, an apt metaphor can convey an abstract truth to an audience, i.e. an appropriate metaphor can be indispensable to the initial intelligibility of an abstract truth. Thus we can say that Aristotelian rhetoric is concerned with authentic persuasion in the sense of the correct and effective instruction of an audience. Consequently, it must combine both style and deliberation and the latter clearly presupposes method. In our terminology Aristotelian rhetoric is local.

Finally, it is instructive to contrast Aristotelian rhetoric with Aristotelian poetics. This division is interesting precisely because McCloskey does not present a sharp division between rhetoric and literature in advocating a rhetorical approach to the philosophy of economics. Certainly, McCloskey is correct in noting that metaphor occurs in both. However, as Ricoeur notes, the Aristotelian division between rhetoric and poetics is interesting precisely because metaphor belongs to both. The Aristotelian division between these activities reflects varieties of domains of discourse. In particular, it reflects a diversification in the use of speech as well as in the situations of speaking. As we have already seen, Aristotelian rhetoric is the art of persuasion in specific contexts. Poetics has a different concern: one may characterize it as the art of composing tragic poetry or drama. Rhetoric and drama occupy two distinct universes of discourse, the latter being concerned with the tragic 'imitation' or representation of human life, while the former is concerned with the politico-legal world of instruction and persuasion. In Wittgensteinian terminology, rhetoric and poetry are distinct language-games. In particular, the rhetorical use of metaphor occurs in the context of instruction/persuasion/conviction and its effectiveness is measured in that context, whereas the literary use of metaphor occurs in the entirely different context of poiesis/mimesis/catharsis and its success is evaluated relative to that language-game. As Ricoeur says, 'poetry does not seek to prove anything at all: its project is mimetic' (Ricoeur 1986: 13) and hence the Aristotelian division, contrary to McCloskey's assumption, reflects significant differences. The language-game of Aristotelian rhetoric, contrary to McCloskey, is not subsumed under literary criticism. In short, McCloskey's economic rhetoric fails both to recognize the local character of Aristotelian rhetoric and to acknowledge that there are distinct language-games with criteria of evaluation other than those of literary criticism. On these grounds it is clearly defective.

ECONOMIC RHETORIC AND CONTEMPORARY HERMENEUTICS: KLAMER'S CONTRIBUTION

As we have already seen, Rorty is perceived by economic rhetoricians as an important post-modernist, articulating a general philosophical position consonant with economic rhetoric. For our present purposes Rorty's philosophy may be viewed as an original, imaginative attempt at synthesizing the post-modern hermeneutical and the pragmatist traditions. The post-modern hermeneutical tradition, however, is sceptical about the very possibility of the science of human beings or of any sequence of human actions. Our question is whether or not this sceptical attitude towards any science of the human world is presupposed by economic rhetoric? Alternatively, are economic rhetoricians sceptical about economics as a science for much the same reasons as post-modern hermeneutics is sceptical about the possibility of any human science, and are they merely alluding to specific factors in economics which bear out this general scepticism *vis-à-vis* any science in the realm of human affairs? In this connection it is useful to briefly consider the manner in which this scepticism is articulated in post-modern hermeneutics.

Hermeneutics was traditionally concerned with the very limited task of interpreting classical texts as well as exegetical studies of the Old and New Testaments. In exceptional cases some passages proved difficult to understand and hermeneutics served as a pedagogical aid in deciphering these exceptional passages. The tacit assumption was that correct understanding is natural and normal or, alternatively, misunderstanding is exceptional or abnormal. In this context hermeneutics was a series of techniques which enabled classical scholars to avoid misunderstanding these exceptional passages. Schleiermacher (1959), who was influenced by the Romantic movement, questioned this tacit assumption. According to Schleiermacher, the correct understanding of a traditional text is not evident: on the contrary, it is hidden. The correct understanding mirrors or reveals what the author of the text had in mind – her or his intentions, for instance – when writing the text. A central task for hermeneutics is to reconstruct the mind of the author from the written work. In order to accomplish this, hermeneutical scholars must transcend their own prejudices and conceptions and become immersed in the mind of the author.

Dilthey broadened the scope of hermeneutics from the narrow domain of the interpretation of texts to that of the human sciences or, more precisely, *Geisteswissenschaften*. Thus hermeneutics is extended to any situation in which we encounter meanings that are not immediately understood and thereby require interpretation (Dilthey 1976). In this fashion, hermeneutics is extended to the interpretation of works of art, the actions of historical figures, direct conversation and self-understanding. Like Schleiermacher, the true meaning of a piece of historical writing is obtained by reconstructing the subjective intention or mind of its author and the same holds for the other domains. In short, Dilthey emphasizes the *opposition* between *understanding* and *scientific explanation*. Historical understanding, for instance, is not achievable by any method modelled on the physical sciences. Empiricism fails to grasp that understanding is much closer to interpreting a foreign text than to the construction of a scientific theory *à la* physics. The latter is concerned with the purposes of science, the former is concerned with deepening or enriching our understanding of human actions which have both an exterior, i.e. behavioural, and an interior, i.e. mind-dependent, dimension. In general, correct understanding is achieved in proportion to the interpreter's ability to abstract from or set aside her or his own ideas and cultural influences and to penetrate or become immersed in the stream of consciousness of the relevant author.

Post-modern hermeneutics as developed by Gadamer is a post-existentialist philosophy, rather than a methodology, which continues to develop the theme of the opposition between understanding and scientific endeavours

53

such as scientific explanation (Gadamer 1975). Like Dilthey, its central thesis is that human studies are much closer to the interpretation of a foreign text than to the scientific study of, say, an astronomical system as presented in contemporary physics. One might almost say that hermeneutics' basic model for understanding social action is the hermeneutical study of foreign texts. Gadamer, however, does not accept the Dilthey programme. The understanding of a historical text is not a question of entering into the mind of its author. As we have just seen, Dilthey demands that we abstract from the 'horizons' of the present in our quest for understanding. According to Gadamer, this demand is the consequence of the Enlightenment or modernist assumption that a non-historical, a-temporal understanding is possible and this assumption is not justifiable, particularly within the parameters of the existentialist theme of historicity. Rather, in Gadamer's view, understanding a text is governed by three dimensions, namely, the author, the text itself and the interpreter. In the case of a text from an ancient culture the author is not available and hence understanding is a question of the fusion of 'the horizons' of the text with those of the interpreter. The horizons of the text include the tradition to which it belonged or which it shaped and thus is public. In short, understanding an ancient text is not, contrary to Dilthey, a question of reconstructing the private mind of the author; rather, it is a question of mediation or fusion of public horizons. Gadamerian, unlike Diltheyan, interpreters bring to their task of understanding the richness of their own cultural perspectives and fuse these with those of the text to create imaginative, original interpretations.

In this post-modern hermeneutical perspective, each culture creates and renovates its own understandings. Moreover, understanding is a task to be achieved which in principle is open to a plurality of possibilities. This pluralism is not a question of tolerance; it is a logical consequence of this post-modern hermeneutical philosophy. Finally, the key to understanding is not some systematic, methodological approach. Creative imagination, not sterile method, is a crucial element for understanding. A fertile imagination deepens, enriches and shows us new possibilities of understanding. Thus hermeneutics restores imagination to the centre of the philosophical stage after being banned by the Enlightenment in the seventeenth and eighteenth centuries.

Klamer maintains, with good reason, that interviews are very useful in revealing tacit positions or values which an author holds very dearly but may not appear in her or his published works. In line with this sound advice, if we consider Klamer's own recent interview with Young Bach Choi, we will clearly recognize many of the above hermeneutical themes. In this interview Klamer bemoans the fact that 'Economists have lost the skill of reading and interpreting a text not only a written text but also a spoken text' (Choi 1991: 131). Practising economists may well wonder why they should cultivate this skill. Hermeneutics supplies the answer. Economists wish to understand the actions of human beings in the market but their scientific methodology will not serve them well in this regard. Rather, one gains facility in understanding human actions in the market or any other context by reading and interpreting texts – as we noted above this is the central model for understanding actions adopted by hermeneutics. Indeed, the theme of understanding runs right through the whole Klamer interview. For instance, we are told that 'Donald McCloskey and I keep repeating that the rhetorical perspective calls attention to the problem of understanding each other, and the problem of communicating with each other' (ibid.: 132). Again, practising economists may wonder why these problems should specifically concern them. The hermeneutical answer is supplied by Klamer. 'The movement from choice to discourse and to context is simply a recognition that we as individuals operate in context' (ibid.: 134). Post-modern hermeneutics without the constellation of historicity, tradition, discourse and context is akin to Hamlet without the Prince. Indeed, in tune with Gadamer, we are told that the rhetorical perspective does not provide a 'straight forward' method. Rather, Klamer feels a strong need to read in literary criticism and philosophy, while he tells us that McCloskey is studying classical languages. Once again hermeneutics shows us why they are pursuing these approaches rather than simply indulging their unrequited passions for economically irrelevant disciplines.

Klamer also confesses that he is 'flabbergasted' by how easily the rhetorical perspective is misunderstood. 'As if we were only about linguistics or language; as if we were relativistic, and do not care about truth' (Choi 1991: 132). He is clear in his own mind that he is not a relativist. He tells us that the project of economic methodology 'was geared to find some standard'. In this context he refers to Blaug's sympathy with standards and to Caldwell's critical pluralism as follows: 'I am not sure where that leaves us. Anyhow one wants standards but standards cannot be motivated outside of discourse. . . . Standards can be negotiated and renegotiated within the discourse' (Choi 1991: 135). We fully acknowledge Klamer's sincerity in holding that economic rhetoric is not relativistic and is concerned with truth. Nevertheless, the critical question remains, namely, how can the notion of truth function within any economic rhetoric which lives in the shadow of post-modern hermeneutics? Sincerity is not a measure of consistency: one can sincerely hold an inconsistent range or class of beliefs. Economic rhetoric has the post-modern notion of hermeneutical understanding as one of its central preoccupations but it fails to show how the notion of truth can function within this framework. Originality and imagination are the keys to understanding. In this context how is one to decide between two original, imaginative but incompatible interpretations of, for instance, the market? One may feel that there must be some objective criteria for evaluating between them. Klamer concedes that he is 'worried about that. I have no good answer' (ibid.: 135). There is also no satisfactory answer in post-modern hermeneutics. Our suggestion is that, in so far as Klamer's rhetoric is influenced by contemporary hermeneutics, the latter's ambiguity towards truth and method will continue to vitiate the former.

Nevertheless, while McCloskey is ambiguous on whether or not his rhetoric implies global rhetoricism, there is no such ambiguity in Klamer's position. Klamer, in our terminology, is not a global rhetoricist. Like McCloskey, he focuses 'on communication among economists' in order to elucidate 'the nature of economic discourse' (Klamer 1984a: 263). In particular, Klamer addresses the 'argumentative character of economic discourse' in which economists 'argue to persuade their audience of the significance of their ideas or claims' (ibid.: 263). In this connection he correctly notes that any argument consists of a range of backings for the claim being made and, again, like McCloskey, he emphasizes 'the uncertainty of arguments in economic discourse' (Klamer 1984a: 264).

Unlike McCloskey, who advocates a poetics of economics, Klamer focuses on the specifics of economic claims and he analyses these into 'theoretical, commonsense, empirical and epistemological arguments' (Klamer 1984a: 284). He gives concrete examples of these distinct arguments in terms of the new classical economics of Lucas, Sargent and Barro. While a theoretical argument consists of numerous steps 'many of which are not made explicit', it certainly includes a sophisticated 'process of transformation' which in turn requires 'choices of assumptions, functions, variables and so on' (ibid.: 285). These choices cannot be specified in an algorithmetical fashion. On the contrary, such choices are a matter of (controversial) judgements. Moreover, these choices result in a 'binding strategy' in that any other theoretical consideration which violates its fundamental assumptions is either 'alleged to be ad hoc' or is 'not seriously discussed' (ibid.: 270). Furthermore, a theoretical argument (a) explores in its *'fundamental theory'* the basic properties of models, with due emphasis on 'rigor and precision in analysis', (b) deploys *'theoretical exercises'* to modify or extend the model and (c) by *'specific models'* prepares the theory for empirical testing (ibid.: 270–1). The numerous decisions, taken at these various theoretical stages, are once again a matter of refined judgement which simply cannot be conveyed by any set of algorithmetical procedures. Thus a pervasive uncertainty prevails at this level which inevitably leads to a lack of consensus.

Aside from these kinds of theoretical considerations, an economic case is also butressed by a series of common-sense arguments, especially the use of parables. He specifically instances the parable of Robinson Crusoe. The central issue is the various, divergent usages of these parables by different economic theorists. This lack of consensus on how these parables are to be transformed or interpreted theoretically also adds to the uncertainty of the case being made. Third, this uncertainty extends to the issue of empirical testing. At this level there are numerous specific sources of uncertainty. For instance, the manner in which a claim is formalized in a specific model, the manner in which the model is operationalized, the selection of specific econometric techniques, or the adoption of relevant statistical criteria involve numerous choices which are also a matter of judgement rather than algorithmetical method. Thus Klamer concludes that 'empirical discourse is not without controversy. Empirical arguments incorporate judgments which may persuade some but leave others unimpressed. Empirical evidence, therefore, is a misnomer as far as economic discourse is concerned' (Klamer 1984a: 281). Finally, the uncertainty of the economist's case extends to the epistemological argument which includes the economist's conception of science and scientific progress.

Klamer's central point is that when we examine the kinds of cases made by economists, these lack decisive criteria for appraisal and consequently 'judgments are essential in economic discourse: The art of persuasion involves the art of making judgments' (Klamer 1984a: 284) and clearly these judgments are too varied to be summed up in McCloskey's poetics of economics. Thus Klamer's rhetoric is distinct from that of McCloskey's. In his concluding remarks Klamer sums up as follows:

> Economists attempt to persuade. . . . It [Klamer's position] stresses the variety of arguments in economic discourse and the prominent role of judgments. No argument is decisive. The effectiveness of argumentation is dependent on the promise of the convention that it embodies. But the assessment of such a promise is in the end also a matter of judgment.
>
> (Klamer 1984a: 285)

He concludes by making a plea for openness.

> The plea for openness does not imply a call for the abandonment of all rules and conventions and a justification of the 'do whatever you please' approach. . . . Moreover the uncertainty of economic arguments demands a certain tenacity on the part of economists; an argument may have problems, but persistant research along the same lines may lead to a break through.
>
> (Klamer 1984a: 287)

In the final chapters of this book we will argue that, despite the fragility and fallibility of economic facts and economic testing, empirical evidence is the final arbiter for the science of economics and thus, contrary to Klamer, empirical evidence is not 'a misnomer as far as economic discourse is concerned' (Klamer 1984a: 281). By pursuing the challenge of empirical or descriptive adequacy, the economist can learn the sophisticated skills required to make a mature, informed judgement on the correct identification of the observable causes of economic events and happenings which permeate our socio-economic world and thereby learn to assess economic models on the ground of the empirical evidence available. In the following section, however, we will limit the scope of hermeneutics and thereby open the door to the possibility of an empirical science of economics.

HABERMAS: A WAY FORWARD

Classical Positivism is characterized by many significant factors. One of these is what Ricoeur calls a universalization thesis, namely, that there is one and only one method of attaining knowledge in all domains, i.e. the physical sciences. Post-modern hermeneutics, however, counters this universalization claim with another: there is one and only one approach to any issue concerning understanding, namely, hermeneutical philosophy. Once again it is important to note that in this formulation of the universalization of hermeneutics the term 'method' is dropped: the notion of a method is inappropriate to the quest for understanding. As we saw in the preceding section, the keys to understanding are the fusion of horizons and imagination. Moreover, even the domain of the physical sciences can now be brought within the scope of hermeneutics. The scientific enterprise is a human one concerned with understanding and thus interpreting the physical world and any such understanding comes within the parameters of the philosophical framework of hermeneutics. McCloskey's central rhetorical thesis that 'all science is humanism' (McCloskey 1985: 57) discussed earlier, is clearly articulated in contemporary hermeneutics' universalization claim.

Habermas, despite the fact that he agrees with the hermeneutical rejection of the Enlightenment approach to philosophy and, in particular, its positivistic universalization thesis, also rejects the universalization thesis of hermeneutics. According to Habermas, human knowledge can be divided in accordance with the human interests it serves and he specifies three domains, namely, science, hermeneutics and critical theory (Habermas 1981). Science serves the interest of prediction and control and within this interest the scientific method is not reducible to either hermeneutics or critical theory. Hermeneutics is concerned with the human interest of understanding ourselves and others and is not reducible to the other two. Finally, critical theory is concerned with our emancipatory interests, in particular, the kind of society which facilitates the realization of unrestricted, non-distorted communication and also this domain is not reducible to the others (ibid.). We have already seen how the hermeneutical tradition has constituted part of the 'background knowledge' to economic rhetoric. In our opinion, a neo-Habermasian threefold division is a more accurate and subtle background for focusing on economics and its methodology: it has the advantage of recognizing the futility of replacing the universalizability of science by the universalizability of hermeneutics or rhetoric. But this is precisely what McCloskey fails to do in his articulation of economic rhetoric. As things stand at the moment, Habermas has identified three major concerns of contemporary Western human beings and, as far as we can tell, none of these domains can be studied by means of a static, algorithmetical sequence of methodological rules.

These three domains constitute, in Wittgensteinian terminology, a web of different, though interconnected, language-games. Moreover, in connection with science, we maintain that it not only serves the interests of prediction and control. It also serves our interest in describing the world. A central task of science is to furnish appropriate and as accurate as possible descriptions of the world. Our principal source of evidence for adding this latter interest lies in the history of science itself. The progress of science has contributed enormously to our store of factual knowledge and this is clearly acknowledged by Habermas himself. While much of the attention of philosophers of science is devoted to the theoretical and/or explanatory dimensions of science, the descriptive dimension is normally not denied. Rather, philosophers find the other dimensions more interesting.

What one might call economic studies – a discipline as yet to be specified – spans all three Habermasian interests. Human actions do not occur in a social vacuum. Rather, they occur in a network of social institutions ranging from the political to the economic. Thus economic institutions may either facilitate or hinder the realization of our human ideals of justice, freedom or emancipation. Hence they are open to an ethical scrutiny. Such an ethical scrutiny constitutes an integral part of economic studies which one might call emancipatory economics. Emancipatory economics would range from ideological investigations, revealing the sectional interests being served by particular economic institutions or theories, to a radical ethical critique of existing economic structures.

Economic studies would also encompass a science of economics in the sense of furnishing accurate descriptions of economic actions of individual agents at one end of the spectrum and equally accurate descriptions of economic structures and institutions at the other end. Indeed, the furnishing of such descriptions is presupposed by emancipatory economics in that the ethical critique of economic structures presupposes the correct identification and description of such structures. This science of economics would also include the history of economic thought in the conventional sense and the archaeology and genealogy of economic knowledge in the Foucaultian sense. These partially complementary historical activities would enable us to describe more accurately the historical course of economic institutions and, in particular, their historical interconnectedness with other social institutions such as those of law or politics. Finally, economic studies would also have a heremeneutical dimension. Without human agents and human actions, the market and firms would cease to operate and hermeneutics offers us a rich reservoir of wisdom and knowledge about human beings and their actions which should throw additional light on economic agents and their actions. At one end of the economic spectrum, the hermeneutical approach could tellingly complement the standard scientific-survey approach when, for instance, a firm is launching a new product onto the market or when an advertising company is investigating how best to advertise a product. At the other end of the spectrum, originality and imagination may be required in the initial construction of a new economic theory or for devising specific methodological techniques, analogous to those used in the econometric investigation of causal claims, to be used in furthering our knowledge of economic causes.

McCloskey's rhetoric, under the influence of the universalization thesis of post-modern hermeneutics, fails to recognize that the domains which Habermas associates with our distinct human interests constitute, in Wittgensteinian terminology, distinct but overlapping language-games, with distinct but again overlapping criteria for evaluation used in the different language-games. In a substantial proportion of economic actions all three are ontologically intermingled. None the less, if we are to make progress in investigating such economic actions, the wisdom of the past suggests that (a) we abstract out from reality these different dimensions, (b) in so far as is possible study them in isolation, (c) investigate how they interact and have interacted with one another.

In summary, our critique of economic rhetoric can be adumbrated as follows. Contemporary economic rhetoric lingers in the shadows of both Aristotelian rhetoric and post-modern hermeneutics. However, the shadow of the former entails method while the shadow of the latter excludes it. Hence the paradoxical nature of economic rhetoric emerges. We suggest that this paradox can be resolved in the case of local economic rhetoric by limiting the range of the shadow of hermeneutics and by recognizing other sources of shadows. However, the paradox remains intractable in the case of global economic rhetoric with an irreconcilable tension between the themes of truth and method borrowed from Aristotelian rhetoric and the themes of conversation and imagination borrowed from post-modern hermeneutics. In particular, we have outlined a prima facie case for giving economic rhetoric a local rather than a global interpretation. With due irony, we have focused on Aristotle, Feyerabend, Habermas and Rorty, philosophers whom McCloskey sees as having a positive influence on his economic rhetoric, to illustrate the ambiguity of McCloskey's own position and to construct our prima facie case for, first, isolating a domain for science within the broad spectrum of language-games which constitutes ideal communication and, second, for locating economics as a descriptive discipline within that scientific domain.

In the following chapters we will focus on what we called above the science of economics, its aims, and its methods. In particular, we will dwell on the descriptive dimension of this science and especially its use of scientific models. In this connection our sympathies are entirely with McCloskey's and Klamer's emphasis on economic models. However, we do not agree with McCloskey's assimilation of models to metaphor. When we have fully articulated the roles of models in science in general and economics in particular – a task which takes us through the remaining chapters – we will finally undermine this central thesis in McCloskey's position. Moreover, in the course of our analysis of the descriptive adequacy of economic models, we demonstrate that empirical evidence, contrary to Klamer, is not a misnomer in a properly constructed science of economics.

3

CONTEMPORARY PHILOSOPHY
OF SCIENCE
Methodology revisited

In defending economic methodology from the challenge of global economic rhetoric we adopted a neo-Habermasian threefold division and specified appropriate and accurate description as a principal task for the science of economics. It may be felt, however, that such a defence is too narrow or limiting. The aim of any science, we are frequently told, is twofold, namely, to furnish accurate descriptions of the events, happenings or facts in the actual world, the dimension which we have focused on, and, second, to explain these facts by recourse to theory, the dimension which we have ignored. In this not uncommon view, the facts are presented in a non-problematical observational language which is theory-neutral. For instance, we may say that it is a fact that the car was travelling at 30 km/hour when it crashed or that the temperature was 65°F at 3 p.m. at a specific location in Dublin on the 31 May last. There is no apparent reference to Newtonian or kinetic theory in these observational statements.

The explanatory move, however, eventually leads us to theory. For instance, gravitational theory explains the falling apple, or atomic theory explains the observational events in a cloud chamber. Frequently this explanatory, theoretical move entails the use of non-observational terms, called theoretical terms, such as gravity, quark or field. Moreover, there appears to be a sharp, clear-cut dichotomy between observational sentences, such as the thermometer is reading 65°F, and theoretical sentences, such as any state of electron spin is a linear superposition of two orthogonal states. In the terminology of Newton-Smith observational terms appear to be *semantically privileged*: we can teach children such terms ostensively, by demonstration, whereas we could not do the same for theoretical terms. Observational terms are also apparently *epistemologically privileged*, since we can apply them more easily and can have more confidence in the judgements we form using them rather than those using theoretical terms (Newton-Smith 1981: 23).

These differences between observational and theoretical sentences were seen by many as indicating a difference in kind rather than simply one of degree. In this view the facts are presented in a theory-neutral, observational language. This theory independent or purely observational language furnishes the terms appropriate to the discovery and accurate description of the empirical facts. Indeed, the meanings of these observational sentences would remain stable or the same, even though the high-level theoretical language could be radically altered. Thus high-level, theoretical language is not used in factual statements or observational reports. It is confined to explanatory purposes.

Let us briefly look at both observational and theoretical terms with Frege's distinction between sense and reference in mind. Observational terms, such as 'car' or 'velocity', have both a sense and a reference in the actual world. A fictitious term, such as 'leprechaun' or 'mermaid', has a sense but lacks a reference in the actual world. What of the theoretical terms of a well-confirmed theory? These certainly have a sense. The pertinent question, however, is whether or not they have a reference? According to naïve or common-sense realism, they have: these theoretical terms refer to the hidden mechanisms of nature. The gravitational pull is the real, though unobservable, mechanism behind the observable event of the falling apple. In this common-sense realist perspective the aim of science is twofold: to describe the observational events of the real world in a purely observational language and second, by recourse to the best confirmed theory, to discover the hidden unobservable, essential mechanisms causing the observable events. In this common-sense realist view nature is like a clock, the facts are like the observations of the clock's face and nature, like the clock, has hidden mechanisms. The major difference is that, unlike nature, the hidden, mechanisms behind the face of the clock are observable ones. This difference is not fatal: the theoretical terms of our well-confirmed theories succeed in referring to the hidden, unobservable mechanisms of nature. A successful theory isolates the hidden unobservable events behind the observational phenomena in that its theoretical terms refer to the unobservable entities which generate the observational events. This common-sense realist perspective can frequently inform the tacit methodological perspective of numerous physicists, chemists and biologists on the one hand and sociologists, psychologists and economists on the other.

EMPIRICISM AND THEORETICAL TERMS

A classical empiricist, especially one influenced by its most sophisticated eighteenth-century exponent, David Hume, has grave reservations about the common-sense realist thesis that theoretical terms refer to unobservable entities. For the empiricist, scientific knowledge begins with observation but, more significantly, it is confined within the boundaries of what is observable. In particular, the realist notion of explanation in terms of the unobservable referents of theoretical terms is suspect because it smacks of metaphysics. There are other more specific reasons for this empiricist thesis confining scientific knowledge to within the boundaries of the observable and for its rejection of the unobservable referents of theoretical terms. One such reason may be illustrated by means of the following example.

In our study we hear a light, patterned, fast flowing sequence of noises coming from directly above the ceiling. What is wrong with explaining this noise pattern by postulating a mouse or mice running across the other side of the ceiling as the cause of this pattern? According to empiricists, within the limits of their understanding of the notion of cause, there is no reason why we should not do just that. Yesterday when we lifted some floor boards we noticed some mouse droppings. In view of this and other facts it is reasonable to assume that a mouse or mice caused the recent noise. The common-sense realist fails to understand why a similar kind of argument cannot be applied to theoretical entities. We observe the Balmer series and we postulate electrons 'jumping' from different orbitals to explain that series. The explanation parallels the mouse paradigm which is accepted by empiricists. Are not empiricists taking their metaphysical qualms too far? Empiricists respond that they are not. The principal difference resides in the fact that in the noise example, the *explanans*, i.e. mice, are in principle observable, whereas in the Balmer series example electrons are said to be entities which are in principle unobservable. The Humean rhetorical question is the following: how can one specify any characteristic of an actual entity which is in principle unobservable and know that one is correct in ascribing the said characteristic? The common-sense realist is articulating two propositions, namely, (a) x is unobservable in principle and (b) x has such and such theoretical characteristics. The classical empiricist sees no rational justification for (b), given (a). The domain of empirical evidence, which is all we have at our human disposal, is confined to the observable and no amount of knowledge about this domain can legitimate any inference about the characteristics of the unobservable in principle.

In view of their basic positivist beliefs or commitments, empiricists maintain that, where the common-sense realist holds that such and such a theoretical term in a well-confirmed theory refers to hidden, unobservable entities, such terms do not refer to any such entity in the actual world. Consequently, they reject the common-sense realist's thesis that high-level theoretical sentences containing such theoretical terms are integral to scientific explanation. In short, according to classical empiricism, theories do not explain at all. The rationally correct aim of science is to describe the actual, observable world and to discover as many facts as possible about that world. The common-sense realist's additional aim, namely, discovering, via well-confirmed theories, the hidden, unobservable mechanisms which cause the observable phenomena, is not an epistemologically viable end at all.

Anyone looking at science, however, can clearly observe the pervasiveness of theoretical terms in that range of extraordinarily successful disciplines. Obviously, the empiricist challenge is to give a coherent, rational account of the role of theoretical terms without recourse to the common-sense realist thesis. In the first half of the twentieth century two such empiricist accounts were constructed, namely, descriptivism and instrumentalism.

DESCRIPTIVISM AND INSTRUMENTALISM

In section two of his 1953 paper on economic methodology, Milton Friedman presents a key descriptivist picture of the role of theory in science, namely, 'the filing system or filing cabinet' metaphor. According to this picture, the aim of science is not merely to describe the actual world and discover new facts. It also wishes to organize these facts into a coherent system. Science aims at an economical, systematic organization of the facts and a scientific theory is the normal way of accomplishing this additional organizational dimension. In this view, a theory is an elliptic or compendious way of presenting the observable facts. This descriptivist view was intimately associated with and systematically elaborated by logical positivism. According to the descriptivist, a theory is translatable into a complex or set of factual statements. Hence there is no question of theoretical terms referring to actual unobservable entities. On the contrary, such terms are definable in terms of our purely observational vocabulary. These definitions were to be effected by so-called correspondence rules or co-ordinating definitions. For instance, if we assume that the statement 'there is an electric current in the circuit' is a theoretical sentence, this could be translated into a series of observational facts about optical, thermal, chemical and magnetic events, such as 'if a galvanometer were introduced into the circuit its pointer would be deflected from its present position' and so on. In this descriptivist approach theoretical terms are guaranteed to be compatible with the verifiability criterion of meaning while simultaneously eliminating any consideration of reference to entities which are unobservable in principle.

The descriptivist thesis gave rise to the logical positivist programme of effecting the translation of theoretical sentences into observational ones. This is not the place to discuss the history of descriptivism and the various modifications of the correspondence rules which resulted from the various attempts at translation. Suffice it to say that the best minds of the logical positivist tradition attempted this programme and failed. The difficulties encountered were varied and the programme was abandoned even by its founding fathers such as Carnap (Suppe 1977: Chapter 2). In the history of economic methodology Terence Hutchison appears to come quite close to the above descriptivist position. Bruce Caldwell tells us that Hutchison, while lecturing in Bonn from 1935 to 1938, studied logical positivism and was very much influenced by its concern to make economics and other disciplines 'truly scientific'. In particular, Hutchison acknowledges that, while the postulates of pure economic theory seem to refer to real objects, they are in fact only 'relations between definitions – a "fact" of linguistic usage if one likes' (Caldwell 1982: 108) . In view of Hutchison's immersion in logical positivism, it is not unreasonable to read such suggestions in a descriptivist way.

Be that as it may, the abandonment of the descriptivist conception of theoretical terms did not result in the widespread acknowledgement of a scientific realist approach. Empiricists, consonant with their basic belief that scientific knowledge is limited by the boundaries of the observable and with their allied view that the aim of science is to describe and not explain, developed the instrumentalist conception of the role of theory in science. Unlike scientific realism, theories are not explanations and, unlike descriptivism, theories are not summary descriptions. Rather, despite the fact that theoretical sentences appear to be propositions, i.e. sentences which are true or false, and that they appear to function as major premises in scientific inferences, these appearances do not stand up to critical scrutiny. Theoretical sentences are not propositions at all: they are neither true nor false. Consequently, they simply cannot function as major or minor premises in scientific inferences and hence there is no question of theoretical explanation. Rather, they are linguistic or conceptual instruments for making transitions from one set of facts to another. They are heuristic devices which enable scientists to discover new facts or 'inference tickets' which license the movement from one set of experimental data to another. We call this position philosophical instrumentalism.

The philosophical instrumentalist thesis has been formulated in a variety of ways and, although there are important differences between some of them, it is beyond the scope of the present work to pursue these differences. For our present purposes, we wish to emphasize the manner in which philosophical instrumentalism differs from both descriptivism and scientific realism. In this instrumentalist approach, the pertinent question about the acceptance of a theory relates, not to truth or falsehood, but rather to its heuristic effectiveness. Just as some instruments are better than others for specific purposes, some theories are more effective heuristic devices than others. The central issue is how well theory effectively directs experimental inquiry or how well it exhibits relationships between observable phenomena which otherwise would be regarded as unrelated. The appropriate question about a theory is whether or not it is an effective technique for representing or inferring observational or experimental facts. Clearly, there is no question of translating theoretical terms, via correspondence rules, into observational ones. Neither is there any question of theoretical terms referring to actual unobservable events or happenings. Moreover, philosophical instrumentalism offers a very compelling account of the role of idealizations in science in general and economics in particular. Nevertheless, in the history of the philosophy of science, this instrumentalist reading of the role of theory was eclipsed by numerous other developments. Among these was the Hempelian approach, which once again placed explanation at the centre of the scientific stage: Hempel's works were very persuasive in re-establishing explanation as a central aim of science.

HEMPEL AND THE RE-ESTABLISHMENT OF EXPLANATION

In 1948 Hempel and Oppenheim published their paper 'Studies in The Logic of Explanation' (reprinted in Hempel 1965). In this and subsequent papers Hempel placed explanation at the centre of the stage of the philosophy of science. Science is to be taken at its face value: the aim of science is both to describe and to explain. Hempel identified two distinct patterns of explanation in the physical and human sciences, namely, the Deductive-Nomological pattern and the probabilistic pattern. The Deductive Nomological pattern consists of law-like universal statements, a number of particular or singular statements, called initial or boundary conditions, and the logical deduction of the event to be explained. For instance, if one wishes to explain the length of the shadow of a particular flagpole, one first states the laws of geometrical optics, second, one ascertains the boundary or initial conditions, such as the actual height of the flag pole, the angle of elevation of the sun and so on and, finally, one deduces from the former the length of the shadow. Thus the laws of geometrical optics combine with the initial conditions to explain the length of the shadow.

This Hempelian conception of explanation demands that the premises in a deductive pattern must meet certain epistemic requirements. If these requirements are not met then the deduction, though valid, is not a genuine explanation. In the first place, the initial or boundary conditions must be true. This requirement captures the intuition that a falsehood does not explain. For instance, if we explain the fact that a certain piece of substance expanded on being heated by means of the following premises: copper expands on being heated and this is a piece of copper, but it turns out, on chemical analysis, the piece of substance is not copper, then the purported explanation is not a genuine explanation. Second, the universal law-like statement must not be known to be false. More positively, the universal statement should be compatible with the established empirical data and also adequately confirmed or supported by independent evidence. These requirements are intended to rule out *ad hoc*, trivial or circular explanations. Let us suppose that one wishes to explain the static noise from one's radio on a given day. Let us further suppose that the explanatory premises contain the statement that there were, on that same day, violent magnetic storms in the atmosphere. If the sole evidence for the latter claim turned out to be the presence of static noise on the radio in question, the purported explanation would be spurious. On the other hand, if we possess independent evidence for this premise then, all other things being equal, we have a reasonable explanation.

Finally, the universal propositions must be nomic rather than accidental.

If the initial conditions and the universal propositions are true and the event to be explained follows necessarily from these premises we may, none the less, have failed to explain. This can happen when the universal premise is merely accidentally true. For instance, our friend Peter has a rather old car and it is factually true that all the screws in Peter's car are rusty. We find a screw from Peter's car but we fail to explain the fact that it is rusty by deducing this from the accidentally true universal proposition above combined with the true initial conditions. The proper explanation for the rust on the screw from Peter's car has recourse to nomic universal statements concerning the process of oxidization. The laws of oxidization are nomic rather than accidental. Accidental or *de facto* universals, though true, cannot serve as genuine explanatory premises; rather explanatory universals must be nomic. A crucial question in the Hempelian D-N approach concerns how one should differentiate between nomic universals, like all copper expands on being heated, from accidentally true universals, like all the shrubs in Jane's garden are over one metre high. However, before briefly adumbrating the empiricist and realist accounts, let us remind ourselves what Hempel has apparently established or upon which there was apparent consensus, namely, nomic, rather than accidental, universals are a *sine qua non* for a satisfactory D-N explanation.

The empiricist wishes to give an account of this nomic dimension of the required universals in terms of subjunctive or counterfactual conditionals and other quasi-syntactical criteria, such as unrestricted scope. Thus the unrestricted, nomic universal 'copper expands on being heated' supports the subjunctive conditional that if this piece of copper were heated it would expand, whereas the restricted, accidental universal that all the screws in Peter's car are rusty do not leave us with the same kind of confidence in the corresponding subjunctive conditional, i.e. if this were a screw from Peter's car, this would be rusty. Similarly, the above nomic universal supports the counterfactual conditional, say where a piece of copper has actually been destroyed by acid, if that piece of copper had been heated it would have expanded, whereas the corresponding counterfactual to the accidental universal does not enjoy the same degree of confidence.

In short, in the Hempelian D-N approach to explanation, we are directed to nomic universals and from there onto true counterfactual conditionals. The question now is one of giving a strict logical account of the distinction between true counterfactual conditionals supported by nomic universals and false counterfactuals. The standard concepts of truth-functional logic, such as material implication or its explication of a logically necessary inference in terms of a tautologous material implication, do not suffice. A material implication, by definition, is true when its antecedent is false and hence will not supply the required distinction. Moreover, a false proposition necessarily implies any proposition. Obviously there is little hope of drawing the required distinction between true and false counterfactual conditionals down this cul-de-sac. The culmination of the various attempts to articulate a persuasive account of either nomic universals or true counterfactual conditionals, compatible with the aims of either classical empiricism or logical positivism, was clearly inconclusive. Hempel put the spotlight on scientific explanation but he and others failed to give an account of this activity in terms compatible with the empiricist approach. An alternative account was required and this account was furnished by scientific realism.

The scientific realist succeeds in accounting for nomic universals in terms of essences, powers and capacities. This particular approach to scientific realism is clearly and cogently presented by Harré and Madden (1975). The notion of power, however, has not faired well in empiricism: the attribution of power to a substance or system is perceived by empiricists as the ascription of some mysterious or occult kind of quality which serves no useful scientific purpose. The attribution of a *virtus dormitiva* or dormitive power to opium, which in turn is used to explain the fact that opium induces sleep, is a standard empiricist example of the absurdity of such power ascriptions or the complete vacuousness of such explanatory hypotheses. This pseudo-explanation is replaced by the scientific account of the chemical constituents of opium, how these react with certain chemicals in the body, and how these biochemical reactions are regularly associated with sleep.

According to Harré and Madden, the attribution of a power to a substance, system or entity is not a quality attribution at all and *ipso facto* does not attribute an occult quality. Their interpretation follows from Ryle's famous analysis of dispositional properties, such as brittle, in terms of subjunctive conditionals, e.g. to say 'glass is brittle' is to say that 'if it is maltreated, it will break' and so on. However, they point out that the Rylean analysis of such dispositional properties in terms of predictions about how something would behave if certain conditions were fulfilled is too limiting and also fails to provide any coherent account of the truth-conditions of the subjunctive conditionals used in the analysis – the same problem as that encountered by the Hempelian account of nomic universals in terms of subjunctive conditionals. According to many scientific realists, the key insight is that things have powers even when these powers are not exercised. The difference between a substance which has a power to behave in a specific manner and one which lacks that power, is not a difference between what they will do. Rather, it is a difference of *intrinsic natures*. Thus they propose the following analysis of power ascriptions to things: 'X has the power to A', means 'X can (will) do A, in the appropriate conditions, in virtue of its intrinsic nature' (Harré and Madden 1975: 86). In short, any such scientific realist argues that he or she has a philosophical scheme which, like the Hempelians, accommodates the centrality of explanation without the Hempelian difficulties. In the next chapter we will show how such a realist conception of science informs Lawson's approach to economic methodology.

MODELS AND EXPLANATION

The Deductive-Nomological approach of Hempel and others clearly placed the methodological spotlight on scientific explanation. Other approaches were also used to focus in on this central scientific endeavour, especially the classification and analysis of models. Since the early 1960s the role of models in science has frequently been intimately related to either analogy or metaphor. This intimate relationship is summed up in the title of Max Black's *Models and Metaphors*, first published in 1962. In this work Black outlines four kinds of models. The simplest kind is the scale model, for instance, a model plane. As the name suggests, the key to a scale model is the preservation of relative proportions between relevant magnitudes of the model and that which is being modelled. Clearly, some features of the model are irrelevant or unimportant, while others are pertinent to the representation in question. Also, change of scale may introduce distortion. The sheer change of size, for instance, may upset the balance of factors in the original: too large a model of a housefly, as Black says, may never get off the ground. The obvious moral is that care must be exercised in drawing inferences from the scale model to the original. A similar vigilance must accompany the scientific use of other models.

The next kind of model discussed by Black is called an analogue model. This may also be called a structural model. This kind of model is based on an isomorphism of structure or pattern of relationships. It exploits the truth that the same structure may be embodied in very different systems. In general, an analogue model is some material object, system or process which reproduces in some new medium the structure or web of relationships in the original. Moreover, since identity of structure is compatible with a very wide variety of content, the possibilities for the construction of such models are endless. One may wish to suggest that analogue models are extensively used by Structuralist sociologists and anthropologists. For instance, an anthropologist may form the hypothesis that the structure of the kinship relations in tribe T_1 in location L_1 which one wishes to investigate, is the same as the structure of the kinship relationships in tribe T_2 in location L_2, about which one has a rich reservoir of information. The anthropologist thus uses the latter as an analogue model of the former. In such a case subsequent empirical study will be the final arbiter of the scientific fruitfulness of an analogue model. As Black puts it: 'Any would-be scientific use of an analogue model demands independent confirmation' (Black 1962: 223).

In this connection it may be useful to distinguish between the scientific and the metaphysical use of such a model. According to some economists, neoclassical economics gives the structure of the economic system of both primitive and contemporary capitalist societies. As Black points out, any such structural model requires independent confirmation. Prior to the actual anthropological investigations, the neoclassical model is merely furnishing a possible hypothesis: it does not provide the required evidence. The meta-physical use of such a model consists of imposing onto the actions and economic structures of primitive societies patterns of contemporary society which may not have existed. This makes the terms of neoclassical theory too elastic or all-inclusive, thereby not allowing for independent confirmation. Clearly, the metaphysical application of this model runs a major risk of misinterpretation. Eternal vigilance coupled with sound archaeological, anthropological-cum-historical research is the rule of the day *vis-à-vis* structural economical models claiming to reveal the structure of economies across large regions of both space and time.

The next category of model discussed by Black is the mathematical model. Indeed, he explicitly refers to Kenneth J. Arrow's use of the term 'mathemat-ical model' in noting the choice of name and the extent to which the term is used in the social sciences. Black sums up the use of a mathematical model in six procedures or steps: (a) Mathematical models are used in some later stage in the investigation of a domain. A number of variables are normally deemed as relevant prior to the introduction of a mathematical model. Indeed, one may add that, *ceteris paribus*, a preference is shown for extensive, rather than ordinal, variables. Black uses population studies to illustrate the use of a mathematical model. In population studies it is assumed by common sense that the variation of a population with time depends on the number of individuals born at the time, the number dying, the number entering the area and the number leaving. (b) Empirical hypotheses are framed concerning imputed relations between the selected variables. For instance, in population studies statistics suggest that the number of deaths during a brief period of time is proportional to the initial size of the population. (c) Simplifications or idealizations are introduced for the sake of facilitating the mathematical formulation and manipulation of the variables. As Terence Hutchison once remarked *vis-à-vis* the postulates of equilibrium economics, they are chosen for their 'tractability' (Caldwell 1982: 110). In the case of population studies, the changes are treated as if they were continuous. This follows from the use of differential equations in presenting the original data. (d) The mathematical equations are then solved or, alternatively, one studies global features of the constructed mathematical systems. For instance, the properties of the so-called 'logistic function' in population studies are completely specified. (e) An effort is made to extrapolate to empirical or testable consequences in the original field. In the case of population studies the model is used to predict that an isolated population tends towards a limiting size independent of its initial size. (f) Removing some of the initial restrictions imposed by the tractability considerations at (c) above will lead to increased generality of the model. The development of the general theory of relativity after the special theory exemplifies the latter step.

Like scale and analogue models, according to Black, mathematical models have both advantages and disadvantages. The advantages reside principally in the precision achieved in formulating relationships and the tractability which resides in the mathematical exploitation of the domain. Another advantage is the facility of mathematical analysis to reveal the structures involved. In this connection Black does not raise the question whether or not the mathematical structure of the model should be taken to correspond to the structure of the domain under investigation. However, in view of his balanced empirical attitude towards analogue models, one can easily anticipate his answer. The mathematical structure at best suggests empirical hypotheses which require detailed empirical investigation. Just as one must exercise care not to read a structural model in a metaphysical way, one must exercise a similar care with a mathematical model. The disadvantages of a mathematical model reside in its idealizations or simplifications demanded in the interests of tractability. Black re-echoes Poincaré's advice at the turn of the century, namely, that one should not confuse mathematical accuracy and elegance with empirical verification in any domain under investigation. In this connection Black makes a rather strong claim, namely, 'mathematical treatment furnishes no explanations' (Black 1962: 225). In other words, causal explanations are not very prevalent in mathematical models. The role of mathematics is largely logical, i.e. is concerned with inference from empirical data. The most that Black is willing to concede is that mathematical models provide the form of an explanation.

If mathematical models, in Black's opinion, fail to provide causal explanations, the same is certainly not true of the final category of model, namely, the theoretical model. The wave theory or model of light is a paradigmatic exemplar of a theoretical model. For the sake of clarity of presentation we will combine Black's account of theoretical models with that of Harré (Harré 1967: 86–100). Like the mathematical model, a theoretical model is introduced into the domain of investigation only when a certain amount of empirical knowledge is already available in that domain. There is, however, a perception on the part of the scientist that some regularities require further explanation or that the basic terms require additional explication, or that the original corpus of knowledge requires extension or modification. Thus the scientist constructs a model of the domain in light of 'a parent situation'. The particle theory of light, for example, had as its parent situation material particles, whereas the wave theory had sound as its parent situation. A parent situation is another domain which is already well explored and thus may serve as a fruitful model for the domain under investigation. Predicates are taken from the parent situation and applied, via the model, in the domain under investigation. For instance, in the parent situation of sound, one knows that sound waves have a velocity, wavelength, amplitude, frequency and so on. By means of the wave model of light, these predicates are taken from the parent situation and reapplied in the domain of optics. Physicists thus attempt to measure the velocity, amplitudes, wavelengths and so on of the various light waves. One cannot tell a priori how successful a theoretical model will be but, as more and more favourable empirical evidence is obtained, physicists move from saying light is like a wave to a more metaphorical way of speaking, namely, light is a wave.

Black distinguishes between the existential and the heuristic fictional usages of theoretical models (Black 1962: 228). If we think of light *as if* it were a wave we are in the realm of heuristic fictions. In this heuristic fictional approach we suspend judgement on ontological issues and thereby refuse to make existential statements. According to Black, the price paid for this heuristic fictional approach is the absence of explanatory power. On the other hand, the existential use of theoretical models, which is not lacking in explanatory power, allows for existential statements and he notes that this approach was adopted by many of the great theorists of the physical sciences. The pattern of explanation in this existential use of a theoretical model is spelled out by Harré (1967) as follows:

(a) Description of the fact, event or regularity to be explained.
(b) Description of the appropriate theoretical model.
(c) Statements linking the latter to the former.

In short, theoretical models have existential implications and are central to our explanatory endeavours. This existential focus on theoretical models also made a significant contribution to the development of scientific realism.

A METAPHORICAL VINDICATION OF THEORETICAL MODELS

Black has drawn our attention to two possible readings of a theoretical model, i.e. the heuristic-fictional one and the existential one. Before discussing the merits or otherwise of each of these readings, two points of agreement should be noted. First, theoretical models are extensively used in science and, second, recourse to such models has paid off. These observations are the common background to the dispute between heuristic fictionalists and their realist opponents. Heuristic fictionalists ranging from Duhem to Braithwaite hold that theoretical models are useful psychological surrogates for sophisticated logico-methodological procedures. Thus, in Black's pertinent phrase, theoretical models are 'disreputable understudies for mathematical formulas' or psychological 'props for feeble minds' (Black 1962: 235–6). A theoretical model is merely an imaginary concrete picture of a very abstract mathematical structure or set of equations which can only be grasped by our rational capacities. Logically and rationally, theoretical models are dispensable. They merely serve psychological purposes: they may furnish a feeling of familiarity with the fundamental postulates or they may aid us to intuitively grasp or picture these very abstract mathematical equations. Actual science which uses any such model can be recast in terms of a sophisticated logical structure of an axiomatic system combined with the empirical facts and regularities.

According to Black, heuristic fictionalists miss the central point of a theoretical model and, once we focus on this point, it becomes clearly evident that theoretical models play a distinctive and irreplacable role in scientific investigation. Contrary to heuristic fictionalists, the issue is neither the familiarity nor the intuitive capacity to furnish imaginative pictures of reality, which theoretical models certainly provide. Rather, the key to a novel successful theoretical model consists in the fact that it introduces a new way of *conceptualizing* an existing domain. One cannot in an a priori fashion predict when a new model will be constructed and, once constructed and accepted, one cannot paraphrase out of existence its new ways of conceptualizing the domain of inquiry. Take, for instance, the wave model of light. Prior to its construction scientists conceptualized optical phenomena in a way which made no reference to waves. However, once the wave theory took hold, physicists reconceptualized optical phenomena in radically new ways. These new ways of conceptualizing optical phenomena led to recategorizations and to the establishment of novel connections. Such radical reconceptualizations are indispensable to science. After the introduction of a successful model the old domain is seen in a new way. In short, scientists are forced to construct a new theoretical model when their existing ways of conceptualizing the domain under investigation is not entirely satisfactory. The new theoretical model introduces a new way of talking about the domain under investigation: it, as it were, stretches the language from the parent situation into the hitherto unrelated domain and the two are inextricably fused to form a novel way of reconceptualizing and approaching the domain under investigation.

As Black and others point out, theoretical models, thus understood, resemble metaphors. Indeed, the existential use of theoretical models is frequently explicated in terms of sustained, systematic, powerful metaphors. Metaphorical thought, particularly when construed according to Black's own interactive theory of metaphor, 'is a distinctive mode for achieving insight' and not 'an ornamental substitute for plain thought' (Black 1962: 237). A powerful, i.e. an emphatic and resonant, as opposed to a weak, metaphor brings two separate domains, which for convenience we shall call the primary and parent domains, into a cognitive relationship which cannot be subsequently paraphrased away in terms of some literal reconstruction. Such powerful metaphors accomplish shifts in meaning by selecting, emphasizing, supressing and restructuring the primary domain and thereby transforming it by inextricably merging it through metaphorical predication to a hitherto unrelated cognitive parent domain. These metaphors enable us to conceptualize the subject matter of the primary domain in radically new ways which, prior to the construction of the metaphor, could not be antecedently predicted nor in any way anticipated.

Thus a theoretical model is a sustained and systematic exploitation of a powerful metaphor. This conception of theoretical models establishes their indispensability against the heuristic fictionalists and simultaneously accounts for the novel revolutionary changes in theory so obvious in the history of science. Novel theories result from the scientific exploitation of imaginative, powerful metaphors. Imagination, which was not by any means cognitively recognized within the ambits of empiricism, is now seen as indispensable to the cognitive progress of the scientific endeavour, an insight which, as we saw in the last chapter, is exploited by McCloskey. In the next chapter we will see how theoretical models are interpreted and deployed by realists in their account of economics and in Chapter 7, contrary to McCloskey, we will outline a non-metaphorical vindication of models in the domain of causal holism. Be that as it may, the collapse of empiricism in the guise of logical positivism, initiated by Hempel's reinstatement of scientific explanation, was also accelerated by this Black-type analysis of scientific models. This collapse, however, had other sources, among which Quine's subtle and sophisticated analysis of scientific objectivity is of the utmost importance. We now turn to this analysis.

QUINE'S HOLISM AND SCIENTIFIC DESCRIPTION

Quine's name is not infrequently associated with complex and controversial questions in the domain of ontology, ranging over such issues as the radical indeterminacy of translation, the inscrutability of reference and ontological relativity. This broad range of philosophical issues, though perhaps crucially significant for those interested in the ontological implications of the physical sciences, has no apparent relevance for the philosopher of economics interested in analysing specific methodological issues of this unique social science. Prima facie this Quinian range of issues has nothing to say about, for instance, Friedman's defence of the neoclassical maximization hypothesis, the post-Keynesian critique of orthodox economics or the rhetorical turn advocated by McCloskey. This prima facie impression, however, may need qualification. It could be argued that the realist approach to science and its application to economic methodology as developed by, for instance, Lawson and Mäki, leaves a lot to be desired, precisely because it fails to meet the Quinian challenge articulated in a very sophisticated way in this constellation of issues. After all, Quine (1953) advocated 'empiricism without the dogmas' rather than scientific realism precisely because of his approach to the above range of issues. In this chapter we will not pursue this intriguing line of inquiry. Rather, we will focus on two other Quinian issues, namely, holism and his underdetermination thesis, issues which have a central bearing on our proposed reconstruction of the methodology of economics.

Quine does not base his philosophy on the analysis of the history of science – in this he stands out from, for instance, Buchdahl, Feyerabend, Grünbaum, Hesse, Hanson, Kuhn, McMullin and Lakatos, to mention but a handful. None the less, he has exercised an extensive and penetrating influence on numerous discussions among philosophers of science with a keen eye for the history of science. In the remainder of this chapter we will be concerned with this Quinian legacy. In his short piece, 'The Five Milestones of Empiricism' (Quine 1981) Quine's holistic approach to science becomes clearly evident. The five milestones are (a) the shift from ideas to terms, (b) the shift from terms to sentences, (c) the shift from sentences to systems of sentences, (d) the rejection of the analytic, synthetic distinction, (e) the abandonment of the goal of a first philosophy. Our central concern is with the first three milestones, especially the third. As we approach the end of this century, the first milestone of empiricism, namely, the shift from ideas to words, is frequently taken for granted, especially in the British–American philosophical tradition. In the language of Hacking, much of Western philosophy has moved from 'the heyday of ideas' of Enlightenment philosophy to 'the heyday of meanings' with its specific twentieth-century focus on the the sense or usage of terms (Hacking 1975).

The second milestone, namely, the shift from terms to sentences, can be summed up in Frege's famous dictum, namely, never take the meaning of a word in isolation but only in the context of a proposition. While Frege arguably did not give due weight to this dictum, Quine certainly does. He gives the epistemological primacy to sentences, not terms. This should not be too surprising in a post-Wittgensteinian world of meaning. The later Wittgenstein urged that the meaning of a word is its usage, and clearly words are centrally used in sentences. Thus Quine is insistent and emphatic about the shift to sentences. We all accept the truism that we give advice, admonish, praise, blame, reprimand, tell jokes, pass judgments in courts of law, assert propositions which are true or false and so forth, by means of sentences, not words in isolation from sentences. In our non-philosophical moods we reflect the primacy of the sentence. A person who could neither understand nor formulate any sentence at all, e.g. a person whose understanding of language is limited to the ostensive utterances of words, is, in this Quinian world, severely conceptually incapacitated. Tragically, our worlds of common-sense knowledge and of science, as well as the worlds of literature, poetry, theological speculation, and so on, are outside her or his cognitive abilities. Indeed, according to Quine, when we say that one is using a term ostensively, for instance, using the word 'rabbit' when pointing to rabbits, the more accurate account is to say that such a person is using the one-word sentence, 'Rabbit', in response to the appropriate stimulation of her or his sensory organs. In this view we were not quite accurate in our previous remark where we spoke of a person who could utter no sentence at all: we should have said that a person whose understanding of a language is limited to the understanding of ostensive, one-word sentences is severely cognitively incapacitated. Clearly, Quine is uncompromising in the shift from terms to sentences. Sentences are at the focus of epistemology and philosophy of science: scientific knowledge is conveyed paradigmatically by sentences.

The full extent of Quine's holism becomes evident in the third milestone, namely, the shift from sentences to systems of sentences. Quine is equally emphatic and uncompromising about this shift. Indeed, it is arguable that much of his philosophical position hinges on it. However, this shift is frequently seen as totally counterintuitive and lacking in justification. We will use two examples and Wittgenstein's later philosophy to show that there is at least a prima facie case in favour of this Quinian milestone. Quine himself illustrates this holistic aspect of sentences by means of the following example. Laboratory chemists are asked to ascertain whether or not a given solution is an acid. They observe that it turns blue litmus paper red and they immediately note that it is an acid. This latter empirical judgement or factual report is implicitly dependent on a whole section of chemistry, i.e. the belief that the solution is an acid is located in a web of beliefs in the appropriate chapter of chemistry. Without this intervening web, the factual claim does not stand. In short, factual beliefs do not occur in isolation: they occur in systems of beliefs. The atomistic assumption of the early logical positivists, which postulated sentences in total independence of one another, missed this crucial holistic dimension of our factual sentences or claims.

Perhaps a different chemical example, this time with a historical flavour, will make this holistic dimension more evident. Chemists identify various gases such as oxygen or hydrogen. For instance, if the contents of a gas jar comply with the contemporary chemist's criteria for oxygen, then *it is a fact* that the gas in question is oxygen and not hydrogen or some other gas. However, when Priestly first isolated what chemists today factually identify as oxygen, he identified it as dephlogisticated air. Priestly did not have current atomic theory at his disposal. Rather, he was working with the now defunct phlogiston theory. The point is that his factual identification, like ours, presupposed some theory – he presupposed phlogiston theory, whereas today's identification presupposes current atomic theory. The latter theory supplies the required background web of sentences in the contemporary chemist's identification of oxygen. Without atomic theory such a factual identification could not take place. The factual sentence 'that gas is oxygen' is embedded in the system of sentences of atomic chemistry: it does not stand on its own. The same holds true for our other factual assertions. Our knowledge of the world comes in, or presupposes, holistic systems of sentences.

Finally, this holistic dimension is explicit in the later Wittgenstein's philosophy of language. The meaning of a term, as we already noted, is its public usage in a sentence or sentences. If we wish to ascertain whether or not a person understands the word 'inflation', we indulge him or her in conversation. If he or she uses the word 'inflation' the way it is normally used in the English language then we concede that the person understands it correctly. We check its usage in a multiplicity of sentences. Indeed, the later Wittgenstein explicitly advised us to locate such sentence usages in their appropriate language-games. In this perspective a word which has a meaning in one language-game may be meaningless when transferred to another. For instance, we know what it means when one asks us to prove Pytagoras' theorem in mathematics. However, if one asks us to prove that other persons exist in the language-game of a court of law, one's demand is meaningless. According to the later Wittgenstein, there are different language-games, and meaningful sentences must be located in their appropriate language-games. Clearly, this Wittgensteinian linguistic philosophy butresses Quine's holistic thesis.

In view of Quine's third milestone of empiricism, the conventional conception of descriptive language outlined in section one above, a conception shared by many common-sense realists and traditional empiricists, is in need of radical modification. If Quine is correct, there is no purely factual language adequate for scientific descriptive purposes, a philosophical thesis exploited by Kuhn, Feyerabend and many others who adopt a historical approach to philosophy of science. Indeed, many of the case studies used by these latter philosophers of science furnish concrete historical examples of Quine's holistic thesis. The extent of the methodological implications of this holism can be seen if one inquires about the role of theory in science in the context of Quine's third milestone. In Quine's holism, theory is indispensable for *descriptive* purposes: as far as we can tell it is impossible to describe the external world without recourse to theory. According to the received dogma of logical positivism, description is independent of theory. The logical positivists assumed that there is a purely descriptive language available in which the scientific facts can be presented in a theory-neutral way. In Quine's holistic approach, the *sine qua non* of theory is description. Given the holistic dimension of our natural languages and their extensions in science, a scientific theory is indispensable for scientific or factual description.

This Quinian vindication of theory in the context of factual descriptions clearly demarcates Quine's holism from descriptivism, instrumentalism and common-sense realism. Contrary to descriptivism, there is no question of reducing theoretical terms, via reduction sentences or some other mechanisms, to purely observational terms. In Quine's view the latter category is empty. Neither is there any temptation to go down the instrumentalist road where theory is merely some heuristic device. Furthermore, contrary to common-sense scientific realism, scientific theory is neither paradigmatically nor stereotypically related to explanation. For the first time in the philosophy of science, the descriptive indispensability of theory is unequivocally defended. As far as we can tell, our factual descriptions are parasitic upon some theory or other and thereby the common-sense, intimate relationship between theory and explanation is divorced. In Quine's holism, scientific theory is liberated from its confinement to the shadows of explanation and now basks in the sunlit space of factual description. In short, scientific description is theory-laden. Today, as Laudan for instance notes, positivists, realists, pragmatists and presumably hosts of others accept that observation is theory-laden (Laudan 1990: 34). Although in a short period of time this insight has, in Laudan's opinion, become a 'tired old cliche', we will argue that it continues to have methodological relevance, especially in the context of the critique of the scientific realist conception of scientific explanation in general and of economic explanation in particular. Quine's holism suggests that the deeply engrained tacit assumption held by numerous economists and economic methodologists, namely, that the central function of an economic theory is to explain some economic fact, range of facts or some low-level economic generalization presented in a theory-neutral descriptive language, does not stand up to critical scrutiny.

HOLISM AND THE DUHEM–QUINE
UNDERDETERMINATION THESES

Quine's classical piece, 'Two Dogmas of Empiricism', first published in 1951, contains his famous formulation of what has been called the Duhem–Quine underdetermination thesis. After presenting a novel and challenging critique of logical positivism, Quine sums up his own position as follows:

> The totality of our so-called knowledge or beliefs, from the most casual matters of geography and history to the profoundest laws of atomic physics or even of pure mathematics and logic, is a man-made fabric which impinges on experience only along the edges.
>
> (Quine 1953: 42)

In the course of this piece, Quine is at pains to point out that statements about the world face 'the tribunal of sense experience not individually but only as a corporate body' (Quine 1953: 41). As Mary Hesse, for instance, pointed out over twenty years ago, for Quine scientific knowledge does face the tribunal of experience (Hesse 1970: 195). We pointed out in the last section that our descriptions are theory-laden. It immediately follows that no observation statement taken in isolation can mirror-image or correspond to an identifiable portion of the external world. However, our factual statements do come before the bar of experience holistically: Quine is advocating an empiricism without the dogmas and not some form of idealism where sensory experience has no significant role. Moreover, Quine spells this out in numerous other works. In his 'Epistemology Naturalized', for instance, he maintains that the proposition 'whatever evidence there is for science is sensory evidence' remains as an unassailable 'cardinal tenet of empiricism' (Quine 1969: 75). Part of Quine's originality lies in his intriguing account of how scientific knowledge does come before the bar of experience in a holistic fashion.

In this connection we will follow Laudan's distinction between Quine's holism understood as a theory of meaning, which we briefly discussed in the last section, and his holism understood as a theory of testing (Laudan

1990: 70). A significant dimension of the Duhem–Quine underdetermination thesis is focused on the latter theory of testing. In this context we distinguish between three versions of this theory. As already noted, the underdetermination thesis holds that single descriptive propositions are never tested in isolation; rather empirical testing presupposes complexes or systems of sentences. We call this the weak version of the Duhem–Quine underdetermination thesis. This weak thesis at the level of testing follows from the meaning dimension of Quine's holism. Since meaning is characterized as existing within a system of sentences, it follows that, at the level of testing, a single descriptive sentence cannot be tested on its own. More precisely, the assertion of Quine's holism at the level of meaning and the denial of the weak Duhem–Quine underdetermination thesis at the level of testing is inconsistent.

A second and stronger underdetermination thesis is also implicit in Quine's work. Hesse formulates this stronger thesis as follows. 'No *descriptive* statement can be individually falsified by evidence, whatever the evidence may be, since adjustments in the rest of the system can always be devised to prevent its *falsification*' (Hesse 1970: 195, italics ours). The weak thesis simply asserts that single propositions are not tested individually. The weak thesis makes no reference to the issue of adjusting the system for the purposes of preventing the falsification of some preferred proposition or belief. This latter issue is raised and resolved by the formulation of the stronger underdetermination thesis. This stronger formulation asserts that science can dramatically adjust its system in order to prevent the falsification of any descriptive sentence taken by itself.

The acceptance of this stronger Duhem–Quine underdetermination thesis, as Hesse perceptively points out, appears to many philosophers to entail the abandonment of any empirical dimension to science. Hesse, however, does not accept this conclusion. This stronger Duhem–Quine (D–Q) underdetermination thesis explicitly allows for the bar of experience at a holistic level. It is a scientific system as a whole, rather than individual propositions, which comes before the tribunal of experience. Nevertheless, even if one grants this, Popper, for instance, is arguably correct in pointing out that actual science can and does refute definite portions of a theory and this stronger version of the underdetermination thesis cannot coherently account for this fact (Popper 1963: 243). Popper is drawing our attention to the scientific practice of empirically testing individual propositions which is as old as science itself. While the stronger D–Q thesis challenges this practice, we maintain that the weak D–Q thesis does not. Rather, the latter retains the scientific practice but fully acknowledges its fragility and fallibility.

Let us briefly look at some usual ways in which it has been suggested that an isolated proposition may be refuted. The first concerns the Popperian notion of testing *vis-à-vis* background knowledge. According to some Popperians we can hold the background knowledge stable and thereby refute an isolated hypothesis. Weak Duhem–Quine theorists have no objection to this pragmatic approach. On the contrary, they quickly draw our attention to the fact that such an acceptance or retention of the background knowledge is, even by Popperian standards, provisional. Consequently, this Popperian strategy is not incompatible with the weak Duhem–Quine thesis. Indeed there is nothing in the latter approach which rules out this kind of pragmatic strategy. The weak D–Q thesis underlines both the delicateness of this strategy and its pragmatic character. Second, it is logically possible that a theoretical system may be axiomatized in such a way that the consequences of a single axiom can be identified. If any of these consequences is falsified then the single individual axiom is clearly in difficulty. Like the previous situation, weak Duhem–Quine theorists are not in difficulty. In view of Quine's holistic theory of meaning, the single axiom and its isolated consequences are themselves theory-laden. Moreover, no axiomatic system on its own can account for a scientific theory. Any axiomatization of a piece of science requires both axioms and so-called 'correspondence rules' or other conditions required for its application to an empirical domain. The latter rules or conditions could in some suitable set of circumstances be revised but once again weak Duhem–Quine theorists have no objection to holding these stable in normal circumstances. Clearly, there is a provisional dimension to this pragmatic decision rendering it compatible with their holistic position.

Finally, practising scientists tend to divide their theories into high-level and low-level parts and they frequently hold that the lower-level is better corroborated or confirmed than the higher-level. Consequently, if a scientific theory is falsified by some evidence, the scientists, quite correctly, tend to locate the responsibility in the less confirmed parts of the theory. Without prejudice to the complexities of confirmation theory, weak Duhem–Quine theorists have no difficulty either with this practical strategy. In short, weak Duhem–Quine theorists do not make a fundamental or epistemological distinction between the theoretical and observational aspects of science. This, however, does not mean that they do not accept the wisdom of various pragmatic procedures developed during the course of the history of science. Their point is that these pragmatic approaches have no grounding in some absolutist foundational epistemology. The fifth milestone of empiricism, namely, the abandonment of a first philosophy, comes into play at this juncture. Our epistemological endeavours are much more fragile and modest than those sanctioned by the reconstruction of the whole edifice of knowledge from indubitable foundations.

We now turn to the Duhem–Quine underdetermination thesis in its third and strongest version. This is summed up in Quine's dictum: 'Any statement can be held true come what may, if we make drastic enough adjustments elsewhere in the system' (Quine 1953: 43). This strongest thesis is very radical. It applies to every kind of statement – descriptive, theoretical, law-like, a priori, analytical, logical laws and so on, whereas the stronger thesis merely applies to descriptive statements. The fourth milestone of empiricism, namely, the famous Quinian rejection of the analytic/synthetic dichotomy, is a principal player in this extension to every kind of statement. Since the whole of our knowledge is a man-made web which touches reality only along the edges, there is no foundational epistemological way of neatly dividing this web into purely analytical and synthetic dimensions or, if one prefers, into logical and empirical dimensions. Hence the thesis is extended to every kind of statement. Moreover, unlike the stronger thesis, it goes way beyond the issue of the falsifiability of an individual descriptive statement or scientific hypothesis. The focus is on the truth of such statements or hypotheses, rather than their probability or falsifiability. The strongest thesis maintains that any statement can be held true by adding sufficiently drastic adjustments to the rest of the system. Clearly, this strongest thesis sails very close to the winds of relativism.

Quine himself endorses all three theses. Indeed, since the weak and the stronger theses are implied by the strongest underdetermination thesis, the three theses are frequently not clearly distinguished from each other. For our purposes, however, this distinction is vital. We are not starting with the D–Q thesis in its strongest version. Rather, we are starting with Quine's holism at the level of meaning, especially the thesis that all scientific descriptions are theory-laden, and thereby we have no reservations about the first three milestones of empiricism as adumbrated above. Our question is: what price must be paid at the level of testing for accepting this holistic thesis at the level of meaning? Quine himself, at least as commonly interpreted, wants to extract the highest price, i.e. the strongest underdetermination thesis. We have argued that there is no need to pay such a high price. The weak underdetermination thesis is necessarily implied by Quine's holism at the level of meaning, but this in turn does not necessarily imply either the stronger or the strongest thesis. In particular, in view of the fifth milestone, i.e. there is no prior philosophy, the weak D–Q underdetermination theorist holds that the age-old scientific strategy of testing statements in isolation is not grounded in some absolutist foundational epistemology. According to the fifth milestone, there is no such epistemological vantage point. However, that does not imply that this age-old strategy, when properly used, is not a wise practice. The weak D–Q underdetermination theorist retains it as such and thereby draws our attention to its sheer contingency and fallibility. In principle, science has the option of questioning the results of the empirical testing of individual sentences. Wisdom, however, teaches science not to exercise this option except, first, where there has been abuse of its conventional well-tried operational procedures and, second, when normal science is undergoing a revolutionary change. In the latter eventuality there is no algorithmetical way for deciding whether or not the option should be exercised. For our purposes we are rejecting the stronger and the strongest underdetermination theses and thereby limiting our interest in Quine to the holistic theory of meaning and to the weak underdetermination thesis. It is these aspects of Quine's philosophy of science which we wish to exploit in the methodology of economics from the causal holist perspective.

4

SCIENTIFIC REALISM
Methodology reinstated

According to numerous commentators, ranging from Davidson to Laudan, Quine's work, especially the strongest version of the D–Q underdetermination thesis, has unmistakable relativist implications, though these implications are expressly rejected by Quine himself. This rejection is not seen as surprising: with notable exceptions, such as Margolis, contemporary philosophers who occupy the conceptual space of relativism emphatically reject any attachment of a relativist label to themselves. Be that as it may, it could be argued that much of the relativism which is said to vitiate Quine's more intricate writings is given a more tangible, historical expression in the works of Kuhn. Aside entirely from Kuhn's explicit acknowledgement of an intellectual debt to Quine in his *Structures of Scientific Revolutions*, (Kuhn 1962) a Kuhnian paradigm can be seen as a specific historico-scientific explication or a novel original articulation of Quine's milestones of empiricism. In the Kuhnian historico-sociological approach to philosophy of science, scientific description is theory-laden, the emphasis is on the location of sentences within paradigms, which can be viewed as concrete historical exemplars of Quinian conceptual schemes, and the Duhem–Quine underdetermination theses appear to reign supreme. Hence, since Kuhn spells out these central Quinian themes in more concrete historical terms, their relativistic implications are more patently visible there than in Quine's more abstract approach.

RELATIVISM AND REALISM

This relativism becomes clearly apparent in, among others, the issue of theory choice. As we already noted, in a Quinian world the Popperian conception of theory choice does not apply. According to the Popperian view of scientific progress, a fallible theory, T_2, is better than any rival fallible theory, T_1, when (a) both T_1 and T_2 have consequences $C_1 \ldots C_n$ and each C_i is true, (b) T_2 has consequence C_{n+1} and T_1 has a contrary of C_{n+1} as its consequence and (c) C_{n+1} is true. This Popperian conception of scientific progress at the theoretical level totally fails to accommodate the Quinian thesis that all factual statements are theory-laden. T_1 and T_2, contrary to Popper, cannot be assumed to have the same consequences C_i in common. On the contrary, to use the standard terminology, there is meaning variance across the theoretical divide: the consequences of T_1, even if they contain the same tokens or words as those of T_2, are different in meaning. This meaning variance is implied by Quine's holism and is explicitly spelled out in its full historical richness by Kuhn. For instance, Kuhn, completely in keeping with the Quinian milestones, reminds us that the terms 'mass' or 'energy', though common to both Newtonian and Einsteinian relativity theories, are used differently in both and hence have a different meaning or sense. Such meaning variances are integral to the Kuhnian thesis of incommensurability, a thesis which in the eyes of many of its opponents inevitably leads to relativism.

This issue of meaning variance is exploited by Kuhn in an original fashion which, as Newton-Smith for instance remarks (Newton-Smith 1981: 119), gives the impression that Kuhn subscribes to some kind of non-objectivist, idealist doctrine. The infamous quote goes as follows:

> I have so far argued only that paradigms are constitutive of science. Now I wish to display a sense in which they are constitutive of nature as well. In a sense that I am unable to explicate further, the proponents of competing paradigms practise their trades in different worlds.... Practising in different worlds, the two groups of scientists see different things when they look from the same point in the same direction.
>
> (Kuhn 1970: 150)

Many commentators have found this passage, which re-echoes Quine's thesis of the inscrutability of reference and which suggests an ontologically different world following a change in paradigm, both enigmatic and exaggerated. However, if we view it in the following Frege–Wittgenstein–Quine way, the radical incommensurability of Kuhnian paradigms becomes plausible and thereby contemporary relativism more resonant.

The first Fregian thesis consists of the hypothesis that the term 'meaning' is equivocal and should be replaced by two distinct concepts, namely, sense and reference. In other words, if one takes any common noun or adjective one can ask (a) what is its sense? and (b) does it refer? The fact that a term has a sense does not guarantee that it has a reference or referent in the actual world. For instance, the term 'gold' has both a sense and reference while the term 'phlogiston' has a sense but lacks a reference. Moreover, many terms with different senses have different referents, such as, triangle, square, circle, cow, cat or whale. However, some terms with different senses may have the same referent. The positive square root of eighty-one and the notion of seventy-two divided by eight have different senses but they refer to the same number, i.e. nine. In this mathematical example the ascertainment of the identity of reference is a question of proof. In other cases the ascertainment of identity of reference is a matter of empirical investigation. For instance, the expressions 'the largest city in England' and 'the city located on the mouth of the Thames' have different senses but the same reference. In the absence of such a proof or discovery we cannot rationally assume that terms with different senses refer to the same entity or entities. In particular, abandoned descriptions, i.e. descriptions which are not true of the referent, and descriptions used in their place clearly do not co-refer. For instance, the abandoned descriptive term 'possession by a devil' and its replacement 'suffering from epilepsy' do not co-refer: we want to say that there is no such thing as the former but clearly epilepsy is real.

The second thesis is also due to Frege, namely, we ascertain the reference of a term through its sense or, for short, the sense determines the referent. For example, how do we know that the geometrical object drawn on the blackboard is a triangle? We know that the sense of the word triangle is a plane figure enclosed by three straight lines and we observe that these characteristics apply to the figure on the blackboard. Without grasping the sense, we could not ascertain whether or not the term 'triangle' could be truly predicated of the blackboard figure. In this fashion the sense is said to determine reference. The third thesis is the Wittgensteinian truism that the sense of a word consists of its correct usage in the appropriate language-game. In a Quinian context this entails locating the sense in a conceptual scheme or scientific theory. To take an example from the history of science, the way the early Greeks used the word 'sun' and the way it is used in contemporary physics is clearly different. Hence the sense of the term 'sun' for such a Greek would be different to its sense for a contemporary physicist.

If we apply these three theses to, say, the term 'atom' as used in the first decade of this century and that used by scientists today, we arrive at the counterintuitive Kuhnian claim that, despite the fact that both communities of scientists use the same word 'atom', its sense or usage is clearly different. Moreover since the sense determines the reference, we have no good reason to assume that, say, Thomson or Rutherford were referring to the same entity as Hawking or Penrose are referring to today in using the same token 'atom'. This is particularly the case when we take into account that the manner in which Thomson and Rutherford described the atom is, by our standards, false. As we already noted, abandoned descriptions and descriptions used in their place do not co-refer. Thus the issue of meaning variance across theoretical divides raises fundamental problems about the referents of terms. Our holistic epistemological conceptions give us no guarantee of the same world across theoretical divides. Though to say that scientists are working in different ontological worlds is not sufficiently precise, the issue of meaning variance does raise fundamental problems about the commensurability of rival theories at the level of reference. Given a Quinian, holistic epistemology, we have no guarantee that the same token or term used in different ways, in different theories refers to the same class of entities. Our common-sense presuppositions on this matter, though deeply engrained, do not stand up to critical scrutiny.

This meaning variance in turn leads to another central relativist thesis, namely, that truth is relative to a specific paradigm, system or conceptual scheme. The basic notion of truth must read something like this: 'proposition 'p' is true in system, or paradigm or conceptual scheme S if and only if . . .', and hence the correspondence theory of truth no longer holds. It is beyond the scope of this work to explore these challenging issues. For those interested, the contemporary tapestry of relativism is ingeneously reconstructed by Margolis (1991) in his *Truth about Relativism*. This challenging work bears out Laudan's claim that 'one simply cannot address contemporary relativism and ignore how central Kuhnian and Quinian themes have become for that tradition' (Laudan 1990: xi). Hence, it could be argued that any recourse to Quine in the methodology of economics as a means of rejecting rhetoric is merely going from the proverbial frying pan into the fire. The consensus is that Quinean themes are central to the tapestry of contemporary relativism, a fate which is at least as bad if not worse than that of rhetoric. We shall see in Chapter 7 how the causal holist resolves the issue of meaning variance without embracing a self-defeating relativism.

In the meantime, however, we wish to focus on an entirely different issue, i.e. the manner in which scientific realism deconstructs the tapestry of contemporary relativism while it simultaneously vindicates the objectivity of the scientific endeavour. In particular, scientific realism, as articulated by the early Putnam and other causal theorists of reference, either totally eschews or resolves the relativist issues of meaning variance. Just as scientific realism gives a more cogent account of scientific explanation than that offered by the empiricist tradition, it also succeeds in avoiding the pitfalls of relativism. The widespread consensus about a realist approach or approaches to the philosophy of science which has emerged since the 1970s is not just some passing fancy. Rather, it is based on realism's perceived successes in a wide range of issues which have engaged the contemporary philosopher of science. It is not surprising that realist themes are now being articulated in the methodology of economics. Indeed, the surprise resides in the fact that this has not occurred much earlier and has not been more extensive.

The causal theory of reference was introduced by Kripke and Putnam. It applies to proper names, natural kind terms, such as gold or lemon, artefactual terms, such as pencil or computer, physical magnitude terms, such as electricity and to theoretical terms. For expository purposes we shall sketch this theory for proper names. First, the introduction of a proper name, N, requires an act of initial baptism. In this initial baptism an individual is segregated from all other individuals and is thus pinned down for the establishment of a direct, non-attribute mediated, connection between N and its referent. Second, a speaker who uses sentences containing N need not witness nor in any way participate in the initial baptismal act. Rather, a speaker using N succeeds in referring to N's referent only if there is a causal chain of events linking the initial baptism to the speaker. It is both the initial baptism and the causal chain which explains how we succeed in referring to, say, Adam Smith or other historical figures using proper names. We belong to a collective or community, namely, historians of economic thought, who can trace this causal chain back to the introducing event. It is not necessary that the user of the name be in any way familiar with the manner in which the causal chain is established. All that is required is that such a chain exists. Third, the designation of a referent by a proper name is *rigid*. In other words, in any possible world discussed containing the proper name N, N has the same referent. Thus, for instance, when speculating what would have happened if David Ricardo had not entered the London Stock Exchange, the name 'Ricardo' refers to the same person as referred to by historians of political economy who use that name.

The causal theory of reference for proper names has many advantages over the Fregian view that the use of a proper name presupposes a criterion of identity for the name's referent. It accounts for the fact that different speakers can and do use the same name to refer to an entity without these speakers sharing some common definite description. It also accounts for the fact that very poor history students succeed in referring to, say, Alfred Marshall, without having any true beliefs about the referent of that name. Thus the Fregian principle enunciated above in connection with the issue of meaning variance, namely, that the sense determines the reference and that false descriptions associated with a term prohibit that term from having a rigid referent, are not correct at least in the case of proper names.

According to the causal theory of reference as developed by Putnam, the same holds true for natural kind, physical magnitude, artefactual and theoretical terms. The referents of natural kind terms, such as gold, are also established by direct demonstration or ostension in a kind of 'baptismal act' or introducing event in which a natural kind term is posited. The initial baptism is a kind of 'inaugural referential use' (Leplin 1988: 498). However, in the original baptismal act, 'the principle of Benefit of Doubt' (Putnam 1975a: 274) must be applied to the original dubber or the relevant expert. We give the original dubber the benefit of the doubt in certain cases by assuming that he or she would accept reasonable modifications of his or her criteria or descriptions used in the inaugural situation. For instance, we can imagine an original dubber pointing out whales to a child and saying that whales are fish. In short, the original dubber is fallible. Second, we, the contemporary users of natural kind words need not witness nor in any way participate in the initial inaugural event. Rather, it suffices that we belong to a community which, through a chain of causal events, relates back to the initial introduction. Moreover, like the original dubber, we too are fallible. The Principle of Reasonable Ignorance applies to our usage of natural kind terms. Thus, for instance, we know how to use the word 'gold' correctly, despite the fact that we are unable to distinguish between genuine gold and fool's gold: we are reasonably ignorant about the criteria of genuine gold. Once again the Fregian principle, which was at the root of the referential relativist difficulties raised by the problem of meaning variance, namely, the sense determines the reference, does not apply to natural kind words. Rather, in our usage of the natural kind word 'gold', its reference is determined by the fact that we belong to a collective or group, some expert members of which establish the causal link or chain to the inaugural introducing event.

Third, like the case of proper names, natural kind words are rigid designators: they refer to the same kind of thing in every possible world. What is of crucial significance for us is the fact that such rigid designations are intimately connected to essential properties. In the last chapter we saw how the realist account of scientific explanation articulated the view that science, by its theoretical endeavours, reveals the hidden essences of nature. In the causal theory of reference, essences are also a *sine qua non* of science. In this case the recourse to essences is mediated by the theme of the rigid designation of natural kind words and, as we shall see in a few moments, by theoretical terms. In short, the referents of natural kind words have essential properties, i.e. properties which an object could not possibly lack in any possible world in order to be a thing of that kind. Thus, to take Putnam's example of water. The rigidity of the designation of this natural kind term is evident in the following analysis. In every possible world W, and for every x in W, x is water if x bears a certain sameness relation to the stuff we refer to as water in the actual world W_1 (Putnam 1975a: 231). Since mature science informs us that the nature of water is H_2O we will not count anything as water unless it bears this sameness relation to our water. Moreover, as the example clearly illustrates, sameness relationships which hold between the referents of natural kind words are theoretical ones. Indeed, Putnam is explicit on this point: these sameness relationships are ones which theoretical science discovers (Putnam 1975a: 225). The causal theory of reference as applied to natural kind terms also undermines the referential paradoxes or difficulties engendered by the problem of meaning variance. Moreover, it reinstates essential characteristics of natural kinds and it sees science through the development of its theories as approximating to these essences. Science, and not metaphysics or philosophy of language or whatever, discovers the hidden essences of natural kinds.

The causal theory of reference is extended to theoretical terms such as 'quark' or 'electron' by slightly modifying the account of the inaugural situation. In the case of natural kind terms there is an indispensable ostensive element involved in the initial baptism: water refers to, for instance, the stuff in the river at hand or in the glass in front of us or some other clear exemplar. However, we cannot point in this way to electrons or quarks. Putnam readily admits this but maintains that we can adjust the causal theory to such cases by noting a related way of introducing some theoretical terms. We can imagine a scientist saying that he believes that there is a particle, which is responsible for such-and-such observable effects and that he is calling this an electron. In such inaugural cases the Principle of Benefit of Doubt will apply to the expert. Thus Putnam draws our attention to the fact that there is nothing in the world which exactly fits Bohr's description of an electron. However, there are particles which cause the key effects identified by Bohr and his contemporaries. The Principle of Benefit of Doubt dictates that we treat Bohr as referring to these particles when he used the term electron.

Once again the causal theory of reference undermines the referential qualms of the relativist. It acknowledges that science is fallible but it sees science as hunting for the hidden essences of nature. As Leplin puts it:

> After all, according to CTR (causal theory of reference) it is science that tells us what properties are essential, and science makes mistakes. Then CTR allows revision of attribution of essential properties. . . . In effect CTR appeals to "final science" for determinations of essential properties. As we lack final science, we could be wrong about essential properties. Yet we have evidence and probably satisfy the conditions for knowing what are [some] essential properties, although perhaps not for knowing that we do.
>
> (Leplin 1988: 500)

SOME CENTRAL THEMES OF SCIENTIFIC REALISM

In the previous section a very schematic account of the causal theory of reference was introduced with the intention of furnishing some conception of how scientific realism emerged in the seventies as a dominant philosophy of science. When this is taken in conjunction with the previous chapter, scientific realism, in its historical development, is seen as an alternative to various empiricist-positivist approaches to science on the one hand and as an alternative to varieties of relativism on the other. However, in view of the vast number of realists, one would expect that scientific realism would not consist of a monolithic fixed set of dogmas. A quick survey of the literature bears out this expectation. There are varieties of realism ranging from variations of the causal theory of reference at one end of the spectrum to variations of Hooker's evolutionary naturalist realism at the other end. Indeed, as Hooker correctly points out, there is 'a certain taxonomic disarray at present' (Hooker 1987: 258). Horwich, Hellman, Leplin, Mäki and Newton-Smith, to mention but a few, attempt to introduce some order into the contemporary disarray. In this section we do not propose any such effort. Indeed, we are not convinced that any such taxonomy will do justice to the full complexity of the situation. Rather, to use Putnam's terminology, we will list some of the 'stereotypes' of scientific realism, noting with Putnam that propositions expressing stereotypical characteristics are not analytic truths. In other words, any actual scientific realist may not accept the full package of stereotypes but would accept a substantial number of these stereotypes or some reasonable modifications thereof.

89

Newton-Smith remarks that all scientific realists share a minimal common factor, namely, that, contrary to philosophical instrumentalism, the sentences of a theory are true or false and, second, contrary to relativism, these sentences are true or false in virtue of how the world is independently of ourselves (Newton-Smith 1981: 21). A central ontological thesis of the latter is further explicated to read as follows. The actual world exists independently of any and every knowing subject. In Hooker's more apt terminology, 'existence is logically and conceptually independent of epistemic conditions' (Hooker 1987: 156). Moreover, contrary to Kantian idealism where the object in itself is not knowable, the independently existing world is knowable. Indeed, many realists are committed to knowable, unchanging objects or natural kinds or essences, where natural kinds have essential properties which exist independently of us and we are capable of knowing these. These constitute four stereotypes of scientific realism.

The question can now be raised as to the means by which we come to know these real subsistent objects or essences. However, before addressing this, the logically prior question, i.e. by what means do we come to know that there are unchanging objects or essences, may be asked. Realists diverge on this. Some, such as Kripke, will have recourse to the philosophy of logic combined with a philosophy of language. Others will argue from a naturalistic standpoint in which there is no rigid sharp boundary between philosophy and science. Hooker would fall into this category. Others, such as Bhaskar, will reject this variety of naturalism and argue that philosophy is distinct from science especially in its use of some kind of Kantian-type transcendental arguments. With respect to the means by which we come to know what these unchanging objects or essences are, a variety of answers is also possible. Logically, one could opt for a position rather close to Kantian idealism by maintaining that there must be such objects or essences but these remain unknowable to us. Another logical possibility is that we come to know what these objects or essences are through either metaphysics or transcendental arguments or philosophy of logic or philosophy of language or some other non-scientific means such as intuition, tacit knowledge or some 'lumen naturale'. We will take it as a stereotype of scientific realism that it is through science, rather than any of these other means, that we learn what we can know about the actual world and its unchanging objects or essential characteristics. In particular, theoretical science reveals these to us. In other words, the principal aim of science is to reveal the unchanging objects of nature or their hidden essences and this aim is achieved in mature theoretical science.

In this fashion, theories are central to the realist account of science. In this account, however, theories are neither filing cabinets nor heuristic devices nor sets of mathematical equations in a mathematical model. As we already said, theoretical sentences are propositions, i.e. they are true or false, and their theoretical terms are not reducible to observational ones. Rather, the former refer to the unobservable generative mechanisms of nature. The realist thus emphatically embraces the distinction between explanation and prediction. Theory not only aims at prediction, it is also centrally concerned with explanation. This in turn can give rise to the notion of explanatory power as a distinct criterion for theory choice. Moreover, mature scientific theory deepens our understanding of the actual world in that its explanations culminate in revealing the unchanging objects of nature or their hidden essenses. Thus, as we saw in the last chapter, mature scientific theory discovers unobservable entities which act as the generative mechanisms or basic causal processes of the observable phenomena in a domain. This in turn gives rise to the realist theme of causality. Contrary to many interpretations of Hume, in the realist view causes exist in the actual world and entities by virtue of their natures have causal powers or capacities. This in turn gives rise to the realist theme of natural necessity. These constitute another range of stereotypical characteristics of scientific realism. Again, let us repeat: we are not introducing various categories of scientific realism. Rather, we are outlining stereotypical characteristics in Putman's sense of this term.

Let us now move on to the issue of the grounds for this realist conception of science. As we already noted, according to the realist, the conditions under which a proposition is true are distinct from, and should not be confused with, the conditions under which it is known to be true. In view of this basic distinction, a theoretical sentence could be true but we may not know it to be such. Hence how do we know that the theoretical terms of a mature theory refer to the generative, hidden, unchangeable objects of nature or that these reveal the hidden essences? The history of science makes this question very pertinent. We learn from it that, historically, earlier theories than ours have been falsified and clearly those falsified theories do not convey the hidden essences. Thus how can we claim privilege for our theories? Certainly, they are more mature relative to some earlier theories but, if the human race survives, will not future generations view our theories with much the same jaundiced eye as we use when viewing older theories? Surely Hesse, for instance, is correct in enunciating a principle of no privilege for contemporary science? A pessimistic, though correct, inductive argument over the history of science legitimates Hesse's principle. One common realist response is to acknowledge with Popper, Quine, Kuhn and others that scientific theories are fallible. However, some theories are more epistemically valuable than others in terms of predicting and controlling the environment. Furthermore, some theories are better corroborated or, in some non-algorithmetical way, epistemically more excellent than others. In short, there is progress in science in the sense that, though current theories are fallible, they are closer or nearer to the truth than their historical predecessors. As scientific theories progress through history they become more mature in the sense of approximating more and more to the truth. Newton-Smith calls this view 'the thesis of verisimilitude' (Newton-Smith 1981: 39) and it is undoubtedly another stereotypical characteristic of scientific realism. As science progresses at the theoretical level it is moving closer and closer to the correct characterization of the actual world as it is in itself. This thesis is in turn buttressed by the Kripke–Putnam causal theory of reference or some variations as suggested by, for instance, Leplin (1988) or Newton-Smith (1981).

Another stereotype is derived from the crucial centrality and pervasiveness of theory, summed up in the contemporary truism that all description is theory-laden. Indeed, this theme of realism could be summed up in the phrase 'let's be realist about holism'. After all, holism teaches us that our cognitive capacities consist of abilities to both perceive and to theorize which are inextricably linked. Whether or not one follows Hooker in locating these in a literal evolutionary context or whether we follow Quine in locating them in a learning-feedback model, there is no good reason why one should be sceptical about theory and, as suggested by the empiricists, give the epistemic laurels to observation. Empiricism gave priority to perception and neglected reason's contribution to the content of human knowledge whereas rationalism did the opposite. These two dimensions are inextricably linked in contemporary holism. The so-called epistemological privilege of observation terms, noted in the previous chapter, is nothing but an empiricist prejudice. Hence Hooker's rhetorical question, 'Why reserve scepticism for just one?' sounds convincing. In this holistic context Churchland's realist thesis, namely, 'the excellence of a theory is the measure of its ontology' (Churchland 1979: 43) or Sellars' claim 'to have good reason for holding a theory is *ipso facto* to have good reason for holding that the entities postulated by the theory exist' are very plausible indeed (Sellars 1962: 97). A unified realist account of our cognitive capacities does not supply any rational means for giving precedence to theory-laden observation over the basic theoretical ontology. Any such precedence is due to the failure of laying to rest the ghost of empiricism.

Finally, we come to the related realist theme of inference to the best explanation. A simplified version of this principle may be stated as follows. If we are considering two or more explanations of some event or happening or regularity, all other things being equal, we opt for the best explanation available. We certainly apply this principle in ordinary life, for instance, when deciding on the cause or causes of a rail accident or a change in the weather pattern. This principle has served us well. In the context of contemporary holism, if the best explanation of some event is some theoretical entity then there is no good reason for not continuing to apply this principle to any such unobservable entity. The theoretical terms of a mature science which serve as the best explanation of the observable events, by this principle, can reasonably be taken to refer to actual entities in the world. There is no good reason why we should not be as ontologically committed to these as we are to theory-laden entities of our observable world.

Indeed, there is nothing to stop us from expanding this theme of inference to the best explanation to philosophy of science itself. We are all aware of science and its fruits. The question is: which philosophy of science gives the best explanation of actual scientific practice? Depending on how this question is answered, one could possibly categorize realists as assertive, dogmatic or transcendental. The assertive realist holds that among the philosophies of science currently on offer, ranging from varieties of empiricism to varieties of relativism, realism offers the best explanation: it is the least problematical of the competing views. If we were realists we would be assertive ones. Many realists are either dogmatic or portrayed as such. According to Laudan (Laudan 1990: 12), scientific realists hold that realism is the *only* epistemology of science which provides a cogent alternative to relativism. Newton-Smith is much more explicit. He argues 'that we cannot make the scientific enterprise intelligible except on the assumption of realism' (Newton-Smith 1981: 180). Realism is not only the best explanation, it is the only one. In a similar vein Hooker maintains 'indeed without the metaphysics and semantics of realism one cannot develop an adequate theory of cognition' (Hooker 1987: 275). Harré and Putnam also argue along similar lines. The transcendental realist is a specific kind of dogmatic realist. To be more precise, transcendental realists are not expressly concerned with the best explanation. Rather, they ask a Kantian question, namely, 'what are the conditions of the possibility of science?' and realism is the answer. This approach to realism is adopted by, for instance, Bhaskar and Lawson. Thus Lawson tells us that realists are disposed to asking the transcendental question: 'what must be the case given that X occurs?' and, in particular, maintains that a condition of possibility of science is 'that objects exist and act independently of their identification' (Lawson 1994a). Bhaskar systematically elaborates a sophisticated transcendental realism in *The Possibility of Naturalism*. 'A *transcendental refutation* [of an account of science] is obtained if it can be shown to be inconsistent with the possibility of science' (Bhaskar 1979: 153).

The above stereotypes do not constitute an exhaustive list of the themes of realism and their subtle, but perhaps crucial, variations. For instance, we made no attempt to locate scientific realism *vis-à-vis* the history of realism in Western philosophy ranging from that of Plato or Aristotle to the anti-nominalist realists of the Middle Ages. Neither do we intend to discuss the relationship between post-Kantian idealists and realism and the degree to which one feels it is wise or prudent to categorize these as either realist or non-realist. Rather, we focused on some of the major stereotypes of scientific realism as articulated in contemporary philosophy of science, with a view to furnishing the reader with some small appreciation of the richness and heterogeneity of this philosophy of science and thereby providing the broader background to the scientific realist approach to the philosophy of economics, especially that of Lawson and Mäki.

CRITICAL REALISM AND ECONOMICS:
SOME PRELIMINARIES

Scientific realism is primarily a philosophy of the physical sciences and the issue immediately arises as to whether or not any such philosophy can be correctly applied to economics. The possibilities are numerous ranging from a straightforward yes, through a wide spectrum of qualified agreements or rejections – the qualifications being required by the fact that economics is a rather unique social science – to a categorical no. In this connection Lawson points out that, generally speaking and with some stretching of the history of economic methodology, philosophy of economics has oscillated between two poles, namely, naturalism at one end and anti-naturalism at the other. The naturalistic tradition, with its principle of unity of method, (i.e. there is one and only one method which applies to both the physical and human sciences and that is the method of the physical sciences), has, in his opinion, dominated most orthodox substantive positions in economics and especially econometrics. Indeed, if one keeps a close eye on econometrics, this natural-istic tradition becomes identified with Humean positivism, which rejects any notion of natural necessity and focuses on a regularity or constant con-junction of events as its conception of causality.

The Humean regularity view reduces causes to correlations or constant conjections of events without any residue whatsoever. Thus, for instance, when a patient at a casualty department tells the doctor that an acid solution burned his hand when its container accidently spilled over, he is claiming that the acid solution was the *active* ingredient in the burning of his hand. Moreover, he is, on realist terms at least, asserting that acid *necessarily* causes skin burns provided other countervailing conditions do not obtain. The Humean rejects both of these claims. The causal relationship is merely one of regular succession: when acid and skin come in contact skin burning regularly follows. The alleged physical necessity between the causally related events is psychological or mind-based and is projected onto the world of events by the perceiver. In other words, the physical necessity ordinarily attributed to causal production is illusory. In short, the Humean is main-taining that causal relationships can be reduced to non-causal laws of association.

This Humean analysis may appear completely misguided. As any first-year social science student will insist, correlations do not imply causation. For instance, an established covariation between Ireland's budget deficit and subsequent Irish inflation does not necessarily mean that the former causes the latter. In other words, the Humean regularity view of causality gives rise to the problem of how to distinguish causal connections from mere cor-relations. A Humean response to this challenge could be developed from the following insight. Uncorrelated quantities are not causally connected, but any two correlated quantities are directly causally connected unless the correlation disappears when further factors are taken into account thereby 'screening off' the effect from the alleged cause. For instance, if the correlation between the budget deficit and inflation disappeared when, say, increase in the money supply is taken into account, we would maintain that the increase in the money supply 'screened off' inflation from the budget deficit. This is the insight which governs Suppes' neo-Humean reduction of causation in which an earlier event A is a cause of a later event B if, and only if, A is correlated with B and there is no earlier C such that the partial correlation of A with B, given C, is zero.

According to Lawson, aside from 'time-varying' parameter models and the determination of means and growth rates, the vast majority of econometric work is characterized by the search for Humean regularities. Moreover, within this Humean framework, econometrics has experienced numerous advances and its limits have been explored. This latter work is not the immediate, principal concern of Lawson. Rather, his immediate concern is the tacit or implicit assumption of econometrics which it has 'borrowed' from the Humean empiricist analysis of the physical sciences, namely, that science is constituted by *empirical regularities between discrete events*. Experiences of these atomistic events and their conjunctions exhaust our knowledge of nature. This Humean approach to all scientific knowledge has been subjected to rigorous scrutiny by realist philosophers of science, such as Bhaskar, Harré, Madden and Secord, and is found to be wanting. This realist critique, however, accepts the principle of unity of method advocated by naturalism but totally rejects the Humean positivist conception of scientific knowledge and its method. Lawson, following Bhaskar, calls this version of scientific realism 'transcendental realism'.

Lawson gives us a flavour of this transcendental realist critique of Humean positivism in developing Bhaskar's analysis of experimental activity. He introduces this analysis by pointing out that significant invariant empirical regularities have not been observed in the domain of economics. In this connection he draws our attention to Haavelmo's remark in justifying a probability approach in econometrics that economics, so far, has not led to very accurate and universal laws like those obtaining in the natural sciences, and adds that the situation today is not apparently much better: econometricians are constantly puzzled by the fact that their 'estimated relationships' constantly break down in light of new observations. One may feel that the absence of such regularities in the domain of econometrics is due to the vast multiplicity of causal factors operating in the economic world – a point which was clearly appreciated by J.S. Mill and explicitly endorsed by Lawson. Be that as it may, the laboratory sciences do furnish empirical regularities in their experimental results and, when this experimental activity is properly analysed, serious limitations of the Humean regularity view are exposed. Lawson draws our attention to two central observations about this kind of scientific activity. First, most of these regularities in fact only occur in experimental situations. To use Lawson's own example, the fall of an autumn leaf does not typically conform to an empirical regularity. Many factors, including gravitational, inertial, thermal and aerodynamical, are operative. The laboratory situation, however, engenders a closed system in which some of these influences are either eliminated, marginalized or these influences are built into the calculations and thereby a uniform regularity is obtained. Thus Lawson concludes that, in general, closed systems, i.e. those in which event regularities obtain, are not spontaneously occurring. For the moment we are focusing on how this analysis is used to undermine the Humean positivist approach to science which in turn underpins econometric practice. Lawson's conclusion is that, if a closed system emerges, it is typically highly localized and occurs in part as a result of human agency. This conclusion when combined with Humean positivism, which identifies causal laws with a constant conjunction of events, leads to the absurd or at least counterintuitive conclusions that, first, Humean causal laws of nature are not universal and, second, they are dependent on human agency. As Bhaskar puts it: 'Notice that, as human activity is in general necessary for constant conjunctions, if one identifies causal laws with them one is logically committed to the absurdity that men, in their experimental activity, cause and even change the laws of nature' (Bhaskar 1979: 12). Clearly, an alternative account is required and this is furnished by transcendental realism.

The second observation concerning experimental activity which Lawson wishes to exploit is that the knowledge thereby acquired is successfully applied outside the experimental situation in what Bhaskar calls 'open' systems. Once again it is important to recall that in any such open system no constant conjunction of events obtains. In this connection the Humean regularity approach is also totally wanting, in that it fails to address the question of what governs events outside of experimental situations, and hence fails to offer any valid explanation of the fact that we successfully apply the knowledge acquired in closed systems to open ones. The transcendental realist conception of science, however, faces no such embarrassment. Indeed, transcendental realism is fashioned in part by its analysis of the experimental situation. The patterns or regularities produced in the laboratory under meticulously controlled conditions enable scientists to identify or discover unchanging objects which are typically structured and intransitive, i.e. scientists in no way invent or construct them. These unchanging, structured objects persist in the actual world and these generate or cause the events which we experience. Contrary to Humean empiricism, the primary focus of science is not the flux of events at all. Rather, the primary focus is the identification of enduring natures, structures or mechanisms in virtue of which things have causal powers to generate the observable phenomena. Thus Lawson tells us that once we understand the nature of copper or trade unions, for example, we can deduce their respective powers to conduct electricity well or to defend conditions of workers. In this realist setting a central objective of experimentation is to intervene in order to isolate a generative causal mechanism by, as it were, 'holding off' all other potentially interfering mechanisms.

Let us briefly focus on the realist's non-Humean conception of causality, understood on the picture of powerful particulars, such as magnets or trade unions, actively producing effects in virtue of their natures. These powerful particulars in the form of generative mechanisms can produce new states of affairs. As we saw in the last chapter when scientific realists say 'X has the power to A' they mean 'X can/will do A, in the appropriate conditions, in virtue of its intrinsic nature'. In this connection it is important to note that in ascribing a power to a thing one is saying something about what it *will* or *can* do but one does *not* assert any specific hypothesis about the nature of the thing in question. The question of the specification of its nature is left open to scientific enquiry. Moreover, one could distinguish, *à la* Harré and Madden, between the intrinsic enabling conditions and the extrinsic stimuli conditions. The intrinsic enabling conditions ensure that the thing is of the right nature and in the right state for the exercise of a certain power. The presence of an engine in a proper state is an intrinsic enabling condition for a car to have the power to move. The actions performed by the driver to set the car in motion are extrinsic stimuli conditions. Finally, a power may be exercised over and over again or be diminished or augmented or not exercised at all. Hence the possession of a power is different from its exercise. Bhaskar sums up as follows: 'causal laws must be analysed as tendencies, which may be possessed unexercised and exercised unrealized, just as they may of course be realized unperceived (or undetected) by men' (Bhaskar 1979: 12). This realist conception of causality, rather than that of Humean empiricism, is the one required for econometrics in particular and economics in general. This realist conception of causality is indispensable to Lawson's transcendental realist approach to economics.

In this transcendental realist view the central aim of economic theory is to provide explanations in terms of hidden generative structures. Moreover, explanatory power is clearly distinct from predictive capacity. The tendencies which economic entities have by virtue of their essences may not furnish accurate predictions in the actual world due to the influence of other countervailing factors. In other words, predictive accuracy prevails in closed systems. The economic world, however, is an open system and in this case predictive accuracy is normally not available. The issue for Lawson is the degree of predictive accuracy required. He notes that if a policy of tax-cutting is introduced it is possible at best to predict its immediate impact on, say, consumer spending. His point is that the actual level of consumer spending will typically not be predictable due to the influence of a complex combination of counteracting mechanisms. Indeed, if additional countervailing mechanisms were simultaneously induced, the impact of this policy could be totally unpredictable. In short, economics must be seen as essentially explanatory and typically non-predictive. Finally, Lawson speculates that, if a closed system were to emerge in the actual economic world, it would most likely be 'highly localized', of limited endurability and would occur, at least partially, as the result of intentional agency. In such a case the limited predictability of economic phenomena is in some part made to happen through the knowledge, motivations and capabilities of economic agents.

A Lawsonian scientific realist views the physical and social worlds as open systems where multiplicities of countervailing causal factors are both sequentially and simultaneously active and presumably the degree of openness of the socio-economic world is much more intricate and complex than that of the physical world. This vast intricate web of causal mechanisms renders accurate prediction a rarity. The Lawsonian realist, however, unlike Hayek and other neo-Austrians, is optimistic about unearthing the generative causal mechanisms behind or underpinning the complex, non-predictive flux of observable economic events. Economic theory, if properly constructed, unearths the generative structures underpinning this flux of economic phenomena. In this connection it is crucially important to note that the scientific theorist is not limited to the standard empiricist-cum-Popperian methods or modes of inference, namely, induction and deduction. The theorist's distinctive mode of inference is called abduction, retroduction or retrodiction or inference to the best explanation. One rationale for this crucial distinctive method can be seen from the following. How do scientific theories or theoretical concepts originate? Clearly, neither induction nor deduction can be of any assistance. Rather, theoretical concepts come about by abduction which consists in studying facts and devising a theory to explain these. According to Lawson, some of the key notions allligned to this mode of inference are analogy and metaphor, notions which we briefly discussed in the last chapter. A central justification for this distinctive mode of inference 'is that if we are ever to understand things at all, it must be in that way' (Peirce as quoted by Lawson 1989a: 68) – the transcendentalism of Lawson's scientific realism emerges here.

In order to complete this preliminary discussion of the Lawsonian application of scientific realism to the domain of economics, let us briefly return to Newton-Smith's minimalist realist thesis, namely, that the physical world exists independently of human minds or language or consciousness. Clearly, the socio-economic world does not possess this independence. If all human beings were to disappear from the face of the earth, the realist is convinced that the cosmos would continue to subsist. However, local, national and international markets would cease to exist in such an event. The socio-economic world simply has not the same ontological independence of humanity as the physical world. The socio-economic world is not a natural given, it is, rather, a human construct.

Hermeneutical anti-naturalism focuses on this ontological interdependence. As Lawson points out, hermeneutics emphasizes that economics, unlike the natural sciences, deals with a pre-interpreted reality. In local markets, lay, i.e. non-scientific, agents perform many actions and transactions. The very nature of these actions includes an indispensable reference to some conceptual scheme or other. For instance, the same behaviour, such as handing over a signed cheque, can constitute different actions: in one instant the agent is paying off a debt and in another he or she is defaulting on a payment. Without the *concepts* of bank accounts, legal contracts, purchasing in advance, etc. these actions cannot be properly *identified*. There are obvious parallels between this hermeneutical position and Quine's third milestone of empiricism discussed in the previous chapter. Be that as it may, Lawsonian economic realism embraces this essential interpretative dimension of the actions of economic agents. Thus Lawsonian realist economists clearly acknowledge human agency as a causal power. However, they reject the argument that, just because everything which happens in the social world consists of changes in, or brought about by individuals, all causal forces are essentially reducible to individual agency. Socio-economic structures, though dependent on human agency in general, exist prior to any individual act or action or transaction and either enable or constrain the individual agent in performing her or his actions. Clearly, Lawson is suggesting that some kind of neo-Bhaskarian or neo-Giddens conception of social structures should be embraced by transcendental realism as applied to the socio-economic world. If, for instance, the action of paying a debt by cheque could not exist without the concept of a bank account, neither can it exist without a banking system. Social systems or structures as well as individual agents have causal powers. Individual agency presupposes social structures and vice versa; neither can be reduced to the other.

Finally, Lawson's realism is also opposed to the hermeneutical anti-naturalist tradition which argues that the human sciences, by virtue of their distinct subject matter, i.e. human, mind-dependent action rather than behaviour, and its distinct aim, namely, understanding rather than scientific explanation, requires a distinct method from that of the physical sciences. Lawson's sympathies are entirely with Bhaskar who maintains that hermeneutical accounts of natural science are very positivistic and hence it is not surprising that they reject naturalism. However, when a transcendental realist account of science replaces this unjustifiable positivistic view, the hermeneutical rejection of naturalism loses its force. Lawson calls this application of transcendental realism to the social world critical realism. Before we proceed to further articulate Lawson's critical realist approach to economic methodology by presenting his challenging interpretation of Kaldor's methodological critique of equilibrium economics, let us sum up by locating his critical realism in relation to the various scientific realist stereotypes introduced earlier. As we already noted, Lawsonian realism includes the stereotype that the world exists independently of our knowledge of it. Indeed, his realism is much more specific in that he holds that the world consists of, in Bhaskar's terminology, intransitive, structured objects. By structured he means mechanisms, powers and tendencies which are ir-reducible to Humean events and by intransitive he means that these objects exist independently of our knowledge of them. Second, Lawsonian realism is a transcendental realism. In answer to the question of: how do we know the world is so composed? Lawson, also in tune with Bhaskar, answers in terms of a Kantian type transcendental argument, i.e. scientific practice (especially the application of the laboratory results acquired in closed systems to open ones) would be incomprehensible if this were not the case. In other words, he poses a Kantian type transcendental question: what must the world be like for scientific practices of the form experienced to be possible? and answers it by postulating an ontology of structured objects (Lawson 1989a: 68). Third, although Lawson says that the term 'realism' signals 'a concern to elaborate the nature of the objects of natural and social science' (Lawson 1992c: 2), his use of the words 'nature' and 'essence' should not be taken to imply that he accepts the Leplin–Putnam realist stereotype that theoretical science either reveals or approximates to the hidden invariant or ultimate essences of nature. This is related to what Bhaskar calls the transitive dimension of science (Bhaskar 1979: 14–17). This transitive dimension refers to our scientific knowledge which is constructed, trans-formed or radically altered in specific social contexts. Lawson's own example will help us here. He maintains that the essence of copper is given by its atomic structure. This structure, however, is not ultimate. His idea is as follows. Once the atomic structure of copper is identified, it becomes the subject of further scientific investigation which may result in postulating deeper structures which in turn are investigated and so on. Thus when Lawson speaks of essences, he is not postulating anything ultimate or invariant. His notion of essence is embedded in our transitive knowledge and there is no guarantee that the essences of final science will approximate to the actual structures of intransitive objects. The Leplin–Putnam stereotype of scientific realism, namely, that the theoretical terms of mature science refer to the real invariant essences or, in Lawson's terminology, structures of intransitive objects, does not hold in Lawson's realism. In short, onto-logically an essence is taken by Lawson to be an intransitive object but our knowledge of it is transitive.

Lawson's realism is, as it were, dualistic in nature. On the one hand *philosophy*, especially a Kantian-type transcendental argument which re-flects on the conditions of the possibility of science, grounds an ontology of structured intransitive objects. On the other hand, given the transitive nature of *scientific* knowledge, our scientific conceptual schemes or frame-works are in a state of flux in that they are fallible and constantly open to revision. In view of this dualism of an intransitive world guaranteed by philosophy and transitive scientific knowledge, where does Lawson stand *vis-à-vis* the scientific realist stereotype of verisimilitude, i.e. mature scientific theory furnishes approximately true descriptions of the structures of the intransitive objects postulated by philosophy? If he does not accept this stereotype or some reasonable modification of it, his realism is in danger of being caught on the horns of the following dilemma. We know by a philosophical transcendental argument that there are structured intransitive objects but these structures may not be known by any science since the essences of the latter are not invariant. In other words, the real essences of today's science will become the nominal essences of tomorrow's science and so on, which implies that the structures of intransitive objects may not be revealed by any mature science. The other horn is Kuhnian relativism as outlined in the opening section of this chapter. As we move from one scientific conceptual scheme to another how do we know that the theoretical terms in the various schemes continue to refer to the structures of intransitive objects? As we already noted, the Leplin–Putnam stereotype, namely, that the theoretical terms of mature science approximate to the real invariant essences in nature or, in Lawson's terminology, to the actual structures of intransitive objects, resolves this difficulty, but Lawson, by locating essences in transitive knowledge, appears to distance himself from this Leplin–Putnam move.

While Lawson does not expressly address this issue, the following additional theses of his transcendental realism may help to resolve it. According to Lawson, there are three domains of reality, namely, *'the empirical'* – this includes human experience and sense impressions – *'the actual'*, which includes events and states of affairs given in direct experience, and the *'deep'* or *'non-actual'* which include the structures, mechanisms, powers and tendencies of intransitive objects (Lawson 1994d: 8). In light of this threefold division, the aim of science is to 'identify' and 'illuminate the structures and mechanisms, powers and tendencies, etc. that govern or facilitate the phenomena of experience' (Lawson 1994d: 10). The aim of scientific explanation is to move from some 'surface phenomena' to some 'deeper' causal mechanism or power. However, the mere fact that, in Lawsonian realism, science has this aim does not imply that this aim is realizable. The horns of the above dilemma remain. Lawson may attempt to extricate himself from these horns by means of his account of scientific explanation in terms of 'abduction' or 'retroduction' (Lawson 1994d: 11). As we already noted this mode of inference is neither inductive nor deductive. It is an inference, based on analogy or metaphor, from observational results to a theoretical mechanism which is postulated as either generating or facilitating the actualization of the observable phenomena. In this fashion, the scientific realist stereotypes of explanation and causal powers noted earlier come into play in Lawsonian critical realism. We now proceed to Lawson's intriguing and engaging application of his critical realism to Kaldor's critique of equilibrium economics.

101

THE REALIST INTERPRETATION OF KALDOR'S CRITIQUE OF EQUILIBRIUM THEORY

The equilibrium approach to economic theory has in the postwar period been subject to a searching critique which was spearheaded by a group of economists at Cambridge University of which Nicholas Kaldor was one of the outstanding contributors. Notwithstanding the profound methodological implications of the Cambridge critique in general and of Kaldor's contribution in particular, little has been written within the economic methodology literature which has attempted to provide a coherent framework to interpret and assess the methodological basis which informed this critique of equilibrium economics. However, Lawson has provided what is in effect the first authoritative philosophical interpretation of Kaldor's important methodological contribution. Lawson's stimulating and challenging interpretation is timely since Kaldor's methodological writings have remained largely unexamined, certainly by Anglo-American economic methodologists, notwithstanding the fact that they represent a comprehensive and penetrating critique of orthodox neoclassical equilibrium theory which, as noted by Thirlwall in his outstanding analysis of Kaldor's life-work, 'will remain one of his most important legacies' (Thirlwall 1987: 316). Kaldor's critical incursion into methodology dates arguably from his altercation with Samuelson and Modigliani in 1966, where a number of the major themes central to his later critique were initially identified (Kaldor, 1966). His increasing dissatisfaction with orthodox theory and its methodological foundations was reflected during the 1970s and 1980s in a number of critical contributions which culminated in the 1983 Okun Memorial Lectures and the 1984 Mattioli Lectures (Kaldor 1984, 1985). Taken as a whole, Kaldor's postwar writings on methodology represent one of the major critiques of orthodox economic theory and methodology produced this century.

While Kaldor went on to identify a number of major areas of economics where orthodox theory was in his estimation seriously inadequate and erroneous, the main target of his critique was what he termed 'equilibrium economics' and, more particularly, the general equilibrium variant of this mode of theorizing. Kaldor's critique of equilibrium economics follows from his conception of science, which provided the foundation for his overall methodological critique of orthodox economic theory. The dominant theme of this critique was centred on the empirical inadequacy of orthodox theory in its failure to accurately represent the reality of the contemporary economic system of the developed market economies. Nothing short of an 'act of demolition' of the basic conceptual framework would satisfy Kaldor's relentless critique of equilibrium economics. While this position represents a fundamental and radical rejection of the methodological basis of equilibrium economics, as Lawson correctly points out, Kaldor did not provide a systematically formulated alternative methodology for economics. Instead

102

we find scattered among his empirical writings various suggestions that indicate the possibility of constructing such an alternative methodology. But this extended articulation and coherence is not provided by Kaldor himself. Consequently, we are left with the task of reconstructing a coherent explicit economic methodology from the various methodological insights provided by him. Lawson has provided one such reconstruction by arguing that critical realism provides the most compelling philosophical interpretation of Kaldor's methodological contributions. We concur with Lawson in his rejection of the orthodox approaches to economic methodology, particularly instrumentalism. We also agree with him that critical realism presents a superior approach to economic methodology than the current orthodox approaches, but we differ from him in arguing that critical realism represents the most plausible philosophical interpretation of Kaldor's contribution. Instead we will argue in Chapter 8 that causal holism represents an alternative methodological framework for systematizing Kaldor's important insights.

Lawson, in developing a critical realist reading of Kaldor, focuses on the latter's notions of tendencies and stylized facts. The following quote is typical of Kaldor's methodological remarks.

Hence the theorist, in choosing a particular theoretical approach, ought to start off with a summary of the facts which he regards as relevant to his problem. Since facts, as recorded by statisticians, are always subject to numerous snags and qualifications, and for that reason are incapable of being accurately summarized, the theorist, in my view, should be free to start off with a 'stylised' view of the facts – i.e. concentrate on broad tendencies, ignoring individual detail and proceed on the 'as if' method, i.e. construct a hypothesis that could account for these 'stylised facts' without necessarily committing himself to the historical accuracy, or sufficiency, of the facts or tendencies thus summarised.

(Kaldor 1978: 2)

In his critical realist reading Lawson connects Kaldor's 'as if' method to abduction, in that the entities or generative structures postulated may be real and should be subjected to further scientific investigation. None the less he concedes that Kaldor argued for the superiority of induction over deduction and thus to some extent either obscured or distracted attention from this distinctive abductive mode of inference favoured by the critical realist. The principal issue of course is not a historical one, i.e. whether or not Kaldor was a critical realist. Rather, Lawson's interpretation articulates how critical realism is to be formulated in the domain of economics. Moreover, it also intended to provide a straightforward, coherent account of Kaldor's methodological remarks which explains and justifies the nature of Kaldor's objections to equilibrium economics.

The critical realist interpretation of Kaldorian tendencies is effected by recourse to the notion of causal powers adumbrated earlier. Entities, structures and economic agents have powers to act in certain ways in various circumstances by virtue of their enduring natures. As we pointed out above, we may not have knowledge of these natures. This is a matter for scientific investigation. However, once economists discover the nature of a thing we can deduce its causal powers. For instance, once we know the nature of trade unions or private enterprise we can deduce their respective powers to defend conditions of workers or to seek profits. Moreover, as we have already seen, entities may possess these powers without exercising them or they may be exercised without being manifest in the observable events of the actual world. By virtue of their natures, entities have tendencies to do certain things but these tendencies do not, in the case of economics, result in uniform regularities because they are embedded in a network of countervailing tendencies due to other generative structures or natures. Here Lawson draws our attention to Mill who was at pains to point out that in political economy effects are commonly determined by a multiplicity of causes and consequently people often make the error of predicting actual results when what they should have predicted was a tendency to that result. Also the notion of liability, as when we say a boy is liable to catch a cold, is a kind of 'passive power' in that we mean that the boy, if placed in certain extrinsic circumstances, has a tendency to suffer a cold in virtue of some aspect of his nature, such as his low immunity. Kaldorian tendencies are thus powers or liabilities of entities or structures, which because of the multitude of countervailing mechanisms in operation, may be exercised without being manifest in actual economic outcomes. The scientific realist notions of power, tendency and liability form a constellation of ideas which are intimately connected to the notion of specific natures. These natures are often hidden and hence these tendencies are, in Lawson's own words, 'non-empirical features of causal structures' (Lawson 1989a: 65). The generative structures or natures on which these tendencies are based are unobservable but these are the real causes of the observable economic facts.

An analysis of Kaldor's work shows that he sometimes conflates the notion of tendency with that of a stylized fact. In Lawson's challenging presentation these two notions are related but not conflated. As we saw above the laboratory sciences can discover genuine causal laws and thereby identify the natures and tendencies of entities in the physical world. The closed system of laboratory experimentation facilitates this kind of discovery. In economics, however, such a situation typically does not arise. Economists have no laboratory – they are field researchers operating in open systems. The effects of the tendencies of an economic agent, entity or structure will frequently be modified or hidden by the effects of countervailing mechanisms and hence uniform regularities are rarely observed. Nevertheless, all is not lost. Some degree of uniformity, persistency or generality may and does 'shine through': total chaos does not reign at the level of economic observation. The presence of some degree of uniformity or persistence provides a prima facie case for postulating some enduring generative economic mechanisms. Conceptualizations of these partial regularities, which in Kaldor's phrase 'ignore individual detail', are explicated by Lawson as stylized facts. In this explication a stylized fact is a theory-laden description of a partial, broad, but by no means universal, regularity among events. According to Kaldor the claim that the UK productivity rate in the postwar period has been less than that of comparable industrial economies is an example of a stylized fact. In summary, the economist begins his theory building with stylized facts, i.e. theory-embedded descriptions of partial regularities among observed economic events and, by means of abduction, postulates generative non-empirical mechanisms, the natures of which have tendencies or powers to regularly produce events or are liable to undergo certain happenings in suitable external circumstances.

In his critique of general equilibrium theory Kaldor summarizes his position as follows:

My basic objection to the theory of general equilibrium is not that it is abstract – all theory is abstract and must necessarily be so since there can be no analysis without abstraction – but that it starts from the wrong kind of abstraction, and therefore gives a misleading impression of the nature and manner of operation of economic forces.

(Kaldor 1978: 202)

Unfortunately, Kaldor does not elaborate on the criteria for distinguishing between the right and the wrong kinds of abstraction. In this connection Lawson draws our attention to a traditional Aristotelian-Thomistic realist interpretation of abstraction, namely, that concepts are abstract in the sense that they are derived by focusing on certain aspects of real things and neglecting or ignoring others. Thus, for instance, the concept of a cat is abstract in that it is acquired by ignoring the size, colour, position, etc. of a range of cats and focusing on their shared common characteristics. According to Lawson's realism, abstractions are indispensable to the initial analysis of economic phenomena. Concretely economic reality is a complex combination of diverse features, components, etc. and abstraction at the conceptual level separates these into distinct elements. Also, abstraction is used in the examination of the mechanisms which generate economic phenomena. For example, the economist can isolate certain powers or tendencies from others and thereby abstract economic structures. In this realist view, abstraction obtains knowledge of the real structures or mechanisms of the real phenomena of the economic world thereby eschewing artificial, though convenient, fictions or idealizations advocated by numerous methodologists in their defence of orthodox economics, such as Friedman.

Lawson suggests two guiding realist principles which in effect enable us to distinguish the correct or appropriate kind of abstraction from the misleading, inappropriate kind. In the first place, an abstract conception must be concerned with the real, rather than some ideal convenient fiction. Realists aim at discovering the real causal mechanisms and in this context idealized fictions should be avoided. Clearly, this principle rules out such idealized notions as universal perfect competition, rational expectations and perfect foresight which are conceded by many of their advocates as unrealistic assumptions. We will be returning to this topic in more detail in the next chapter when we come to discuss the realism of assumptions issue in the context of Friedman's classic essay. For the moment, suffice it to say that, according to Lawson's first realist principle of an acceptable abstraction, the idealizations of neoclassical economics constitute inappropriate, misleading abstractions.

Lawson's second principle states that the correct kind of abstraction 'must be concerned with the essential rather than merely the most general' (Lawson 1989a: 69). This, prime facie, is a surprising contrast since all abstractions entail generality. Lawson is clearly aware of this. The point of the contrast is to focus our attention on the prevalent practice among a substantial body of orthodox economists of formulating economic axioms of their discipline in relatively contentless generalizations which consequently have little explanatory power, in that they fail to explore the essential natures of the economic mechanisms and structures which govern the observable stylized economic facts. The point of abstraction here is to abstract from that which is not essential to the correct explanation of some phenomena in order to focus on what is essential. In direct conflict with this realist approach Hahn (as quoted by Lawson 1989a), for instance, uses the very general truism that 'agents have preferences' as one of his axioms. Such a truism is certainly uncontentious but, as Lawson points out, it has little explanatory value being, as such, effectively contentless. Indeed, one may be tempted to add that it is this recourse to such broad generalizations which gives orthodox economics its persuasive power: anyone can see that its axioms are true. Lawson correctly points out that in such axiomatic approaches to economics the real work is done by powerful assumptions added to the axioms. Again Hahn tells us 'that people have preferences and try to satisfy them we treat as an axiom while universal perfect competition, for instance, must count as an assumption' or that 'managers have preferences is an axiom; that they take a particular form, for instance that they are linear in expected profit is an assumption'. Lawson's point is that these assumptions are not even intended to convey the mode of operation of real economic mechanisms. Rather, many of them are introduced to achieve mathematical tractability. Moreover, this axiom-cum-assumption approach to economic theory gives the impression that the assumptions will at some future time be removed. Just as some of the assumptions of the special theory of relativity developed by Einstein in 1905 were dropped in his general theory of 1915, future economics will also succeed in dropping these assumptions for more realistic ones. However, as Kaldor remarks, the process of relaxing these unreal but basic assumptions has not yet started in general equilibrium theory and, furthermore, one suspects that their relaxation would not leave orthodox economic theory intact.

Perhaps the best case for the axiom-cum-assumption approach to economics is made by Hahn himself. In his view such economists are engaged in the programme of enquiring 'how far observed events are consistent with an economy which is in continuous Walrasian equilibrium'. They may also be engaged in the programme of specifying the conditions under which such a theory would be applicable. This programme, however, would utterly fail to offer any explanation or deepen our understanding of the mechanisms which govern the events in our non-equilibrium economic world. Moreover, there is no valid reason why it should feature in policy analysis or decision-making processes. It is not surprising that Lawson concludes that, if a commitment to critical realism is accepted, this whole basic approach seems misconceived.

The perceptive reader may wonder why we did not include any reference to abstraction in our presentation of the stereotypes of scientific realism in the previous section. This exclusion is not based on some definite conviction that a realist theory of perception and, in particular, the thesis of abstraction is not logically required by a scientific realist. Contrary to Hooker, we are inclined to the opinion that some kind of realist theory of perception constitutes a stereotypical characteristic of scientific realism. Many scientific realists, however, do not *expressly* commit themselves to the doctrine of abstraction – Bhaskar, for instance, hardly mentions it – and consequently we felt it more prudent not to include it. This exclusion in no way affects the validity of our presentation. We did not claim that the central themes presented in the previous section were an exhaustive list of the stereotypical characteristics of scientific realism. Clearly, abstraction is an integral part of Lawson's articulation of that position.

5

THE PLAUSIBILITY OF
ECONOMIC ASSUMPTIONS
Realist perspectives

Since its initial publication in 1953, Friedman's seminal paper has been a central focus of attention for a vast number of economic methodologists. Consequently, it is not surprising that both Lawson and Mäki, the two major contemporary exponents of scientific realism in the domain of economic methodology, have engaged Friedman's position. This realist engagement explicitly serves the dual purpose of, first, articulating the manner in which scientific realism is to be applied to economic methodology and, second, furnishing a realist critique of Friedman's theses.

As we have already noted, Friedman puts the methodological focus on the predictive success of an economic theory: an economic theory is centrally tested by an examination of its consequences. In particular, any economic theory with unrealistic assumptions is scientifically acceptable provided its consequences are in conformity with the observable facts. Contrary to this position, many realists, including Lawson, draw a sharp distinction between the explanatory power and the predictive success of a theory. The example from geometrical optics used in Chapter 3 is quite helpful here. The reason why the correct prediction of the height of the flagpole from the principles of geometrical optics combined with the length of its shadow is not explanatory, though predictively accurate, is that the generative causal mechanisms which actually determined the height of the pole are not specified in the prediction. Thus, for the Lawsonian realist, the aim of economic theory is to discover generative causal mechanisms based on the powers and tendencies of specific economic agents and structures. A theory with un-realistic assumptions may be predictively accurate but fail to facilitate the discovery of the generative causal mechanisms operational in an economy.

LAWSON'S REALIST CRITIQUE OF FRIEDMAN

In Friedman's methodological framework the reason why neoclassical eco-nomics fails to fulfil this basic realist aim is intimately connected to his famous 'as if' method. According to Friedman, business firms behave *as if* they were fully informed, rational calculators aiming at the achievement of profit maximization, even though clearly these assumptions do not apply to actual firms. In this respect neoclassical theory is similar to the hypothesis that leaves on a tree are:

> positioned as if each leaf deliberately sought to maximize the amount of sunlight it receives, given the position of its neighbours, as if it knew the physical laws determining the amount of sunlight that would be received in various positions and could move rapidly and instantaneously from any one position to any other desired and unoccupied position.... Is the hypothesis rendered unacceptable or invalid because, so far as we know, leaves do not 'deliberate'.... Clearly, none of these contradictions of the hypothesis is vitally relevant.... The hypothesis does not assert that leaves do these things but only that their density (around the tree) is the same *as if* they did.
>
> (Friedman 1953: 19–20)

In short, according to Friedman this hypothesis is tested by the correctness of its predictions and not by the realism of its clearly false assumptions. In Max Black's terminology (of aforementioned Chapter 3) Friedman is a heuristic fictionalist. Nevertheless, as Lawson notes, there are some similarities between Friedman's 'as if' method and the realist abductive/retroductive account of method. Both approaches view economic theory as attempting to explain by introducing explanatory hypotheses which must include some generalizations. Despite this, both methods are basically very different. Friedman's 'as if' method limits the testing of explanatory hypotheses to the investigation of their consequences and thereby not only allows but positively encourages the positing of known fictitious entities in our explanatory hypotheses. The realism of these explanatory assumptions is irrelevant in the Friedman 'as if' method. Thus, as Lawson also points out, the causal mechanisms that actually govern the density of the leaves on the tree is not an issue at all for Friedman but it is of central importance for the realist. In general, Friedman rules out what is of paramount importance to the critical realist, namely, the scientific activity of checking out the nature and reality of any posited theoretical entity in terms of its generative causal mechanisms. The neoclassical account of the business firm totally fails to carry out this scientific investigation which is essential to critical realism and this failure is, we might say, built into the core of Friedman's 'as if' method. Surely Lawson is correct in noting that not all theorizing in mainstream economics is so restrictive.

Lawson develops this theme in terms of his two principles of appropriate abstraction noted in the last chapter. Both of these realist principles are completely ignored and clearly violated by Friedman's 'as if' method. The first principle requires that an appropriate abstraction must be concerned with real mechanisms, rather than some idealized convenient fiction. In Friedman's 'as if' method such real abstractions are not the objective at all.

In this connection Lawson quotes Friedman's remark about his first analogue of neoclassical theory, i.e. bodies falling in the atmosphere behave as if they were falling in a vacuum, to argue that the objective for Friedman is merely to specify the empirical conditions in which such hypotheses are found to hold:

> The important problem in connection with the hypothesis is to specify the circumstances under which the formula works or, more precisely, the general magnitude of the error in its predictions under various circumstances. Indeed ... such a specification is not one thing and the hypothesis another. The specification is itself an essential part of the hypothesis.
>
> (Friedman 1953: 18)

The realist's first principle of abstraction draws the economist's attention to the scientific probing of the real generative intrinsic mechanisms governing the observable economic phenomena, while Friedman's 'as if' method puts the spotlight on idealizations or heuristic fictions and the extrinsic empirical conditions beyond which they fail to apply.

If Friedman's 'as if' method violates the first realist principle of apt abstraction, it actually proposes the contrary of the second in that it explicitly puts the methodological premium on high-level generalizations rather than on the essences or natures of the events, agents and structures which produce and underlie the observable economic world. Idealized fictions, such as 'deliberating', 'mobile' leaves which are tacitly presented as paradigmatic exemplars for economic theory, hinder economists from scientifically probing the natures and tendencies of the powerful economic particulars and structures which generate the flux of economic life in our non-equilibrium world. Lawson's critique thus suggests that Friedman either reduces economic explanation to correct prediction or fails to adequately distinguish between them. The Friedman 'as if' method aborts the birth of genuine economic explanation which, first, abstracts out of the flux of economic phenomena the essentials of our economic world and which, second, scientifically probes these. In Kaldor's terminology, it is working with the wrong kind of abstraction, or, in Max Black's terminology, it fails to acknowledge the existential use of economic models.

Lawson's penetrating critical realist critique of Friedman's methodological account of positive economics is not limited to the above considerations. It also extends to Friedman's views on how economic theories or hypotheses are tested. As we have already seen, in Lawson's realist approach neither spontaneously occurring nor artificially created closed systems, i.e. those in which invariant regularities among events hold, exist in the actual economic world. In the economic world which is subject to a multiplicity of countervailing generative causes invariant regularities are very rare. Inductively based generalizations will at best result in statistical, partial regularities understood

110

as stylized facts. However, as Friedman himself readily admits, economists, like other social scientists, have not laboratory based controlled experimentation available to them. Artificially created closed systems are practically impossible in economics. Now since predictive accuracy prevails primarily in closed systems and, in Friedman's 'as if' method, predictive accuracy is the crucial way of empirically testing economic hypotheses, in Lawson's opinion, Friedman is assuming that spontaneously occurring closed systems exist in the actual economic world but this assumption is false.

The assumption of a closed system is clearly evident in Friedman's first paradigmatic exemplar of his 'as if' method, namely, that bodies in the atmosphere behave as if they were falling in a vacuum. Lawson correctly intimates that a vacuum is a typical, laboratory engineered, closed system in which invariant regularities of events are observed to occur. However, when we consider the motion of leaves or feathers in the actual atmosphere, other countervailing factors exert definite influences on these motions. Hence, to claim, as Friedman does, that leaves and bodies move in accordance with this Newtonian law, is *ipso facto* to implicitly assume a closed system. Moreover, if the analogy between economic theory and this paradigmatic exemplar is developed, since Friedman acknowledges that the artificial, laboratory engineered, closed system is not available to the economist, there must be an implicit assumption that spontaneously occurring closed systems exist in the actual economic world. Furthermore, the same implicit reference to spontaneously occurring closed systems can be unearthed by a thorough analysis of Friedman's other paradigmatic exemplars. Nevertheless, as we have already seen, according to Lawson's critical realism, actual economies are open. The untenability of Friedman's position can be expressed in the following elementary fashion. Economic theory is tested by its predictions which are Humean regularities. Humean regularities occur in closed systems or when mechanisms act in isolation. Actual economic systems are open and the economist cannot engender laboratory based, artificially closed systems. Since these are the only possibilities available to the economist, he or she cannot, on Friedman's account, test any economic theory. Lawson, however, stops short of drawing this conclusion in this elementary fashion.

Instead he focuses on the tacit reference to closed systems in Friedman's exemplars of economic explanation and, in a transcendental realist vein, poses the quasi-Kantian question of how this assumption is to be rendered intelligible? As we have already seen, a Humean analysis of causality or causal laws in terms of a constant conjunction of events will not render the actual use of closed systems in the physical sciences intelligible. The only viable option is transcendental realism. Thus transcendental realism is a condition of the possibility or intelligibility of Friedman's exemplars of economic explanation. Transcendental realism demonstrates how invariant laws can be sustained in open systems by rejecting the Humean reduction of such laws to constant conjunctions of events and simultaneously by conceptualizing these laws 'as designating the [generally non-empirical] ways of acting of generative structures independently of any particular pattern of events that may ensue' (Lawson 1992a: 22).

Finally, Lawson maintains that Friedman's position is confused in that it contains conflicting elements of realism and anti-realism. Since Friedman's anti-realism is well known, we will focus on how Lawson identifies realist tendencies in Friedman's piece. As we have already seen, according to Friedman, the scientist must investigate and specify the conditions under which scientific hypotheses work. For instance, when the physicist carries out this investigation in the case of a falling leaf, Friedman suggests that such factors as air pressure or aerodynamic forces are real causal entities actually acting upon the feather, and reference to these must be explicitly included under the title of 'conditions under which scientific hypotheses work'. In such cases Friedman is clearly not denying the possibility of establishing the reality of putative causal mechanisms and neither is he denying that their natures cannot be scrutinized. To this extent he is a scientific realist. Indeed, if we look more closely at what Friedman says about testing economic or scientific hypotheses by investigating the realism of their assumptions, he does not rule this out in an a priori fashion. Rather, as Lawson perceptively notes, Friedman's central thesis is that such an investigation does not constitute 'a test of the validity of the hypothesis *different from* or *additional to* the test by implications' (Friedman 1953: 14). In other words, any scientific hypothesis, including those which postulate hidden natures, can be investigated by only one means, namely, testing its implications. Thus Lawson concludes that, contrary to the not uncommon assumption, Friedman is not arguing that generative structures cannot be established and, we may add, to that extent he is a scientific realist. Rather, 'he is suggesting that economists should not bother with such matters because to do so is unnecessary and not the way in which science proceeds' (Lawson 1992a: 20). Science proceeds by one and only one method, namely, testing implications. In this latter assumption Friedman is, according to Lawson, patently wrong. As we saw in the last chapter, according to Lawsonian realism, there is much more to scientific method than the deductive testing of theories. Nevertheless, we should not lose sight of this realist dimension to Friedman's position. Indeed, this realism is not surprising. If we focus on what economists and other scientists do, i.e. on how they practise science, rather than on what they say they do, scientific realism is seen to be implicitly at work. This implicit realism combined with Friedman's instrumentalist remarks constitutes the confusion in his methodological position.

MÄKI'S INCONSISTENCY CRITIQUE OF FRIEDMAN

While Lawson views Friedman's position as both confused and erroneous, Uskali Mäki, another adroit exponent of the impact of realism on the philosophy of economics, holds that it is inconsistent. In the rest of this chapter we will focus on Mäki's contribution, which certainly should not be equated with Lawson's critical realism. Indeed, Mäki's project appears to be, on the whole, expository or elucidatory, without criticizing specific economic theories or disciplines, whereas Lawson's explicit intention is to criticize neo-classical theory by exposing its unacceptable positivistic basis. While Mäki's contribution is not as explicitly directed, it constitutes another engaging realist interpretation of economics and we propose to introduce some of the basic tenets of this contribution by focusing on Mäki's analysis of Friedman.

By combing through Friedman's famous methodological piece, Mäki identifies at least three mutually incompatible tendencies, namely, realism, positivism and contemporary pragmatism such as that of Feyerabend, Kuhn, Rorty or Quine (Mäki 1986: 127). Furthermore, Mäki holds that Friedman's basic position, which he calls 'the F thesis', namely, '*The realism of assumptions is irrelevant, and predictive power is relevant to the acceptance of economic theory*', is ambiguous and obscure in that it can, on the grounds of solid textual evidence from Friedman's own piece, be explicated in these mutually incompatible ways (Mäki 1986: 127). Finally, he suggests that these inconsistencies are part of Friedman's rhetoric and that the only way of avoiding these inconsistencies is to extend the pragmatist attitude to encompass economic methodologies and thereby read Friedman as a modified epistemological anarchist.

In our opinion the Friedman 1953 piece succeeds in speaking to an extensive range of philosophers of science, including instrumentalists, Kuhnians, logical positivists, Popperians and scientific realists, in the sense that those committed to any one of these philosophical positions could clearly specify significant passages from Friedman which would re-echo their own respective positions. Friedman, at least prima facie, appears to juxtapose various elements emphasized by conflicting methodologies or philosophies of science and one may wonder whether or not this is a genuine synthesis or, as Mäki holds, an inconsistent *mélange*. The principal concern here is not what Friedman intended or actually had in mind when writing this challenging piece. Rather, one is concerned with what the piece says independently of what its author may have wished to say. Hence, for instance, one is at liberty to recognize a Kuhnian dimension or tendency, even though Friedman himself could not have known of Kuhn's work at the time of writing. In other words, we, like Mäki, are viewing Friedman's piece through the microscopes of various twentieth-century methodologies.

It may be useful to devote a few paragraphs to these various trends in Friedman's piece. The following is by no means an exhaustive analysis. Its intention is to recall to mind how Friedman speaks in various methodological tongues. The logical positivist dimension is very evident in Friedman's division of any positive science into two elements, namely, an empty language with no substantive content on the one hand and a body of substantive hypotheses on the other. The former element serves to highlight the function of science as a 'filing system', i.e. it is concerned with systematic organization. The latter element is concerned with the 'meaningful empirical' dimension of science and factual evidence alone can show whether or not an 'analytical filing system' possesses this dimension. The logical positivist's tools are further evident in his later discussion of the use of 'assumptions' in stating a theory. Here he explicitly says that we can regard a hypothesis 'as consisting of two parts: first a conceptual world or abstract model . . . second, a set of rules . . . specifying the correspondence between the variables or entities in the model and observable phenomena' (Friedman 1953: 24). He goes on to point out that the model pertains to the domain of mathematics and logic, a central thesis of logical positivism. On the other hand, the correspondence rules connect the model to the observable world, another central thesis of logical positivism. Furthermore, he uses the standard logical tool of axiomatization in approaching scientific theory, an approach also exploited by the logical positivists. In particular, he assumes, with the logical positivist, that any piece of scientific theory can be axiomatized, i.e. formulated according to the rules of a logical deductive system consisting of primitive terms, nominal definitions, axioms and theorems. Indeed, he fully recognizes that a piece of science can be axiomatized in more than one way and hence the list of basic axioms is relative to a particular deductive system: what are axioms *vis-à-vis* one deductive system may be theorems in another. In short, in these passages Friedman, like the logical positivists, presents us with a logical, as opposed to a historical, picture of the science of economics. In F. Suppe's (1979) terminology, Friedman in these passages is expounding 'the received view' of scientific theory, inherited from logical positivism.

The Popperian dimension emerges in Friedman's brief discussion of what he calls the '*validity*' of an hypothesis. According to Friedman:

> the only relevant test of the *validity* of a hypothesis is comparison of its predictions with experience. The hypothesis is rejected if its predictions are contradicted . . . great confidence is attached to it if it has survived many opportunities for contradiction.
>
> (Friedman 1953: 8–9)

This is simultaneously a clear articulation of Popper's conception of the method of science as the deductive testing of theories combined with both his falsificationism and his theory of corroboration resulting from risky predictions. Friedman also articulates the Popperian vision in the following:

> given that the hypothesis is consistent with the evidence at hand its further testing involves deducing from it new facts capable of being observed but not previously known and checking these deduced facts against additional empirical evidence.
>
> (Friedman 1953: 12–13)

This is a clear statement of the Popperian principle that an acceptable theory must have new and testable consequences which correspond to reality. There is also a clear statement of the Popperian criterion of progress, namely, one theory is better than another when it yields better predictions and of the Popperian thesis that the construction or discovery of a hypothesis is a matter of inspiration or intuition and not of logic. Clearly, from the above and other passages Friedman's methodology speaks to the Popperians as well as the logical positivists, despite the fact that Popper himself is clearly antagonistic to the latter school.

As we already noted, however, Friedman also speaks the language of the philosophical instrumentalist. This is most clearly articulated in his reference to Marshall's *Principles of Political Economy* when he says: 'Marshall took the world as it is; he sought to construct an "engine" to analyse it, not a photographic reproduction of it' (Friedman 1953: 35). Engines are instruments: they neither sum up nor explain and they are neither true nor false. Rather, they are instruments for going from X to Y. Similarly, theories are heuristic intellectual instruments which neither sum up nor explain. On the contrary, they enable us to analyse reality in an efficient, effective way. Moreover, we discard an engine when it looses its effectiveness. Similarly, we discard a theory when it looses its effectiveness, i.e. when it ceases to work as a heuristic instrument for the discovery of novel facts or when we have a better instrument to use in its place.

Friedman, however, continues to be all things to all methodologists. His piece has at least two other dimensions, namely, that of scientific realism and Kuhnianism. This realist dimension is expressly stated in Friedman's alternative formulation of the second element of any scientific theory, i.e. 'it is a body of substantive hypotheses designed to *abstract essential features* of complex reality' (Friedman 1953: 7). According to numerous realists, science, at its theoretical level, reveals the hidden essences of nature. In other words, it abstracts the essential, rather than the accidental, features of reality. Indeed, this quest for the hidden structures or essences is raised by Friedman to the status of 'a fundamental hypothesis of science'.

A fundamental hypothesis of science is that appearances are deceptive and that there is a way of looking at or interpreting or organizing the evidence that will reveal superficially disconnected and diverse phenomena to be manifestations of a more fundamental and relatively simple structure.

(Friedman 1953: 33)

In other words, the appearances are manifestations of the essential structures of the world which in turn are revealed by scientific theory. Indeed, in the manner of Putnam, Friedman points out that the test of this realist hypothesis lies in 'its fruits – a test that science has so far met with dramatic success' (ibid.: 33). In Putnam's terminology, without scientific realism the predictive success of science is miraculous. Whatever the origins of scientific realism in that scientific psyche, there is no doubt that it has penetrated through to Friedman's paper.

Perhaps the most refined sophistication of Friedman's paper is evident in what we call its Kuhnian dimension. As we already mentioned, Kuhn was very influential in gaining recognition of the truth that all descriptions are theory-laden, a thesis subsequently taken on board by many contemporary realists. This same thesis, however, is clearly, though briefly, articulated by Friedman. He says 'a theory is the way we perceive "facts", and we cannot perceive "facts" without a theory' (Friedman 1953: 34). Moreover, in the issue of theory choice Friedman envisages a more complex situation than that discussed within the Popperian framework. The possibility envisaged by Friedman is the following: 'when there exists a theory that is known to yield better predictions but only at a greater cost. The gains from greater accuracy ... must then be balanced against the costs of achieving it' (ibid.: 17). Here, as Friedman says, there is a question of 'balancing' various interests and presumably there is no mechanical, algorithmetic way of effecting such decisions, a central thesis of Kuhnianism. Similarly, when Friedman comes to discuss the rules for the application of an abstract model, unlike the logical positivists and like Kuhn, he maintains that 'no matter how successful we may be in this attempt, there inevitably will remain room for judgement in applying these rules. Each occurence has some features peculiarly its own, not covered by explicit rules' (ibid.: 25). Once again scientific method is not reducible to a logical algorithm. It is a matter of mature, wise judgement. Indeed, like Kuhn, it is not possible to *teach* these kind of judgements in the way one can, for instance, teach students to evaluate the validity of an argument in formal logic. Rather, as with Kuhn, it is a matter of experience and maturity. Indeed, he sums up one of the central Kuhnian theses in the clearest of terms. 'There is never certainty in science, and the weight of evidence for or against a hypothesis can never be assessed completely "objectively"' (ibid.: 30). In short, Mäki's case that Friedman's position is inconsistent does not sound implausible.

Mäki now speculates as to why Friedman appears to be inconsistent. One possible answer is to interpret Friedman's methodological essay as an ingenuous piece of rhetoric. It is likely that Friedman's intention in writing the piece was to *convince* anyone who may be having doubts or reservations about neoclassical economics that its critics were misguided. To achieve the aim of persuading his readers Friedman would have to address a wide range of individuals occupying various positions on the methodological spectrum. In this connection, however, one must distinguish between what Mäki calls 'first-order rhetoric', which *à la* McCloskey views rhetoric as part of the actual method of economics and 'second-order rhetoric' which refers to rhetoric in philosophical methodology (Mäki 1986: 139). Friedman's piece is an ingenious piece of second-order rhetoric. In this connection, however, one might wish to argue that Mäki's additional claim, i.e that the F thesis is ambiguous, may not hold in this interpretation. The argument is that the F thesis applies, irrespective of which methodological position one adopts across the philosophical spectrum: its content will remain the same, despite its location in different, incompatible philosophies of science. In other words, Friedman does not infer or deduce his F thesis from some preferred philosophy of science such as that of Popper or instrumentalism. Rather, the F thesis concerns a specific problem in the methodology of economics and the arguments for it are, as it were, topic neutral *vis-à-vis* these different philosophies of science. Mäki, however, does not pursue this possibility. Instead he tells us that 'what is important is that here we have rhetoric plus unjustified inconsistency in methodology' (ibid.: 139). In other words, at this level, the inconsistency continues to permeate the F thesis.

According to Mäki, one way of making Friedman's piece coherent is to interpret Friedman as an epistemological anarchist along the lines developed by Feyerabend or, more precisely, as a modified constrained anarchist. He very aptly adumbrates this interpretation as follows:

> Just as there is ontological indifference on the nature of a particular firm, there is indifference on the nature of economic science: what it is about, how it is or should be structured and exercised. . . . Everything – how we understand facts, theories, methodologies, etc. – would become a matter of purposeful decision. . . . Perhaps he (Friedman) is simply in love with certain visions, theories, and policies which he wants to defend – and, as we know, everything is allowed in love (and war).
>
> (Mäki 1986: 139–40)

This anarchistic interpretation of Friedman would certainly account for the various tendencies in his provocative piece and would make his view coherent. Mäki leaves us with three choices: Friedman is an anarchist, or the inconsistencies are merely deceptive appearances, or Friedman is a bad methodologist. Mäki (1992: 1) himself apparently does not favour the second option: he tells us the essay is 'plagued with obscurity . . . lacks coherence and often puts its points ambiguously' and hence he leaves us, as far as the rationality of Friedman's position goes, with a choice between the frying pan and the fire.

VARIETIES OF REALISM, AND THE F THESIS

Like Lawson, Mäki's critique of Friedman is a sophisticated, orchestrated rendition of various realist themes. Indeed, he maintains that the most important set of obscurities in the Friedman position relates to the term 'realism' itself. As we have already seen, negatively speaking, the F thesis states that the realism of assumptions is irrelevant to the acceptance of an economic theory and, according to Mäki, this use of the term 'realism' is hopelessly ambiguous. In the last chapter we noted that there are varieties of realism. The hopeless ambiguity of the F thesis results in part from the failure to acknowledge this variety. In this connection Mäki proposes to insert some taxonomic order into the socio-historical developments of realism and to this end introduces a taxonomy of realisms. The upshot of this taxonomy is that Friedman can be considered as an ontological, referential, representational and veristic realist – distinctions of which Friedman himself is clearly unaware and which render the F thesis ambiguous. Indeed, this ambiguity is frequently carried over into numerous debates on Friedman's position. Moreover, Mäki maintains that one must distinguish between the concepts of 'realism' and those of 'realisticness'. The term 'realism' designates a collection of onto-logical or semantic doctrines which are philosophical in nature, while the terms 'realisticness' or 'unrealisticness' are related to economists' discourse about their theories or their constituent statements. Failure to recognize this distinction also contributes to the hopeless ambiguity of the F thesis. This thesis concerns realisticness rather than realism as such. In this section we will focus on Mäki's classification of realisms, leaving his discussion of realisticness to the next section.

The following Mäki taxonomy of realisms is not exhaustive. Rather, it focuses on those categories which Mäki perceives as being in some sense relevant to the analysis of some central issues in the philosophy of economics. The first category is called ontological realism. Statements of the form 'X exists' or 'There are Xs', where X may designate at the most general level the world right through to specifics, such as Chile's inflation rate last year, exemplify ontological realism (Mäki 1992: 4). Anyone who sincerely utters a statement with this form is an ontological realist. Given this characterization, Friedman is clearly an ontological realist. So too are the Austrian and neo-Austrian economists. Indeed, this category of realism is very extensive. The early Greek philosophers, the scholastics, the nominalists, the rationalists, the classical empiricists, the Kantian and post-Kantian idealists, Marxists, logical positivists, instrumentalists, conventionalists, Popperians, pragmatists, exist-entialists, post-modernists, relativists, rhetoricians, etc. are all ontological realists. One may well wonder who, short of the sceptic who does not speak or write or communicate in any way, is not an ontological realist? The definition of the category renders it too wide to, for instance, enable us to distinguish between critical realists, such as Lawson, and rhetoricians such as McCloskey. Both subscribe to statements of the form 'X exists' and, by definition, are ontological realists. Indeed, in view of its failure to make such discriminations, it should be no surprise that Friedman is both an ontological realist and, say, an instrumentalist.

The next category introduced by Mäki is referential realism. For instance, if one claims that the term 'gold' refers to something in the real world, one is a referential realist. Similarly, if one claims that a theoretical term, such as 'gene' or 'effective demand', refers to a real entity, one is also a referential

118

realist. Referential realism is centrally a semantical thesis. In general, 'to say that linguistic expressions may, should or do refer to entities in the real world is to subscribe to what may be called *referential realism* with respect to those expressions' (Mäki 1992: 5).

As our central concern is with a taxonomy of realisms appropriate to the philosophy of economics, the actual definition of each category is very significant and deserves close scrutiny. Mäki's referential realism is focusing on linguistic expressions. These include proper names, demonstratives, common nouns, adjectives, observational terms, theoretical terms and so on. Second, to be a referential realist one has simply to hold that some such term *may* refer without specifying how the reference is accomplished or achieved, or without giving any description or characterization of its referent. Thus, for instance, despite the crucial differences in their semantical theories of proper names, Frege, Mill, Putnam and Russell are all referential realists. In this connection, given that Friedman presumably believes that the proper noun 'Chicago' has a referent, he is a referential realist. Once again, the category of referential realism is very broad, though perhaps not as broad as that of ontological realism. The former implies the latter, but it is logically possible to be an ontological realist without being a referential realist. Whether or not any philosopher of economics or economic methodologist has espoused such a possibility is a historical question. Be that as it may, there should be no surprise in the claim that Friedman is both a referential realist and an instrumentalist: the category of referential realism is sufficiently broad to capture empiricists, conventionalists, descriptivists, instrumentalists, Popperians, scientific realists as well as hosts of diverging positions within the philosophy of economics ranging from the Austrians to the rhetoricians.

A specific kind of referential realism is called representational realism. If a theory or statement or term represents an entity in the real world and if it tells us what the entity is like or how it behaves, i.e. if it attributes some properties to the referent, then anyone who holds this is a representational realist. Once again, one must note what is being literally said in this definition or characterization. If a theory predicates a property of a referent and this attribution is false, such a position is still a representational realist view. Thus if Friedman were to hold that Chicago is the capital of France he would be a representational realist. Moreover, unlike Frege who holds that the sense determines the referent, representational realists make no such claim. Like referential realists they are silent on how the referent is determined. To be a representational realist it suffices that one asserts that the referent of X is such-and-such, with or without any justification for this predication. Clearly, there is no incompatibility between being a representational realist and being an instrumentalist or descriptivist or whatever in one's philosophy of science.

Semantics also embraces another category of realism, namely, veristic realism. If one holds that a theory or statement is either true or false by virtue of the way the world is, one is a veristic realist. Thus veristic realism is very similar to Newton-Smith's minimal common factor to most scientific realists noted in Chapter 3. Given this formulation of veristic realism, it is logically possible to accept veristic realism and reject referential realism. Anyone who would pursue such a possibility would *ipso facto* explicate reference in terms of truth. In other words, one would maintain that the notion of truth is semantically more basic than that of reference and thus define or explicate the latter in terms of the former. The history of the philosophy of economics could then be examined to see whether or not anyone subscribed to such a semantical thesis. Mäki, however, does not appear to entertain such a possibility. He restates the thesis of veristic realism in terms of reference: 'statements may be claimed to be true or false partly by virtue of what their referents are like, i.e., by virtue of the way the world is' (Mäki 1992: 5). In light of this formulation, how is one to distinguish it from representational realism? If one holds that the referent of X is such and such, where X is substituted by some appropriate linguistic term, one is a representational realist. The latter kind of realist is not specifying the grounds on which the attribution is held to be true or false, whereas the veristic realist is making such a specification. Alternatively, representational realists are silent on their theory of truth whereas veristic realists opt for the correspondence theory. According to this reading, an irrational dogmatist who holds that, say, Chicago is polluted on the grounds that the said attribution is true because everything he says must be true, would be a representational realist but not necessarily a veristic one. In short, given Mäki's characterizations or definitions, if one is a veristic realist one is a representational, referential and ontological realist. However, one could be a representational or referential realist without being a veristic one.

The question now arises as to how informative is Mäki's claim that Friedman is a realist in the four senses above. In order to answer this let us consider the following example of a Kaldorian stylized fact, e.g. the UK's productivity growth in the postwar period was less than that of comparable industrial economies. If Friedman accepts this fact, and there is no reason why he should not, by virtue of holding such a belief he is an ontological, referential and representational realist. He believes that the UK exists, that the term UK refers, and that its productivity rate in the 1950s was less than that of other comparable economies. In so far as he believes that this fact is true by virtue of how the world is, he is also a veristic realist. However, in connection with his philosophy of science and especially of neoclassical economics, he could adopt any of a variety of philosophies of science, such as descriptivism, instrumentalism, pragmatism, Popperianism, scientific realism or constructive empiricism and still remain a realist in Mäki's four senses by virtue of believing the above Kaldorian stylized fact. In other words, these ontological-semantical realisms do not capture what is distinctive of scientific realism as a philosophy of science opposed to, say, empiricist/positivist approaches to science. In this fashion, one might maintain that Mäki's four

120

categories are too wide and consequently are not as informative as they might first appear. They fail to specify the appropriate methodological framework for the science of economics.

Although Mäki's four categories as such are very broad they can be made much more informative by relating them to specific or definite terms, sentences, or theories. Thus instead of asking whether or not Friedman is, say, a referential realist, one could ask the more specific question as to whether or not he is a referential realist *vis-à-vis* a specific term, sentence or theory. In this connection Mäki makes a very interesting comparison between Machlup and Friedman (Mäki 1989: 185–7). Machlup regards the neoclassical concept of the firm as a 'heuristic fiction' or 'imaginary puppet'. According to Machlup the purpose of neoclassical theory is not to explain the behaviour of business firms. Rather, it is a theory of competitive pricing. Thus, with respect to neoclassical firms, Machlup is an ontological non-realist: he believes that neoclassical firms do not exist. With respect to this same notion he is also a referential and representational non-realist. However, *vis-à-vis* business firms, in the ordinary, as opposed to the neoclassical, sense he is an ontological realist, i.e. he holds that there are business firms in the world. Unlike Machlup, Friedman is an ontological realist *vis-à-vis* neoclassical business firms. He is also a referential realist *vis-à-vis* that notion – it refers to actual business firms. He is also a representational realist in that he holds that the assumptions of neoclassical theory attribute properties to those actual firms. These attributions, however, are false and hence *vis-à-vis* the assumptions of neoclassical theory he is a veristic realist. One might speculate that Machlup is quite Fregian in his semantical intuitions: if the attributes contained in the sense of a term are not true of anything, as are the defining attributes of the neoclassical firm, then such a term does not refer, while Friedman's implicit semantics is much closer to Putnam in which terms with false stereotypes succeed in referring. This speculation, however, is moving the focus away from Mäki's use of his four categories of realism. His suggestion is, first, specify what term, sentence, set of sentences, hypothesis, assumption, or theory is under discussion and, second, ascertain whether or not the philosopher of economics or the economist in question is a realist or non-realist in the four senses outlined above.

Friedman is not only a veristic realist *vis-à-vis* the factual claims of neoclassical economics he is also a veristic realist *vis-à-vis* 'the important hypotheses' of economics in that he holds that these are actually false. This realism has some implications for Friedman's philosophy of science. One major implication is that it is inconsistent with philosophical instrumentalism. As we saw in Chapter 3, philosophical instrumentalism holds that theoretical sentences are not propositions, i.e. they are neither true nor false. Friedman's veristic realism *vis-à-vis* significant economic hypotheses is clearly in-compatible with this kind of instrumentalism. However, according to Mäki, Friedman is a *methodological* instrumentalist in that his famous piece is a plea for the use of a false economic theory for instrumental, i.e. predictive or organizational, purposes. Thus Friedman's economic instrumentalism is a mixture of ontological and semantic realism on the one hand and methodological instrumentalism on the other. Mäki calls this combination the Friedman mixture. Finally, when Friedman says that the realism of assumptions is irrelevant to the acceptance of an economic theory, the term 'realism' is utterly misleading: it should be replaced by the distinct, though related, term of 'realisticness'.

MÄKI'S REALISTICNESS AND THE F THESIS

According to Mäki, unnecessary confusion can be avoided by distinguishing between the terms 'realism' and 'realisticness'. Thus, instead of speaking about the realism of assumptions, clarity would be better served by some such expression as the assumptions are realistic or unrealistic in the sense of X, where the appropriate meaning is specified under X. Clearly, the term 'realistic' has a variety of senses or meanings. For instance, it could be claimed that an economic representation is unrealistic in the sense that it is implausible or irrelevant. Furthermore, unlike the semantical concepts of realism outlined above, some of these senses of realistic admit to differences of degree: one representation may be more realistic than another or a representation itself is more or less realistic in being more or less plausible or comprehensive. Generally speaking, the concept of realisticness is a disjunctive one: its definition consists of the logical disjunction of the appropriate senses, such as is plausible or comprehensive or relevant and so on. In short, the concept of realisticness is distinct from that of realism. Finally, in Mäki's approach the term 'realistic' can be predicated not only of economic assumptions but also of other economic concepts, descriptive or theoretical sentences, hypotheses and so on. Indeed, one could hold that a particular philosophy of economics or economic methodology is unrealistic.

One of Mäki's principal theses is that the relationship of Friedman's famous methodological piece to realism crucially depends on how the term unrealistic is understood. Friedman can be read as endorsing several kinds of realism and this range depends on how '(un)realistic' is interpreted. Furthermore, Friedman's piece is also confused in that Friedman himself both fails to note these differences and to appreciate their significance (Mäki 1992: 19). Hence Mäki explores different senses of the term realisticness and their relationships to the different senses of realism. In this connection he distinguishes between semantic and pragmatic senses of realisticness. The pragmatic range of senses includes notions such as plausibility, relevance or usefulness. Mäki, however, does not focus on this range. Rather, he explores the semantic range. In particular, he identifies three semantic senses of the term which are directly related to the senses of semantic realism noted earlier. First, an economic conception may be *referentially* realistic in that it refers to reality and referentially unrealistic if it fails to refer to entities in the actual world. If a conception is referentially realistic, one must be a referential realist *vis-à-vis* that concept. Second, an economic characterization is *representationally* realistic if it represents real features of real things and is representationally unrealistic if it fails to do so. Clearly, any person who maintains that a characterization is representationally realistic must logically be a representational realist about that referent. Finally, an economic sentence or theory is *veristically* realistic if its predication is true of its referents and veristically unrealistic if the predication is false of its referents. Since the veristic realist holds that sentences are either true or false both veristic realisticness and veristic unrealisticness imply veristic realism. This point is quite significant. Friedman holds that important economic hypotheses are veristically unrealistic and hence, as we noted earlier, he is a veristic realist. Mäki's point here is that we know or can infer Friedman's veristic realism from his attitude of veristic unrealisticness towards significant economic hypotheses. This clearly illustrates Mäki's principal thesis outlined above.

Mäki now proceeds to examine the category of veristic unrealisticness. One may say, *à la* Friedman, that specific economic assumptions are unrealistic in that they are false *without any further qualification*. This we may call unqualified veristic unrealisticness. Veristic unrealisticness, however, may be qualified in different ways and these different qualifications are significant. Consider the following statement. The stuff or substance in all the rivers of the earth is vodka. This statement is unrealistic in that it is plainly or simply false. Contrast that statement with the proposition that the stuff or substance in all the rivers of the earth is water. This too is veristically unrealistic but, since most of the stuff running in rivers is water, we may call it an exaggeration, i.e. this is an *exaggerated* [veristic] unrealistic claim. This in turn must be differentiated from an *understated* [veristic] unrealistic claim. Mäki's example of the latter is 'half the surface of the earth is covered with water' (Mäki 1992: 8). This in turn must be distinguished from a veristic unrealistic assertion which is an approximation, such as the distance from Paris to Le Havre is approximately two hundred kilometres. Simplifications, such as the shape of the earth is spherical, are also veristically unrealistic, as are idealizations involving limit concepts, such as the earth is a point mass, but they are unrealistic in different ways. In short, we may ask of any veristic unrealistic assertion whether or not it is an exaggeration, idealization, simplification, understatement and so on, or just simply unqualifiedly unrealistic.

A statement may be unrealistic in that it fails to tell the truth and be qualified along some of the lines just suggested. Alternatively, a statement may be unrealistic in either failing to tell the whole truth or nothing but the truth. These latter senses of unrealisticness are quite important. A representation which fails to tell the whole truth is called an isolation and, as Mäki perceptively notes, isolations do not imply falsehood. Mäki also points out that Friedman's piece fails to distinguish between these different senses of unrealisticness and thereby adds to the confusion. Moreover, this confusion vitiates, at least in part, Friedman's argument for the F thesis. When discussing some recent criticisms of the maximization-of-returns hypothesis on the grounds that businessmen do not behave as the theory assumes they do, Friedman explicitly draws our attention to a completely 'realistic' theory of the wheat market, which would, on the grounds of the whole truth, have to include the chemical characteristics of the soil used, the farmers' education and other social circumstances, the weather and so on. The wheat market example clearly shows that such an economic theory must be unrealistic in that it has to isolate certain factors and ignore others, i.e. it is unrealistic in that it does not present the whole truth. This kind of unrealisticness, however, does not imply anything *vis-à-vis* the unrealisticness of the assumption that wheat producers are maximizers in the entirely different sense of not giving an account which includes 'nothing-but-the-truth'. A less than completely comprehensive account does not imply any kind of falsehood. Hence Friedman just manages to confuse the issue by reference to the fact that economists and other scientists legitimately accept unrealistic theories in the sense of being less than fully comprehensive.

Mäki briefly analyses the neoclassical maximazation hypothesis in order to show some of the senses in which it is unrealistic. The formulation which he works with is the following. Producers and traders pursue maximum expected returns. He points out that Friedman appears to have taken the Hall and Hitch criticism seriously, i.e. that firms are not maximizers in the sense that they do not actually engage in the required marginal calculations and adjustments, and concludes that it is unqualifiedly veristically unrealistic. However, on pursuing the analysis we can see that it is unrealistic in the sense that the hypothesis does not tell 'the whole truth'. If the maximization hypothesis is understood to be referring to the motives, as opposed to the behaviour, of business people it involves an isolation. It isolates the motivation of maximum profits from all other motives, such as altruism, personal satisfaction, maximization of sales and so on. It does not tell the whole truth. Second, it is veristically unrealistic in that it involves an exaggeration. If, as Simon for instance argues, economic agents are satis-ficers, rather than maximizers, and thereby are content with less than maximum returns, the hypothesis is veristically unrealistic in being an exaggeration. This in turn means that it is also unrealistic in the sense that it goes beyond stating 'nothing but the truth'. Friedman failed to keep these distinct and opted for unqualified veristic unrealisticness. This in turn implies that Friedman is an ontological and semantic realist and there is no incompatibility between these realisms and his methodological instrumentalism.

124

COMMON-SENSE REALISM, SCIENTIFIC REALISM AND FRIEDMAN

How are ontological and semantic realisms as characterized by Mäki to be connected to the stereotypes of scientific realism as outlined in Chapter 4? We have already seen that empiricists, relativists, pragmatists and others who oppose scientific realism are in their own specific ways ontological and semantic realists. Mäki makes the connection to scientific realism by, first, looking at what he calls common-sense realism. The ordinary lay person is ontologically committed to apples, oranges, chocolate and the other numerous entities of her or his common-sense conceptual scheme. According to Mäki, a minimalist common-sense realist holds that these common-sense objects exist, while a radical common-sense realist holds that only these exist, e.g. they are non-realists about theoretical scientific entities such as black holes or quarks. The minimalist scientific realist holds that scientific entities exist and, in particular, that theoretical terms refer, whereas the radical scientific realist is a non-realist about the objects of common sense. Essentialist scientific realism is a specific form of scientific realism which holds that scientific theories either reveal or approximate to the truth about the hidden essences of the actual world. In this connection the epistemic acceptance of an economic theory is based on its explanatory power and Mäki notes that in many versions of scientific realism explanatory power, existence and truth are intimately connected in that the acceptance of a theory as the correct explanation entails the belief that its referents are real and that the theory is true or approximates to the truth. Indeed, he notes a particular kind of essentialist scientific realism which analyses the explanatory power of a theory in terms of its capacity to effect theoretical redescription accompanied by ontological unification or reduction (Mäki 1990: 25–7). This form of scientific realism certainly necessitates the rejection of radical common-sense realism and some versions of it, such as Paul Churchland's eliminative materialism, necessitate the rejection of a substantial portion, if not indeed all, of the ontological framework of minimalist common-sense realism. Despite Mäki's claim that a commitment to ontological unification is a 'very natural' one for an essentialist realist, we did not explicitly specify it as a stereotype of scientific realism. Without doubt numerous scientific realists are silent on this matter. However, it could be argued that this commitment is tacitly assumed or logically follows from essentialist scientific realism. We would certainly concur that it is a natural extension of essentialist realism. In, particular, since Mäki focuses on this in both his discussion of Friedman and of the Austrians, a few words about this kind of scientific realism may be in order.

In our presentation of scientific realism we drew attention to the qualification of realism as scientific by pointing out that science, as opposed to philosophy, especially metaphysics, reveals the truth about reality. Mäki, however, draws a different contrast: science, rather than common sense, reveals the truth. Scientific realists hold that the most reliable, and perhaps the only, way to discover what the world actually or really is, including its basic causal mechanisms, is to engage in scientific theorizing. The procedures, conceptual resources and ontology of common sense simply do not stand up to critical scrutiny when compared to those of advanced scientific theory. In particular, science has ontological priority over our common-sense framework. As we have already seen, in scientific realism explanation and ontological commitment go hand in hand: the entities postulated by the best theoretical explanations are the basic entities of the world and, as is clear from the physical sciences, the ontological resources of our common-sense conceptual scheme are completely inadequate and misleading. Hence scientific realism demands the rejection of radical common-sense realism.

According to Mäki, Friedman finds common-sense realism appealing. In this connection Mäki notes that Friedman is like the Austrians: both are common-sense realists about many objects. In the Friedman perspective, the presumed fundamental constituents of economic reality are common-sense entities like business firms, households, consumer goods, money, prices, taxes and so forth. From a radical common-sense realist perspective, none of these common-sense entities look dubious, whereas the entities postulated by a sophisticated scientific theory, like those of quantum physics, are highly suspect. Mäki supplies a penetrating example of how this common-sense realism can function in one's understanding of neoclassical economics. The example is that of the business firm. Business firms are an integral part of the ontological furniture of our contemporary common-sense framework in that these firms actually exist and have observable properties. However, neoclassical theory describes these as fully informed, rational calculators intent on profit maximization. Such a characterization is, from the perspective of common-sense realism, clearly false. In other words, neoclassical economics at the theoretical level, does not accurately describe actual business firms. Nevertheless, this neoclassical characterization is most useful for predicting and organizing economic data. Hence the Friedman mixture of methodological instrumentalism and semantic realism noted by Mäki follows naturally from this (radical) common-sense realism or constitutes a specific economic paradigm of this form of realism.

A radical essentialist scientific realist would view neoclassical theory in a completely different way than the Friedman mixture. Mäki is certainly correct in asserting that such a realist would view the maximization principle or axiom or assumption as revealing the essence of economic behaviour (Mäki 1992: 26). Neoclassical theory has discovered the essential properties of economic behaviour, business firms, prices and so on. What the common-sense realist sees as false, the radical essentialist realist sees as indispensable. For instance, according to the radical scientific realist the common-sense characterization of business firms is both false and misleading in that it

126

conceals the true essence of such firms and hence it must be rejected. The neoclassical characterization of the business firm must replace the false characterization from common sense: the radical realist *theoretically re-describes* the business firm. Moreover, this radical essentialist realist reading accomplishes an ontological unification or reduction of the apparently diverse and disconnected phenomena of the economic world as presented in our misleading common-sense framework. The diverse phenomena of the actual economic world are really the products or the manifestations of the basic, essential factors which have been identified by neoclassical theory. The ontological reduction is effected by a process of redescription. In this process one is maintaining that, for instance, business firms are really, ultimately, at rock bottom, nothing but maximizers as characterized by neoclassical theory. In this way neoclassical theory discovers the fundamental entities of the economic world and economic phenomena are ontologically reduced to these fundamental entities in that they are redescribed and reconstituted in terms of these basic entities. The theoretical redescriptions are conveying what these really are or their authentic generative mechanisms. The radical essentialist scientific realist thus draws a sharp distinction between appearances and reality.

According to Mäki there are notable passages in Friedman's essay which could be read in this radical scientific realist fashion. He concludes that Friedman hovers between this position and the radical common-sense realist position as exemplified in the Friedman mixture of methodological instru-mentalism and semantic realism. This hovering, moreover, is part of the problem with Friedman's piece, especially since these two positions are mutually incompatible. Furthermore, Mäki maintains that the common-sense realist, unlike the essentialist scientific realist, is unable to make a serious distinction between appearances and reality. Consequently, the common-sense realist is unable to perceive the difference between the notion of unrealistic understood as an exaggeration and that understood as an isolation which can convey the essential truth but perhaps not the whole truth. Thus Mäki explains why Friedman fails to differentiate between these two senses in terms of Friedman's attraction to common-sense realism. Friedman appears to think that if an economic theoretical representation does not correspond to the common-sense experience, such a representation is un-realistic in the sense of simply being false. However, unrealistic assumptions, particularly isolations, can serve the pursuit of truth in economics, provided this is understood in an essentialist realist fashion. According to Mäki, this possibility cannot be recognized unless radical common-sense realism is rejected and the different senses of unrealisticness acknowledged.

Mäki expressly declares that his analysis of Friedman serves a dual purpose in that it both clarifies the famous Friedman piece and reveals Mäki's own thoughts about economics. By way of conclusion we shall attempt to briefly address the latter. In the first place he holds that clarity in the philosophy of economics in general, and in connection with the realism of assumptions debate in particular, is served by distinguishing between realism and realisticness. Varieties of realism and of realisticness exist and some of these, though distinct, are interrelated. In particular, the notion of plausibility belongs to the pragmatic rather than the semantic category of unrealisticness. In connection with scientific realism, Mäki's intuitions are strongly realist (Mäki 1989: 195). However, he introduces two qualifications. First, he distinguishes between the acceptance of a theory and believing that a theory is true. A theory is accepted if it is adopted, held, used, applied and so forth. In Mäki's view, acceptance does not imply belief. Economic theory X may be more acceptable than theory Y for creative modelling, whereas Y may be more acceptable than X for the purposes of systematic organization of the empirical data, but neither may be believed to be true. The essentialist scientific realist, however, will pursue economic theories which are both acceptable in some specified sense and believed to provide a true, explanatory account of the essence of the economy.

The second qualification appears to arise from the first. It amounts to the claim that different theories may be accepted on different grounds. Since acceptance entails many dimensions other than belief and indeed may not entail belief at all, clearly there are different standards of appraisal for economic theories relative to the aspect of acceptance under discussion. To this extent Mäki holds that Caldwell's critical pluralism and realism are compatible. The question, however, immediately arises as to whether or not Mäki is also a pluralist *vis-à-vis* the scientific realist acceptance of a theory as the correct explanation? While the notion of acceptance is not univocal, i.e. there are different criteria of acceptance depending on the sense used, the more specific scientific realist notion of acceptance as the correct explanation is univocal and hence does not necessarily accommodate methodological pluralism. How can one rationally assume that divergent methods and conceptual frameworks will succeed in revealing one and the same explanationary hidden structure or mechanism, or essence? Mäki is not very explicit on this matter. On the one hand, he rejects any radical version of fallibilism and on the other hand, he points out that the realist can view the standards of appraisal for economic theories as evolving over time:

> nobody may pretend to hold the final, infallible set of *criteria of acceptance*. Several candidates for the role of a good criterion or set of criteria have to be taken seriously. Only little by little can we hope to learn which criteria serve best our purposes, including the major goal of attaining true explanatory economic theories.
>
> (Mäki 1989: 196)

Finally, we come to a constellation of issues raised by Mäki himself *vis-à-vis* the Austrians' realism. Essentialist scientific realism maintains that economics, by sophisticated theoretical activity, can reveal the ultimate or invariant constituents of the economy. However, any ultimate explanation implies that the theory fulfilling this end is neither in need of nor susceptible to further analysis or change. In other words, the explanatory quest must stop at the real essences and mature economic theory reveals these in the case of the economic world. Mäki, however, appears to voice some reservations. In view of the fact that contemporary economies are embedded in other socio-political structures, Mäki rhetorically asks whether or not any claim about 'ultimate explanation' should be strongly relativized with respect to disciplinary boundaries? Clearly, this question raises crucial issues for the scientific realist's reduction or ontological unification programme. For instance, are contemporary economic theories capable of undergoing revolutionary change like that witnessed in the physical sciences at the hands of Newton or Einstein? If so, how are we to talk of the ultimate explanation at the theoretical level? Is this, as suggested by Leplin, (Chapter 4) to be realized only at the very end of theoretical economic activity? However, in view of Quine's holism and theoretical pluralism, how are we to know that we have reached the end of theoretical economics? In short, which, if any, of the contemporary economic theories succeeds in approximating to the invariant non-empirical economic structures and, in view of Mäki's apparent methodological pluralism, how can we, as fallible theoreticians, know that we have reached such a position? Lawson is clear that econometrics in particular and neoclassical theory in general, fail to attain these real structures. Mäki, however, is not so forthcoming.

There is, in this respect, a remarkable contrast in Lawson's and Mäki's styles. Lawson is criticizing specific philosophical methodologies, such as Humean empiricism and instrumentalism, as well as specific economic activities or disciplines such as econometrics and neoclassical theory. Mäki's style is more expository with the exposition more focused on the philosophico-methodological writings of economists than on specific economic theories. At times one may feel that he is merely using his taxonomy of realisms as tools for interpretative purposes in engaging the history of economic methodology and hence is suspending judgement on the respective merits of specific economic theories. His style could give the impression that his realism is disguising the pluralist's penchant for the *status quo* in economic activity, which ironically would leave us with little hope of coming to a rational conclusion about the competing economic theories. Perhaps this is reading too much into a difference in style. After all, Lawson is an economist interested and skilled in philosophy, whereas Mäki is a philosopher interested and skilled in economic methodology. Whatever the reasons for their differences both Lawson and Mäki adroitly articulate and deftly develop central themes of scientific realism in the philosophy of economics.

6

CONSTRUCTIVE EMPIRICISM
The challenge to scientific realism

The rapid and remarkable expansion of scientific realism in the 1970s sounded the death knell for logical positivism or logical empiricism. While it might be an exaggeration to say that the former had by the end of the 1970s replaced the latter as the dominant philosophy of science, there was little doubt that realism was quickly emerging as the victorious successor for that title. There was an impressive consensus that logical positivism was utterly untenable and had wrought widespread disaster in philosophy of science. In the rush to distance themselves from any contamination by the corpse of this corruptive influence, philosophers of science, of various shades and colour, sought haven in the clearly uncontaminated realm of scientific realism. In the 1980s, however, constructive empiricism, as articulated by van Fraassen, attempted to halt this onrush into scientific realism by arguing that the timely death knell of logical positivism was not ringing for the basic empiricist view that scientific knowledge is limited to what is observable. Empiricism, in the form of constructive empiricism, survives the totally legitimate demise of logical positivism.

CONSTRUCTIVE EMPIRICISM: SOME BASIC TENETS

Constructive empiricism is expressly developed as an alternative to scientific realism. The latter maintains that a scientific theory accounts for or explains the observable phenomena by postulating processes and structures which are not directly accessible to observation. In particular, theoretical science has as one of its principal aims the discovery of true descriptions of the unobservable processes which explain the observable phenomena. Contrary to this realist approach, constructive empiricism puts the focus on construction rather than discovery. One of the principal tasks of science is the construction of scientific models. However, contrary to realism, these constructed models do not lead to the discovery of the truth concerning unobservable entities, processes or structures. Rather, they furnish true or correct descriptions of what is observable and the constructive empiricist suspends judgement on the rest. In general terms we can say that a scientific model, for epistemic purposes, is divided into its lower-level descriptive statements and its higher-level theoretical sentences. If the former furnish accurate descriptions of the observable world, constructive empiricists claim that the constructed model is empirically adequate and thereby suspend judgement on the issue of ascertaining the truth or falsehood of the model's high-level theoretical sentences. In this fashion, the spotlight is clearly focused on the construction of models with a view to furnishing accurate descriptions of the observable events and entities of the actual world. Thus the principal epistemic concern is whether or not a theory is empirically adequate, i.e. whether or not the constructed model furnishes true descriptions of the whole domain of the observable, and this, contrary to scientific realism, has nothing whatsoever to do with unobservable essences, mechanisms, processes or structures. Clearly, constructive empiricism is opposed to both Lawson's tanscendental realism and to essentialist scientific realism as characterized by Mäki.

In addition to claiming empirical adequacy, rather than truth or approximation to the truth, as the principal epistemic characteristic of a scientific model, the constructive empiricist also effects a Copernican revolution in our conception of scientific explanation. Numerous economists tacitly assume that theory is introduced for explanatory purposes. The primary function of a theory is to explain. This conception, as we already noted, is given a challenging explication by scientific realism in general and transcendental realism in particular. The constructive empiricist totally rejects this whole approach. Contrary to scientific realism, the central function of theory is to furnish accurate descriptions of the observable world and this has nothing to do with explanation. As we saw in Chapter 3, Quine is the central figure. According to Quine's holism at the level of meaning, theory is indispensable to our descriptive endeavours. The constructive empiricist unequivocally endorses the Quinian thesis that all scientific description is theory-laden. Our scientific descriptions presuppose scientific theory.

It could be argued that this Quinian thesis does not, as such, preclude the possibility of theory playing the dual roles of furnishing theory-laden descriptions on the one hand and scientific explanations on the other. Any such dual role is expressly ruled out by constructive empiricism. Constructive empiricists develop a challenging analysis of scientific explanation which unequivocally severs its specific links to scientific theory. The upshot of their analysis is the relocation of scientific explanation in the domain of applied, rather than of pure, science. In this connection constructive empiricists draw a sharp distinction between the epistemic and pragmatic dimensions of theory acceptance. The epistemic dimension is solely concerned with the relationship between a model and the world. This is pursued in pure science and, according to the constructive empiricist, this is summed up in the claim of empirical adequacy. Epistemically speaking, pure science is centrally concerned with the construction of empirically adequate theories. In this view theory is indispensable to pure science at the descriptive, as distinct from the explanatory, level. The acceptance of a scientific theory entails much more than this epistemic dimension. It also entails an extensive pragmatic dimension. This pragmatic dimension of theory acceptance is characterized by van Fraassen in negative terms. It includes all aspects of theory acceptance other than the epistemic dimension. For instance, it covers our human concern for technological control on the one hand and our human appreciation of elegance and simplicity on the other. Thus the pragmatic dimension ranges over a wide range of non-epistemic human interests. Moreover, success in the pragmatic dimension has no bearing on the evaluation of the epistemic acceptance of a theory. This unequivocal independence of the epistemic from the pragmatic is central to constructive empiricism. Any pragmatic success has no bearing whatsoever on the issue of the empirical adequacy of a theory. The constructive empiricist's Copernican revolution consists in relocating scientific explanation in this pragmatic dimension, thereby maintaining that the explanatory success of a scientific model has no bearing whatsoever on its epistemic evaluation. Constructive empiricists acknowledge that this relocation is revolutionary. This relocation, however, is absolutely central to their challenging philosophy of science. These two corner-stones of constructive empiricism, namely, the focus on empirical adequacy and the relocation of scientific explanation into pragmatics, which are totally at variance with scientific realism, have major implications for the philosophy of economics. This chapter is devoted to exploring this significance.

EMPIRICAL ADEQUACY: A PRELIMINARY ACCOUNT

Van Fraassen sums up scientific realism as follows: 'Science aims to give us, in its theories, a literally true story of what the world is like; and acceptance of a scientific theory involves the belief that it is true' (van Fraassen 1980: 8). This, in his opinion, is minimal, in that no scientific realist would find any objection to it. In this he is evidently wrong. Mäki, for instance, points out that it is far too strong to be acceptable as a common characteristic shared by all versions of scientific realism. As we saw in the last chapter, Mäki, in explicit opposition to van Fraassen, does not view the acceptance of a theory as necessarily containing an epistemic dimension. Nevertheless, in view of the fact that both agree that the notion of acceptance is distinct from that of belief, Mäki's objection can easily be accommodated without radically altering van Fraassen's summary account of scientific realism. The modified version could read as follows: science aims to give us, in its theories, literal accounts which are true of the actual world and the epistemic attitude of the scientific realist involves the belief that a mature scientific theory is true or approximates to the truth. Moreover, one need not read this as some highest common factor of all versions of scientific realism – it suffices that it be seen as a stereotype of scientific realism. The principal reason for focusing on the above formulation is the fact that van Fraassen sums up constructive empiricism in opposition to it as follows: 'Science aims to give us theories which are empirically adequate; and acceptance of a theory involves as belief only that it is empirically adequate' (van Fraassen 1980: 12). The following is perhaps a more comprehensive summary. Science aims to give us, in its theories, literal descriptions of the observable world, and the epistemic attitude of the constructive empiricist involves the belief that such a mature theory is empirically adequate. Thus the contrast is sharply drawn between belief-as-true and belief-as-empirically adequate. The basic intuition underlying the latter notion is that a theory is empirically adequate if what it says about the observable things and events in this world is true. In holding that a theory is empirically adequate, the constructive empiricist is maintaining (a) that its factual statements about observable entities and events are true or false, (b) that in principle the truth-value of such statements can be rationally ascertained, (c) that its theoretical statements about entities which are in principle unobservable are also true or false but (d) that rationally we cannot ascertain which of these truth values applies and consequently we suspend judgement on them.

In a sense one could say that constructive empiricism is holding some middle ground between philosophical instrumentalism and scientific realism. As we saw in Chapter 3, philosophical instrumentalists do not accept theoretical sentences at face value: they concede that such sentences appear to be propositions, i.e. sentences which are true or false, but this is merely an appearance. Such statements, in van Fraassen's terminology, are not literally construed by instrumentalists. Rather, philosophical instrumentalists re-construe them as conceptual tools or inference tickets or material rules of inference. In Mäki's terminology, the philosophical instrumentalist is not a veristic realist *vis-à-vis* theoretical sentences. In opposition to the philosophical instrumentalist, theoretical sentences are propositions in the eyes of the constructive empiricist, i.e. they are sentences which are true or false. Like the scientific realist, the constructive empiricist is a veristic realist *vis-à-vis* theoretical sentences. However, unlike scientific realists, constructive empiricists have a different aim in mind in constructing a mature scientific theory and a different epistemic attitude towards it. They believe that a mature theory is merely empirically adequate which falls short of the realist's belief that it is actually true or approximates to the truth. The scientific realist holds that theoretical sentences are true or false and that those of a mature theory can be known to be true or approximately true. The constructive empiricist is a Humean agnostic or sceptic *vis-à-vis* the latter but not *vis-à-vis* the former. The most coherent attitude towards the belief that specific theoretical terms can be known to refer to unobservable entities or that theoretical sentences can be known to predicate true descriptions of unobservable objects is simply and unequivocally to suspend judgement on it. Such realist considerations have nothing to do with either the aim of, or our correct epistemic attitude towards, science. According to constructive empiricism, the principal epistemic virtue or characteristic of a pure scientific theory concerns whether or not it is empirically adequate. The philosophical instrumentalist is primarily concerned with whether or not a pure scientific theory is a successful tool or heuristic instrument, the scientific realist is primarily concerned with whether or not it accurately describes the unobservable events, entities, structures or essences of the actual world, whereas the constructive empiricist is centrally concerned with its empirical adequacy, i.e. whether or not it furnishes accurate descriptions of the observable world. It should be noted that, in claiming a theory is empirically adequate, one is referring to all observable phenomena, including those which will occur in the future and hence the claim does involve a degree of risk. As van Fraassen puts it, 'we stick our necks out: empirical adequacy goes far beyond what we can know at any given time' (van Fraassen 1980: 69).

In the specific domain of economics this entails the construction of theoretical models which offer accurate descriptions of all observable economic phenomena. In order to facilitate the realization of this aim, a division of labour whereby some pure economists would devote their complete attention to the construction of mathematical models may be useful. This task could include the construction of axiomatic systems and the invention, adaption or application of mathematical techniques for generating equilibrium solutions for the equations of these models. This in turn could include the investigation of consistency constraints and so forth. Moreover, all of this theoretical work could be done in total isolation from any empirical study of specific economies, such as that of America, the EU or Japan. Within constructive empiricism, however, if pure economic theorizing or activity were to stop at this point, it would not merit the name of pure science. Any pure science, ranging from physics to economics, must present a model of the world. If an aim of pure economics is the construction of a mathematical model, such a model must, in the name of pure science, be investigated for its empirical adequacy. A pure economic theory which is claiming to be scientific must convey observational information about actual economies and economic activity or behaviour. If it does not fulfil this minimum condition it is not an empirical discipline at all. In accepting that an economic model is a part of pure science, rather than simple, elegant or fulfilling certain requirements demanded by the necessity of equilibrium solutions, one is claiming that it furnishes accurate descriptions of real economies. The epistemic concern of pure economics is centrally focused on whether or not it is empirically adequate.

Let us suppose that we are investigating the epistemic status of some specific economic theory, say neoclassical economics, from a constructive empiricist perspective. Let us also suppose, à la Friedman, that its predictive success to date is not in question. The neoclassical economist could remain sceptical about the future and merely claim that, up to the present, the theory has performed very well in providing accurate descriptions of consumers, firms, prices and so forth. If neoclassical economists were radical sceptical empiricists, they would not be willing to accept anything more than that. Alternatively, neoclassical economists could argue, *à la* essentialist scientific realism, that the extensive predictive success of their theory is due to the fact that neoclassical economics, at its theoretical level, is approximating to the fundamental, non-empirical, generative principles of the real world of economic transactions. Constructive empiricism, at the epistemic level, goes beyond radical sceptical empiricism but stops short of essentialist scientific realism. The constructive empiricist would, under the above assumptions, claim that neoclassical theory is empirically adequate, i.e. what the theory says about all observable economic phenomena past, present and future is true, while suspending judgement on the rest. In other words, the radical sceptical empiricist believes that neoclassical economics has accurately predicted what is currently observable and that is all that can be claimed; the essentialist scientific realist believes that the theoretical core of neoclassical economics reveals or approximates to the fundamental principles of the economic world and the constructive empiricist holds that neoclassical economics is empirically adequate to all observable economic phenomena and suspends judgement on what is in principle unobservable. So much for a preliminary outline. Before we articulate how van Fraassen spells out the details of this central notion of empirical adequacy, we will examine his challenging conception of scientific explanation.

THE CONTEXT DEPENDENCY OF SCIENTIFIC EXPLANATION

Numerous economists as well as philosophers unhesitatingly accept the view that scientific theory has a central explanatory role. In particular, the Lawsonian scientific realist articulates this deeply ingrained insight in a unique way: scientific theory, by liberating us from the dazzle of appearances, enables us to comprehend the reality behind these appearances and thereby explains how the latter are causally generated by the hidden structures of intransitive objects. For scientific realism, a mature theory simultaneously describes the hidden mechanisms and explains the observable world ultimately by reference to these mechanisms. Indeed, many of those who are not scientific realists, such as Popper, still hold with the view that scientific theory serves our explanatory endeavours and that this explanatory dimension is integral to any account of the role of theory in science. As we have already seen, Quine challenges this prevalent, deep-seated view. According to Quine, theory is indispensable for scientific description and the constructive empiricist shares this Quinian insight. Quine, however, does not systematically elaborate any novel account of explanation which would do justice to the sociological fact that experts, from physics to economics, seriously engage 'why' questions. Scientific curiosity is not simply limited to discovering and

135

describing the events and happenings of the observable world. Scientists also spend much of their time explaining the observable facts. It is one thing to know that the average EU inflation in 1992 was 4.7 per cent but the person who sincerely asks 'why was this so?' seeks to understand this phenomenon. Constructive empiricism meets this challenge by developing a contrastive analysis of explanation.

Like Garfinkel and others who pioneered this approach, the constructive empiricist starts from the truism that explanations are answers to 'why'-questions. One normally offers an explanation for an event or happening in response to the question 'why did it happen?' Constructive empiricism, however, wishes to exploit another truism, namely, that the request or demand for an explanation is context-dependent. Why-questions do not occur in an intellectual vacuum; on the contrary they occur in specific contexts and these contexts are crucial for the ways in which the questions are understood and the kinds of answers given in reply. The same why-question can be construed in different ways in different contexts. For instance, the question 'why did John buy a computer?' could, according to the context in which it is asked, mean:

(a) Why did John, rather than Peter, buy a computer?
(b) Why did John buy, rather than rent or borrow, a computer?
(c) Why did John buy a computer rather than a television?
(d) Why did John buy a computer yesterday rather than last month?

In each of the above examples a specific contrast is made – hence the term 'contrastive explanation'. Normally these contrasts are implicitly understood from the context in which the question 'why did John buy a computer?' is posed. In this connection the constructive empiricist draws our attention to two significant points. First, there is no one definitive explanation. There are different explanations, each appropriate and accurate relative to different contrasts. Second, the acceptability of a given explanation is evaluated in relation to the contrast made. Thus scientific explanation is context-dependent.

The context-dependency of explanation is not simply limited to tacit or explicit contrasts. The kinds of explanation offered and accepted are context-dependent in another sense, i.e. the interests of the relevant expert or person proffering the explanation influence the choice of salient factors used in satisfactory explanations. The standard example is the various explanations of a specific automobile accident given by different experts. The medical expert confirms that the driver was drunk and thus isolates that factor or event as the explanation of the accident. The mechanic confirms that the breaks in the automobile were defective thereby isolating this as the relevant explanatory factor. The urban geographer determines that the corner at which the accident occurred is dangerous and hence focuses on this as the salient explanation.

136

As van Fraassen perceptively notes, these different answers cannot, in a certain sense, be combined. The urban geographer is, *ceteris paribus*, isolating the corner as the cause, and the *ceteris paribus* clause in this instance includes medical, mechanical and other factors which could be isolated by different experts. Similarly, the medical expert is claiming, *ceteris paribus*, the accident was caused by the drunken state of the driver. In this instance, however, the *ceteris paribus* clause includes the urban geographer's salient factor. What one expert 'keeps fixed' or excludes by means of the *ceteris paribus* clause the other does not, but one cannot do both of these at once. In other words, the selection of the salient cause is a matter of which factor is the most interesting relative to the specific expert. The same holds for the question 'why did John buy a computer?' The neoclassical economist will focus on John's utility function, while the psychologist will focus on John's susceptibility to the television ad used for the brand of computer purchased and his wish to impress his girlfriend, while the sociologist will focus on the structures of modern capitalist urban societies as distinct from, say, pre-capitalist, agri-cultural societies. The legitimate interests of the various experts rule in certain factors as salient and rule out others as not being salient. These interests are also part of the context of explanation. Thus salience is context-dependent in that ranges of possible explanations are ruled out by the contrast made and by the interests of the experts or discussants. The context of explanation thereby influences the choice of relevant factors which goes far beyond the notions of statistical relevance developed by mathematicians.

Finally, in the constructive empiricist approach, there are vast varieties of explanations ranging from scientific, mythical, theological, philosophical, to the vast domain of those of common sense. What makes an explanation scientific, as opposed to mythical or theological, for instance, is that the discussants choose their salient explanatory factors from the domain of science. According to constructive empiricism, the logic of scientific ex-planation is a matter of a three-term relationship between a scientific theory (which, on grounds completely independent of any reference to explanation, is believed to be empirically adequate), the event in question, and a specific context. The context influences the choice of relevant factors. An empirically adequate theory furnishes scientific experts with a range of explanatory parameters from which they can choose the salient explanatory factors in light of a given context.

Scientific realists, Hempelians, Popperians and many others have lost sight of the indispensable role of context in scientific explanation. While Lawson, for instance, briefly notes that scientific explanation is very much an affair of context, he completely fails to perceive how integral context is to this pragmatic activity. Indeed, contrary to Lawsonian realism, this context-dependency demonstrates that scientific explanation belongs to applied, rather than to pure, science. In particular, economic explanation pertains to applied, rather than to pure, economics. This relocation of economic explanation to the domain of applied economics is of paramount importance. It fundamentally challenges the pervasive view that the aim of theoretical economics is to furnish explanations. According to constructive empiricism, pure or theoretical economics is primarily concerned with the construction of an empirically adequate economic theory and the epistemic decision on empirical adequacy makes no reference whatsoever to the explanatory success or otherwise of that theory. The issue of the explanatory success of an economic narrative is a non-epistemic, contextual affair which pertains to applied economics. An economic explanation entails a subsequent and derivative use of an empirically adequate theory in specific, pragmatic contexts. In light of the explicit or tacit contrasts gleaned from the context, the applied economist chooses the relevant or salient explanatory factors from the empirical substructures of the economic theory. The applied economist, in offering explanations, shows how the chosen factor from the theory is relevant to the event requiring explanation in a specific context. The economic theory, however, merely forms the background from which the salient explanatory factor is drawn.

The constructive empiricist's basic picture of economic explanation is as follows. Theoretical economists construct and test their models for empirical adequacy. This epistemic dimension of pure, theoretical economics is distinct from and independent of economic explanation. The latter belongs to the pragmatic, non-epistemic dimension of economics. It is located in applied, rather than pure, economics. Economic explanation comes into play in response to 'why?' questions in specific, pragmatic contexts. In furnishing explanations, economists assume that they already have on their books, so to speak, an empirically adequate model and, in light of a specific context, they choose the appropriate explanatory factor from their model. This is an applied task: it is the application in a specific context of a model which, on independent grounds, is held to be empirically adequate. By relocating economic explanation in applied, rather than theoretical, economics and by distinguishing between the epistemic and pragmatic dimensions of the acceptance of an economic theory, the constructive empiricist furnishes a very compelling account of the ways in which particular events and happenings are explained by economists. Contrary to Lawsonian realism, economic explanation neither pertains to the aim of theoretical economics nor to the criteria for evaluating its epistemic acceptance. Economic explanation, because of its context-dependency, is a pragmatic rather than a purely epistemic, issue.

In this connection it may be useful to re-look at McCloskey's rhetoric. It could be argued that, like constructive empiricists and unlike scientific realists, rhetoricians clearly perceive the full implications of the context-dependency of economic explanation. For instance, when economists are explaining to, say, politicians the recent surprising rise in inflation, they must be fully aware of the context. This includes more than the identification of tacit contrasts. The politicians are not familiar with the theoretical language of the economist's models and some time must be devoted to surmounting this pragmatic problem. The explanation after all must be understood by the audience to which it is addressed. Many rhetorical skills will be absolutely necessary in such contexts. Hence if one accepts the deep-seated assumption that the central role of economic theory is to furnish explanations, given that the latter is context-dependent, then clearly one must acknowledge that rhetoric is integral to the correct philosophical analysis of the former. In this fashion, global rhetoricists are fusing the context-dependency of economic explanation with this deeply ingrained assumption about the central explanatory role of economic theory. The constructive empiricist, however, does not accept this assumption. As we have already seen, the central epistemic function of an economic theory is, according to constructive empiricism, to furnish accurate descriptions. This has nothing to do with economic explanation which is relocated in the domain of pragmatics. In the latter perspective, the economist's skills in presenting explanations are rhetorical in the Aristotelian local sense: the applied economist is adroitly choosing the relevant explanatory factors from a theory which is already accepted as empirically adequate and the criteria for this epistemic acceptance has nothing to do with so-called explanatory power. The global rhetoricist tacitly accepts and consequently unhesitatingly works with this deeply ingrained notion of the basic explanatory role of economic theory which is rejected by constructive empiricism. The global rhetoricist fails to see that the epistemic acceptance of an economic theory is totally independent of the explanatory successes of economists. In short, global rhetoricism confuses the epistemic with the pragmatic and, like scientific realism, fails to appreciate that economic explanation pertains to applied, rather than to pure, economics.

According to constructive empiricism, there is a clear division of labour in the activities of economists. Pure economists are engaged in the activity of constructing models, which epistemically may be legitimated as empirically adequate. The pure economist constructs these models, attempts to justify the belief that they are empirically adequate and thereby is engaged in taking limited epistemic risks. This conception of pure economics is at variance with that of certain practitioners who limit the activity of pure economics to the construction of mathematical models without probing their empirical adequacy. As we have already seen, the construction of a mathematical model may be integral to the task of pure economics. The question whether or not a mathematical model can do justice to the complex historical development of an economy as well as other issues integral to the belief in the model's empirical adequacy are also investigated in pure economics. This investigation, however, contrary to scientific realism, does not extend to the explanation of particular economic events and happenings. The latter is among the numerous pragmatic, as distinct from the epistemic, activities of economists. The context-dependency of economic explanation introduces various interests other than the epistemic interest in empirical adequacy into the reckoning. While the work of offering appropriate, acceptable, relevant and accurate explanations is integral to economic activity, it pertains to applied, rather than pure, economics. This division of labour is not arbitrary: it reflects the independent dimensions of empirical adequacy which is centrally epistemic and of contextual relevance which is pragmatic in character.

An economic explanation is an answer, A, to a why-question, Q, which occurs in a specific context which includes a contrast class, X. Other additional information, especially an economic theory, E, which is held to be empirically adequate, forms part of the scientific background. How does the constructive empiricist arrive at the decision that A is a satisfactory explanation? How is the answer 'because A' to be scrutinized, evaluated or legitimated? Once the question Q is explicated to read why B rather than Xi, where Xi is a member of the contrast class X, the constructive empiricist follows conventional wisdom in suggesting three criteria. The first concerns the evaluation of A itself. If A is false then clearly the proffered explanation is rejected. However, if A is not known to be true, one must examine the probability of A in view of E, i.e. what probability does E confer on A? This in turn is later compared with the probability E confers on other possible answers. Second, one must investigate the extent to which the answer A favours B rather than any Xi. If the contextually specified subsection of E combined with A implies B and also implies that each Xi is false, then A clearly favours B as opposed to Xi. If this does not happen, one must investigate how well A redistributes the probabilities on the contrast class with a view to favouring B as opposed to any Xi. The mere fact that the probability of B is lowered is not sufficient to disqualify that answer as the telling one: its probability may be lowered while it is still way ahead of its alternatives. Finally, one must compare A with other possible answers to the same question. Issues of one event 'screening off' another, etc., will arise here.

When an economic theory is accepted many of its features are held in high esteem: it may be applauded for its mathematical elegance, its scope or its simplicity. It may also be complemented for its capacity to unify disparate domains, its success in making empirical predictions or its explanatory power. In this connection the constructive empiricist separates these into epistemic and pragmatic virtues. The central epistemic virtue is that of empirical adequacy which concerns the theory's relationship to the world and is independent of the other human interests or desiderata. The pragmatic virtues are concerned with these other interests and desiderata. Elegance, beauty, simplicity are attributes which have no bearing on the theory's relationship to the world. Perhaps calling these pragmatic is a misnomer. The constructive empiricist's central point, however, is that, whatever the term used, the range is very wide. It encompasses any non-epistemic use to which a theory may be put on the one hand and its quasi-aesthetic attributes on the other. What these share in common is the fact that they do not impinge on the question of empirical adequacy. Economic explanations of specific events and happenings are located in this non-epistemic, pragmatic dimension of economics. In view of our interest in a specific contrast rather than another, the economist answers why-questions in specific contexts which entails the subsequent pragmatic use of some theory as a background from which the relevant explanatory factor is chosen.

CAUSALITY AND EXPLANATION

The constructive empiricist furnishes a plausible and telling account of the scientific explanation of specific events and happenings. Scientists, however, do not confine their explanatory efforts to such events. They also explain the laws of science. For instance, Boyle's law describes an empirical relationship between the pressure and the volume of a given mass of gas at a constant temperature, whereas the kinetic theory explains this regularity. Van Fraassen maintains that this kind of search for explanation consists, for the most part, in the search for unified theories which are empirically adequate. In other words, the concept of explanation as used by scientists is rich and subtle: it covers the construction of unified, empirically adequate theories which is an epistemic activity, and the contextual explanation of specific events and happenings which belongs to pragmatics. Similarly, any claim that a theory explains a specific event can be reinterpreted as follows. There are facts which explain the event and these facts are embedded in the empirical substructures of this background theory. Indeed, if we look at specific instances of the claim that a theory explains an event, such as Newton's theory explains the tides, our earlier assertion that in scientific explanation one chooses the relevant explanatory factor from a theory which is held to be empirically adequate, is too exacting. In so far as one insists that Newton's theory does explain the tides, one is having recourse, for explanatory purposes, to a theory which is known to be empirically inadequate. The claim that Newton's theory explains the tides is construed by the constructive empiricist as follows. Relative to the background theory of Newtonian physics, the gravitational attraction of the moon is the relevant fact which explains the tides. Once again the subtlety of the scientific notion of explanation is visible.

Despite this subtlety, the common-sense notion of explanation is fundamentally at odds with the constructive empiricist approach. This basic conflict hinges on the role assigned to causality in our explanatory endeavours. Many economists, numerous other scientists and the ordinary person on the street assume that, when one explains an event or happening, one does so by reference to its cause or causes. To correctly explain is to identify the actual causes. The central picture underlying this view may be summed up as follows. Events in the actual world are enmeshed in a historical chain or network of causal relationships. When we present an explanation we are constructing a narrative which specifies some part of this causal chain or web of events which resulted in the event to be explained. The narrative structure of the explanatory account must include some reference to at least one of the causal nodes in the causal network which actually brought about the event in question. The contrasts made and the other factors which result from the context-dependency of an explanation influence the form of the narrative structure and the specific choice of node or some combination of these from the complete causal network which pertains in the real world. In other words, an explanation focuses on a part of the causal chain which is deemed relevant or salient by the explanatory context. In light of the preceding section we could say that the facts used in explanations must, at a minimum, be causally relevant. The constructive empiricist, however, rejects this common-sense approach.

As we saw in the last chapter when articulating Lawson's realism, one of the central philosophical problems arises from the Humean-type question 'what exactly is a causal relationship?' One way, among many, of specifying a relationship is to look at its *relata*. According to Humean empiricists, a causal relationship in not between things; it is between events. The acid did not cause the burn on my hand; rather, it was the event of spilling the acid which caused the burning. We have already seen how this account is rejected by Lawsonian realism. Moreover, many different accounts of causality have been furnished in the philosophical literature. Based on the insight that there is some connection between a cause and a necessary condition – if the acid did not spill on my hand it would not have been burned – J. L. Mackie (1980) concluded that a cause is an insufficient but necessary part of an unnecessary but sufficient condition, while David Lewis (1973) gives an account in terms of counterfactual conditionals with a *ceteris paribus* clause added: all other things being equal, if the acid did not spill on my hand it would not have been burned. As we saw in Chapter 3 one must give an account of the truth-conditions for these counterfactual sentences, and standard truth-functional logic will not suffice. Lewis gives his account in terms of possible worlds. Patrick Suppes, however, as we say in Chapter 4, prefers a neo-Humean account in which the notion of causality is reduced to complexes of statistically correlated events. Faced with these and numerous other accounts of causality, what is the reaction of the constructive empiricist? The key, once again, is the semantic approach to science with its focus on models. Models are human constructs and only sections of them, i.e. the empirical sub-structures, are isomorphic to the observable phenomena. In other words, certain aspects of our models go beyond the observable phenomena and, according to constructive empiricism, these include our causal discourse. In this view causes could be said to describe features of our models rather than features of the world. Van Fraassen explicitly endorses this as a graphic way of articulating his position (1989: 214). In this graphic language, causes do not belong to the observable world. Rather, they are a part of our theoretical models which transcend the observable. Causality is like the notion of absolute space in Newtonian physics. While it is an integral part of the

142

language used in presenting the empirical substructures of physics, we suspend judgement on its reference to anything in the observable world.

In this respect the constructive empiricist accepts the traditional empiricist thesis which acknowledges contingent regularities, while denying deeper reasons for them. In so far as causal discourse is construed in terms of physical necessity or in terms of the semantics of possible worlds, it is merely referring to the internal structure of our models. Causal narratives are answers to why-questions and hence are indistinguishable from explanations. Thus van Fraassen concurs with Hanson that there are as many causes as explanations and thereby maintains that the meaning of the sentence 'X causes Y' depends on the context in which it is uttered. In particular, contrary to Lawsonian realism, the constructive empiricist rejects any answer to a why-question which insists on an indispensable and real role for causal connections, power or propensities, and possibilities or necessities. In the spirit of Humean empiricism, one can distinguish the contingent facts and regularities, which convey information about the actual world, from the rest of this causal narrative. This residual causal narrative may be integral to our models. If so, it is a human construct on which we suspend any judgement about its reference to the actual world. This residual causal narrative is merely reflecting the pragmatic contextual relevance of the empirical facts or regularities to the issue requiring explanation.

In this constructive empiricist interpretation there is no way of establishing an isomorphism between our causal narratives and the world which transcends empirical regularities. Whereas the ordinary person in the street shares with Lawson and many scientific realists the view that any scientific explanation should make some reference to some portion of the actual causal network extending through real time, constructive empiricists reverse this. They explicate causality in terms of scientific explanation, i.e. as context-dependent answers to why-questions which of course, if satisfactory, will isolate some fact or empirical regularity of the actual world. However, since the domain of the observable and hence of empirical adequacy does not extend beyond contingent facts and regularities, any concept of cause which transcends these contingent regularities, cannot be said to refer to anything beyond this contingent world. Like explanation, there is much more to causality than facts and contingent regularities. This additional surplus belongs to the human context and cannot be said to reflect or refer to the observable world. The basic constructive empiricist picture is as follows. The observable world is constituted by contingent facts and regularities. We construct models which furnish theory-laden descriptions of these observable regularities. In so far as these models contain causal narratives, the causes can only be known to refer to empirical regularities. The rest of the causal narrative is merely reflecting aspects of our models which are outside the scope of genuine knowledge. As far as the constructive empiricist is concerned there are no real causal connections in the observable world over and above contingent facts and regularities. The realist ontological picture of an actual causal network is replaced by a Humean world of contingent regularities.

In this connection van Fraassen explicitly rejects the kind of Bhaskarian realist notion of causality espoused by Lawson in his application of scientific realism to economics. In experimental situations scientists isolate regularities and, furthermore, they postulate structured, intransitive, unobservable entities as the generative causes of the observable tendencies in open systems. The laws of science, such as water is H_2O, refer to the structures of these intransitive entities. These laws are not the uniformities or regularities; rather, they refer to the generative causal mechanisms which account for the uniformities. According to van Fraassen, a two-pronged conviction frequently sustains and supports this realist move from experimental regularities to unobservable structures and laws. Although empiricists hold that there are stable regularities, in the eyes of the realist they fail to see that no regularity can result from chance: there must be a reason. The reasons are the structured entities and the laws of nature convey information about these unobservable entities. The second prong argues that, if one holds that regularities are contingent, chance uniformities, there is no good reason for assuming that these regularities will persist. For instance, in this Humean world of contingent regularities, there are no rational grounds for the expectation that Jane will continue to exist into the immediate future as a human being and not, like Lot's wife, turn into salt. Scientific realism avoids such chaos and explains our legitimate expectations about the future. Science, through its laws, reveals the structures of intransitive things and these enduring structures legitimate our rational expectations about their continued existence into the immediate future.

As van Fraassen correctly acknowledges, the conviction conveyed in this two-pronged realist approach is very strong and one which has exercised an extensive influence in the history of philosophy. Constructive empiricists, however, do not share that conviction. In their approach, two events bearing no special relationship to each other could be contingently connected in some regular or uniform way by virtue of the fact that this is just the way things are. Constructive empiricists see the world as ultimately contingent: its regularities have no necessity or probability inherent in them. This is just the way things are. Moreover, constructive empiricists are very much philosophers of the twentieth century living in an intellectual environment which has explored chance and probability in rich and sophisticated ways. In this environment, contrary to the realist's first prong, regular events can come about by chance, without any underlying reasons. Hence constructive empiricists do not accept the realist tacit inference that 'there is a regularity, therefore there must be a reason for it, since no regularity could come about without a reason' (van Fraassen 1989: 20). This brings us to the second prong. Let us suppose that there is a regularity which has come about by chance. According to the second realist prong the fact that the regularity held in the past does not afford us the slightest reason for expecting it to continue into the future, but we do have such expectations and it would be ridiculous to abandon them. According to van Fraassen, this second prong is based on an equivocation concerning the notion of chance. Chance can mean either 'due to no reason' or 'no more likely to happen than its contraries'. A chance regularity in the first sense does not imply a chance regularity in the second. The observed regularity of stones falling, for instance, is a chance event in the first sense in that it is not due to some active hidden causal mechanism. However, it is not a chance event in the second sense in that we can rationally expect that it is more likely to continue to happen than its contraries. We can and do update our opinions using probability theory and this enables us to legitimate our expectations about the future. Such legitimations, do not require the transcendental realist interpretation of laws as specifications of the structural properties of the intransitive unobservable constituents of reality. Rather, they merely require the use of the probability calculus for updating our opinions. The death knell for logical positivism is not ringing for the Humean belief that the observable world is limited to contingent facts and regularities. On the contrary, it is tolling for the transcendental realist account of causality which fails to recognize the proper epistemic limitations to scientific knowledge.

VAN FRAASSEN'S EXPLICATION OF EMPIRICAL ADEQUACY

It is now time to consider in more detail the constructive empiricist's conception of empirical adequacy. Van Fraassen explicates the notion of empirical adequacy by characterizing it as an isomorphism between the observable phenomena and the empirical substructures of a scientific model. In order to clarify this explication or basic characterization, we will briefly outline, first, his conception of the observable and, second, his conception of the empirical substructures of scientific models. As we have already seen, van Fraassen accepts the thesis that scientific language is theory-laden. In other words, we cannot divide scientific language into two separate epistemological categories, the theoretical and the non-theoretical. 'Hygienic reconstructions of language such as the positivists envisaged are simply not on' (van Fraassen 1980: 14). However, van Fraassen does not use the contrast between theoretical and observational. Any talk of an 'observable-theoretical dichotomy' is apparently a category mistake: terms or concepts are theoretical, while entities, not terms, are observable or unobservable. Thus the term 'observable' classifies putative entities: both flying crows and flying horses are observable, whereas the number seventy is not observable. Moreover, the term observable has an anthroprocentric dimension to it, in that it is merely a shorter formulation of observable-to-us or observable to an appropriate epistemic community. Though he does not spell this out, presumably van Fraassen would accept that beings with different sense organs to ours could exist and that what would be observable to them may not be to us. What he does tell us is that the notions of existence and observable do not imply each other. A flying horse is observable but there is no such thing, whereas the number nine exists but it is not observable. Hence van Fraassen, contrary to logical positivism, would accept that the sentence 'unobservables exist' is not meaningless. Indeed, it is true. Moreover, in connection with the physical sciences, he maintains that one of their central tasks is to extend the boundaries of the observable-to-us. Although one must be careful to distinguish between observing and detecting, science, by means of the construction of theory-laden instrumentation, makes an indispensable contribution to human knowledge by extending the boundaries of the observable. Van Fraassen's picture of a mature physical science is the following. The physicist constructs a theoretical model. This model postulates entities which are currently unobservable and may ultimately be unobservable. Also the physicist, by the invention of theory-laden instrumentation, extends the current boundaries of what is observable-to-us. At the end of the scientific extension of these observable boundaries, if the most mature model continues to postulate entities which are unobservable, the scientific realist would believe that what that theory says about these unobservable entities is approximately true. Constructive empiricists, on the other hand, would hold that the theory is merely empirically adequate, i.e. that what it says about what is observable to that final epistemic community of humans is true. They would suspend belief on the rest, even though it is either true or false.

The constructive empiricist, while conceding that any scientific language is, in van Fraassen's own words, 'thoroughly theory-infected', draws a sharp distinction between *observing* and *observing that*. This distinction enables the constructive empiricist to avoid ontological pluralism which, as we saw in Chapter 4, tempted Kuhn. We will use van Fraassen's own example to illustrate how he draws this distinction. A recently discovered Stone Age family, untouched by Western civilization, is shown a tennis ball by an anthropologist. The anthropologist can see from the family's behaviour that its members have noticed the ball; for instance, one member picks it up and throws it to another. Clearly, the family members do not *see that* the object is a tennis ball; that would require some conceptual awareness of the game of tennis as understood by us. However, and this is the crucial point, to claim that the family does not *see* the same entity as the anthropologist is plainly silly. Such a claim is confusing seeing with seeing that. The claim that a person observed the tennis ball does not imply that the same person observed that it was a tennis ball. In short, contrary to the positivists, we have no theory-neutral language available in which we can present our scientific descriptions. Nevertheless, since observing is distinct from observing that, scientists committed to incompatible or different theories have observational access to the same world. Scientific description, in so far as it is describing that, is

146

theory-laden, whereas observation, as distinct from observing that, is not theory-laden. One can reasonably infer from this distinction that the constructive empiricist is sympathetic to a realist theory of observation. In the above preliminaries we have briefly considered van Fraassen's conception of the observable which is integral to his notion of empirical adequacy. Let us now briefly focus on the other term of the isomorphism, i.e. the empirical substructures of theoretical models.

According to van Fraassen, the logical positivists emphasized the syntactical approach to scientific theory. In this approach, any scientific theory is, in the first place, axiomatized, i.e. presented in the form of a deductive system consisting of axioms and theorems. In this connection early twentieth-century logic made astounding progress by furnishing precise syntactical explications of the basic notions of a formal deductive system, such as internal consistency, implication and mutual inconsistency between two or more axiomatic systems. The logical positivists wished to extend this syntactical success by furnishing a purely syntactical account of the empirical import or empirical substructures of a scientific theory which put the focus on a specific body of theorems stated in a specific language, i.e. a purely observational one. As we all know, the latter efforts totally failed: there is more to science than syntax.

The constructive empiricist fully acknowledges this failure. However, early twentieth-century logic had successes other than the syntactical explication of the basic notions of an axiomatic system. Part of this success, ignored by the logical positivists, was the development of a semantical approach which put the emphasis on models rather than the syntax of an axiomatic system. In this semantical approach the emphasis is on the interpretation of an axiomatic system. There is no particular concern with whether a statement in a model is an axiom or theorem of an axiomatic system. Indeed, a statement of a model may be an axiom in one formulation and a theorem in another. This kind of difference in axiomatic status is of no particular concern in the semantical approach. As van Fraassen points out, some of the first examples of this semantical approach were furnished in the study of non-Euclidean geometries. Models were used to establish the absolute or relative consistency of those geometrical axiomatic systems. The basic ideas underlying this were as follows. If a set of axioms could be given a physical interpretation, i.e. if a model of the system could be found in some portion of the real world, the axioms would be true of that segment of the world. Moreover, since the theorems necessarily follow from the axioms, these must also be true. Finally, since truth cannot be inconsistent, the axiomatic system must be consistent. Similarly, if an interpretation could be found for an axiomatic system within another system, the consistency of which is not in question, one could establish the relative consistency of the interpreted system. Furthermore, despite the fact that the axiomatic systems of the Seven Point Geometry and of Euclidean Geometry are mutually inconsistent, the former can be embedded in the latter. Thus an axiomatic system which is inconsistent with another may, nevertheless, be modelled in a portion of the system *vis-à-vis* which it is inconsistent. This illustrates the sophisticated richness of the semantical, as opposed to the syntactical, approach to theory. This semantical approach furnishes constructive empiricists with their basic notion of a model. The empirical substructures of such models are the descriptive or factual statements as enunciated in these models. Practising scientists have little difficulty in recognizing or specifying these. Finally, a model is empirically adequate when its empirical substructures are shown to be isomorphic to the observable phenomena. Thus the model's empirical substructures furnish accurate, theory-laden descriptions of the observable world.

The true business of pure science, namely, the adequate description of observable reality, begins when a purely formal axiomatic system is given an interpretation, thus constructing a model of some portion of reality. Pure science is concerned primarily with the construction of such models. As we have just seen, this use of the concept of model derives from pure logic and meta-mathematics. In van Fraassen's opinion this usage is not too far from, say, Black's notion of a theoretical model, briefly outlined in Chapter 3. Even if van Fraassen is wrong on this, i.e. if theoretical models have distinctive features which differentiate them from the logico-meta-mathematical notion associated with formal axiomatic systems, we can easily reconstrue constructive empiricism as embracing both kinds of models. The basic point is the focus on semantics which includes both the notions of model and that of truth. According to van Fraassen, Patrick Suppes was among the first to realize the crucial significance of models, as opposed to axiomatic systems, for the philosophy of science:

> Suppes's ideal was simple: *to present a theory, we define the class of its models directly*, without paying any attention to questions of axiomatizability, in any special language, however relevant or simple or logically interesting that might be. And if the theory as such, is to be identified with anything at all . . . then a theory should be identified with its class of models.
>
> (van Fraassen 1989: 222)

This family of models may be presented in many ways. Indeed, the theory may not be axiomatizable at all in the logical sense of the term. In this respect, the notion of model is much closer to actual scientific practice than the notions used by the logical positivists.

If an axiomatic system is internally inconsistent it has no model at all, it is not true of anything. It is logically inadequate. However, if two systems are mutually inconsistent, it may still be possible to embed one in the other, and, despite their mutual inconsistency, both may be empirically adequate, a crucially important point which is totally missed in the syntactico-axiomatic approach and by scientific realism. In this semantical case all the observable phenomena could be isomorphic to either the whole of one system or the corresponding part of the system in which it is embedded. The crucial point is that the same class of observable phenomena could be described in radically different ways, even possibly in mutually inconsistent theories. A logically adequate theory, however, may be empirically inadequate. Intuitively, if some observable phenomenon or some range of observable phenomena does not 'fit' the theory, it is empirically inadequate. More precisely, if none of the theory's models accommodate all the observable phenomena, the theory is empirically inadequate. Alternatively, if the empirical substructures of a model furnish a false description of some observable phenomena then the theory is empirically inadequate. In positive terms, a theory is empirically adequate if what it says about the observable phenomena is true. To sum up, in presenting a theory the scientist constructs a model, and certain elements of this model are specified as candidates for the correct representation of the observable phenomena. Van Fraassen calls these elements the empirical substructures. The theory is empirically adequate if these empirical substructures are isomorphic to all the observable phenomena.

This rather abstract account of empirical adequacy is illustrated by van Fraassen with reference to Newtonian physics or mechanics. The Newtonian scientist presents a mathematical model in which bodies are located in absolute space and in which they have absolute motions. The empirical substructures of this model are specified as differences between absolute motions (using standard vector representation of motions). These are the facts or descriptive statements as enunciated in the model. However, what is observed is always some relative motion. In other words, the observable phenomena consists of motions relative to the observer, such as measurements of relative distances, relative time intervals and so forth. If physicists claim empirical adequacy for the Newtonian theory of mechanics, they are claiming that its empirical substructures are isomorphic to the observable data. Clearly, the acceptance of this model as empirically adequate does not entail the belief that everything it says is true. For instance, we can imagine a fictitious scientist, called Leinbiz, who expressly denies the existence of absolute space on non-empirical grounds, but none the less accepts Newtonian physics as descriptively adequate.

Our fictitious Leinbiz, though very close to van Fraassen, is not a constructive empiricist. Let us further assume that the scientific community has no way of extending the boundaries of the observable to include absolute space, i.e. absolute space is an unobservable entity. (In view of the dualism of space and matter used in Newtonian mechanics this assumption is not implausible.) Let us also assume that there is no empirical evidence against the theory. In such a case constructive empiricists, like scientific realists, take a risk by going beyond the empirical evidence available at the moment. Their epistemic risk, however, is more conservative than that of the realist. The constructive empiricist's epistemic risk resides in the claim that Newtonian theory is empirically adequate. Although this claim entails the belief that the proposition 'absolute space exists' is true or false, it also entails the unequivocal suspension of judgement on the issue of which truth-value actually applies. Unlike our fictitious Leinbiz, who says the proposition 'absolute space exists' is false, the constructive empiricist is agnostic on this matter. Moreover, van Fraassen is very clear that it is a question of suspending judgement rather than one of, say, a very low probability of being true. The constructive empiricist is not saying that propositions about unobservable entities have a low probability of being true. To hold such a position is to adopt an opinion of a certain sort. Rather, the constructive empiricist suspends holding any opinion of any sort on such matters. In this fashion, the epistemic acceptance of a scientific theory involves a certain amount of agnosticism or suspension of belief.

Before proceeding to outline the constructive empiricist's general conception of pragmatics it may be useful to further consider how this philosophy of science could be applied to the evaluation of an economic theory, such as neoclassical economics. Clearly, the epistemic evaluation of any economic theory must focus on whether or not it is empirically adequate. In this connection the constructive empiricist will not use any realist notion of explanatory power such as that used by Lawson as a criterion for the epistemic acceptance of neoclassical economics. Explanation has nothing to do with this epistemic evaluation. Moreover, at the epistemic level, the constructive empiricist has no objection in principle to the introduction of Friedmanite hypotheses or assumptions which are 'widely inaccurate'. The construction of a theory which is empirically adequate may require the introduction of theoretical terms, such as idealizations, which are highly implausible or unrealistic. However, the constructive empiricists will not condone any statement in their economic models which is false with respect to some observable economic phenomena. For instance, neoclassical economics says that consumer preferences are stable and transitive, and this statement is either true or false. According to some commentators this claim is factually false. If this is so, then neoclassical economics is empirically inadequate. Moreover, having recourse to some subtle distinction between axioms and assumptions would be failing to face up to its empirical inadequacy. Such a distinction has all the signs of a syntactical, rather than a semantical, approach about it. In this fashion, constructive empiricists distinguish between economic idealizations about entities which are unobservable in principle and which are required for the construction of the theory – their epistemic attitude towards these is one of suspension of judgement – and descriptions which are known to be false of observable economic events, agents or structures. The latter cannot form part of any empirically adequate economic theory.

In short, constructive empiricists specify the empirical substructures of neoclassical economics. These substructures consist of the theory-laden observational statements of neoclassical economics. They then proceed to examine whether or not these empirical substructures are isomorphic to the observable events of actual economies. If neoclassical economics does not account for all the observable economic events then it is empirically inadequate. Thus, for instance, in so far as macroeconomics is not reducible to neoclassical theory, or that institutional economics draws our attention to economic facts not caught in the net of neoclassical models, neoclassical theory is empirically inadequate. This latter kind of empirical inadequacy may be resolved by a suitable extension of neoclassical theory. The extension required, however, cannot be one of simple juxtaposition of conflicting theories, unless a model of one can be found within a portion of another. The reason for this is that such a juxtaposition would be internally inconsistent and, as we have already seen, internal consistency is the minimum logical requirement for the empirical adequacy of any theory. Hence, scientific reduction programmes, whereby the economist attempts to reduce other economic theories to neoclassical economics, serve an important epistemic purpose in the constructive empiricist framework. If such a reduction can be effected, it demonstrates that neoclassical theory can be consistently extended to those domains. If the reduction is not successful, however, neoclassical theory is unequivocally judged to be empirically inadequate to that range of empirical phenomena. Thus the constructive empiricist will force a judgement on the viability of a reduction programme on the evidence available. Given a wide range of contrary evidence, the hope that such a reduction will be accomplished in the future is not sufficient. Moreover, in this setting, reduction plays an entirely different role to that etched out for it by essentialist scientific realism. As we saw in the last chapter, these realists use reduction to effect ontological unification. In their approach, the entities, both observable and unobservable, postulated by the best economic theory are the basic entities of the actual economic world. Constructive empiricists, in light of their notion of empirical adequacy, stop short of this essentialist realist reductionist reading. They suspend judgement on any theoretical entity which is unobservable in principle.

CONSTRUCTIVE EMPIRICISM, RHETORIC AND ECONOMIC POLICY

As the very committed and equally sophisticated scientific realist, Cliff Hooker, points out, van Fraassen has furnished a plausible and powerful articulation of empiricism (Hooker 1987: 165). Indeed, in Hooker's opinion it is more powerful than any of its predecessors. An integral part of its attraction resides in the skilful manner in which van Fraassen deflects the sharpest of the realist's criticisms of empiricism by adroitly synergizing many realist insights with some, but by no means all, of the most treasured doctrines of empiricism or positivism. Nevertheless, as Hooker also points out, constructive empiricism, despite its acceptance of many of the realist's criticisms of logical positivism, is unequivocally opposed to scientific realism in its focus on empirical adequacy rather than truth, in its account of explanation and in its approach to necessity and other modalities. Moreover, it is unmistakably empiricist in its focus on the observable and the contingency of the regularities of nature. Clearly, such an attractive and powerful philosophy of science has important lessons for those interested in the philosophy of economics. We have focused on three of these. The first is the centrality of empirical adequacy. The central epistemic test of any economic theory is whether or not it is empirically adequate. Popperians are concerned with falsifiability, scientific realists are concerned with explanations in terms of unobservable, intransitive objects or explanatory essences, instrumentalists with heuristic usefulness, whereas the constructive empiricist makes empirical adequacy or inadequacy central. In this fashion, constructive empiricism is effecting a challenging reconstruction of economic methodology. As we shall see in Chapter 8, one can sum up Kaldor's critique of neoclassical economics in one phrase, namely, it is extensively empirically inadequate. The second lesson is the shift in economic explanation from the domain of pure economics to applied science. Following Quine's insight that a theory is constructed for descriptive purposes and that all description is theory-laden, the constructive empiricist furnishes a challenging account of economic explanation in terms of answers to specific why-questions in specific contexts – activities which have nothing to do with the evaluation of a theory's empirical adequacy. The context dependency of economic explanations allows for a variety of local rhetorical devices without recourse to global rhetoricism. Finally, the concept of economic cause, like that of economic explanation, must be relocated in the non-epistemic dimension of economics. The economic world is a contingent one in which Humean regularities occur. Constructive empiricists update their opinions about the persistence of economic, contingent regularities by the use of probability theory, thereby rendering the scientific realist conception of causality epistemically redundant.

By way of conclusion, we will briefly consider the constructive empiricist's views on the acceptance of an economic theory and, in particular, its rational-rhetorical implications for the contribution of economists to government economic policy and other applied domains where the emphasis is on deciding what action or actions to take. As we have already seen, the acceptance of an economic theory should have an epistemic dimension: in so far as an economic theory is accepted as scientific, one is maintaining that it is empirically adequate. We have also seen that acceptance is much richer and more complex than mere empirical adequacy. These additional non-epistemic aspects of theory acceptance are referred to by van Fraassen as the pragmatic dimension. As well as encompassing economic explanation, this pragmatic dimension also entails total immersion in the economic world-view or world-picture which is integral to the specific economic theory accepted. This is true of any scientific theory. For instance, by virtue of the pragmatic acceptance of modern science, we are immersed in a world-picture which our ancestors of five hundred years ago could scarcely imagine: water for us is a compound of hydrogen and oxygen, the colour of Kate's eyes is determined by a specific genetic code, we turn on our VHF receivers and so on. We have no other way to describe our world except through the theory-laden language of modern science. As van Fraassen puts it, this is the 'world in which I live, breathe and have my being' (van Fraassen 1980: 81). Similarly, in fully accepting neoclassical economics, an economist becomes immersed in its world picture: firms are maximizers, preferences are stable and well-ordered and so on.

Van Fraassen, while fully accepting this immersion, is at pains to point out that it should not be confused with one's correct epistemic commitment. For instance, let us briefly consider economists immersed in neoclassical economics. If these are constructive empiricists, their position can be summed up as follows. Neoclassical theory says that firms are maximizers and other theories say they are not, but the correct epistemic attitude is that neoclassical theory is empirically adequate. In other words, complete immersion does not preclude the epistemic suspension of judgement on the theory's ontological implications over and above what is actual and observable. In connection with this immersion van Fraassen asks the perceptive question 'After all what is this world in which I live, breathe and have my being, and which my ancestors of two centuries ago could not enter?' His answer is very brief and to the point:

> It is the intentional correlate of the conceptual framework through which I perceive and conceive the world. But our conceptual framework changes, hence the intensional correlate of our conceptual framework changes – but the real world is the same world.
>
> (van Fraassen 1980: 81)

There is one physical world and we conceive that world through the parameters of our theories. Moreover, we know from the history of science that these parameters can dramatically change. None the less, we have no option but to live our lives in an interpreted world, the interpretation being furnished by these same parameters.

Associated with this total immersion in its world-picture, the pragmatic acceptance of a theory also entails a number of other commitments. For instance, scientists make commitments to specific research programmes. In this connection van Fraassen points out that two distinct theories which turn out to be empirically equivalent could give rise to very different research programmes. This indicates that commitment to a theory involves high stakes. In making a commitment the scientist is making 'a wager that all relevant phenomena can be accounted for without giving up the theory' (van Fraassen 1980: 88). These stakes are high. We are mortal, our theories are incomplete and also the vindication of a specific research programme in the foreseeable future may depend more on facts about our present circumstances than on the theory's empirical adequacy. Furthermore, the commitment can run very deep. This depth of the commitment is apparent in the scientist's readiness 'to answer questions *ex cathedra*' (van Fraassen 1980: 88, 112, 202). Thus he compares scientific commitment to ideological commitment. In this connection, however, commitments are not true or false; rather, it is a question of their future vindication.

Let us now speculate on the attitude of constructive empiricist politicians engaged in the demanding task of deciding on government economic policy. Prevailing wisdom suggests that economists are the experts and that any politician who ignores their advice is leading a very perilous life. Constructive empiricist politicians, however, realize that, by virtue of their acceptance of a specific economic theory, economists are immersed in its ontological picture. They realize that economists will talk as if they believed that the whole of their theory is true, i.e. economists speak as if they were essentialist scientific realists, and perhaps some are. Hence constructive empiricist politicians will take the economists' ontological picture with the proverbial grain of salt. Moreover, these politicians will recognize the various commitments made by economists themselves. The economists are playing their own game with, for them, very high stakes. They require funding for their own research programmes, for instance, and the politician realizes that the short term vindication of such programmes does not guarantee the empirical adequacy of the theory governing the research programmes. Furthermore, the economists' commitments may run very deep. Their advice could well be *ex cathedra*.

Having read and absorbed van Fraassen, politicians will be rather wary about this depth of commitment. As we have already noted, commitments are neither true nor false. Economists, however, want to point out that some commitments are rational while others are not. Constructive empiricists readily concede this. In connection with any commitment, the minimal criterion of being rational consists in not sabotaging the possibility of vindication beforehand. In other words, economists are not going to give advice which would create a Dutch Book situation for their own commitments! Economists, in being rational, will give advice which will lead to the vindication of their own commitments. The commitments of the economist, however, may not be those of the politician. When viewed in this fashion, the economist's advice has a sophisticated rhetorical ring about it. In so far as McCloskey's or Klamer's rhetorical approach draws our attention to such factors, the constructive empiricist fully acknowledges their perceptiveness and realisticness. Nevertheless, the constructive empiricist politician also knows that these same economists have the wherewithal to identify empirical regularities or tendencies in the economic world and any rational agent will take these into account in deciding on economic policy. The rationality of such decisions, however, depends on the politicians' commitments which are much more extensive than those of economists. If the stakes are high for the economists, they are even higher for the politicians and possibly even higher still for the rest of the population living within their political jurisdiction. This rhetorical dimension, however, does not impinge on the decision-making process of the pure economist in evaluating the empirical adequacy of a specific economic theory. As we have emphasized time and again, the latter decision pertains to pure economics. Rhetoric with explanation is relocated in applied economics. The constructive empiricist rejects global rhetoric and accepts local rhetoric.

7

TOWARDS A RECONSTRUCTION OF ECONOMIC METHODOLOGY
The emergence of causal holism

The debate between realism and anti-realism continues. As Daniel Hausman puts it: 'Like Muhammed Ali, philosophical positions may occasionally be knocked out, but they always return to fight again' (Hausman 1982: 21). Hausman maintains that, although constructive empiricism has got in some good punches, the current champion, i.e. scientific realism, is not in any danger. In this connection let us briefly review the constructive empiricist's fighting strategy in the rounds thus far and some of the good punches inflicted on its opponent. An integral part of this strategy is to adopt some basic realist positions. Thus van Fraassen, contrary to the philosophical instrumentalist, is, in Mäki's terminology, a veristic realist *vis-à-vis* theoretical sentences, i.e. he interprets theories literally and maintains that theoretical sentences are true or false. Moreover, he accepts the realist critique of logical positivism, especially of its dualistic approach to scientific language, and of its emphasis on a syntactical, rather than a semantical, approach to scientific models. Furthermore, both agree that all factual statements are theory-laden. This common fighting strategy, however, is extended by the constructive empiricist to a sharp distinction between the epistemic and pragmatic dimensions of theory acceptance. The epistemic dimension is focused on the empirical adequacy, rather than the truth, of a scientific theory: a theory is empirically adequate if what the theory says about all the observable phenomena is true, with a suspension of judgement on the rest.

This sharp distinction in turn facilitates the relocation of scientific explanation in the pragmatic, rather than in the epistemic, activities of scientists. Scientific explanation, contrary to scientific realism, is not part of the aim of theoretical science. Rather, it pertains to applied science. In other words, one must distinguish between the quest for empirically adequate theories on the one hand and explanations of individual events and happenings on the other. Both of these are frequently included within the extension of the term 'scientific explanation'. The criteria of empirical adequacy, however, have nothing to do with the so-called explanatory power of a theory. The explanation of individual events is the subsequent and derivative use of a scientific theory. This in turn leads van Fraassen to explicate the notion of causality in terms of explanation rather than vice versa. Like Humean empiricists, constructive empiricists opt for limiting our knowledge to what is in principle observable and do not allow for any kind of necessity other than logical necessity. The knowable world is a radically contingent one and our causal discourse is epistemically limited to contingent regularities. Finally, the pragmatic dimension to the acceptance of a theory entails numerous deep-seated commitments which, in van Fraassen's (1980: 202) own phrase, can lead scientists to speak *ex cathedra*. These commitments, however, are not true or false. Rather, it is a question of future vindication and it would be irrational on the part of those fully committed to act in any way which would sabotage beforehand the possibility of this vindication.

SOME REALIST RESPONSES TO CONSTRUCTIVE EMPIRICISM

We now address some realist responses to constructive empiricism. In this connection we focus on the challenging articulations of the committed and proficient realists, Churchland and Hooker. We choose these accomplished philosophers as clear and elegant representatives of those realists who openly acknowledge that constructive empiricism has delivered some good punches. In particular, we concentrate on Hooker's evolutionary naturalistic realism because of its telling critique of the constructive empiricist's explication of empirical adequacy, a critique which we wish to take on board in developing a causal holist framework for the philosophy of economics. We open this brief account by reviewing some of the good punches of anti-realism as acknowledged by these realists. Both Churchland and Hooker accept the sceptical inductive argument over the history of science which concludes that current science has no privilege. Many past theories, correctly and legitimately accepted as excellent at the time, have been rejected and there is no good reason to assume that a similar fate does not await current theory (Churchland 1982). Moreover, Churchland concedes the Quinean possibility that science could end up with a plurality of rival theories, in that the future journey of theoretical science is not obviously converging on any one theory. Thus Churchland counsels a healthy scepticism with respect to any theory. Similarly, Hooker concedes that if scientific realism is understood to imply that in science we really do come to know the world once-and-for-all with a degree of certainty that warrants the claim to knowledge, such an understanding is mistaken (Hooker 1987). The opponents of scientific realism may feel that these acknowledgements are very damaging to the whole ethos of scientific realism. In particular, these acknowledgements appear to leave little room for any kind of essentialist scientific realism. If we say (a) X is such-and-such which is in principle unobservable, (b) Y is a different, unobservable in principle, such-and-such and, (c) following Quine, that we have no empirical way of differentiating between the theory which postulates X as opposed to that which postulates Y, how can we know that X, rather than Y, refers to some hidden essence? The same type of reservation applies to Lawsonian realism with its focus on abductive inferences to propositions about the unobservable structures of intransitive objects. Quinean considerations show that we have no empirical way of deciding between incompatible theoretical descriptions of these structures. Moreover, Churchland's own 'unorthodox' realism appears to reject any Mäki-type referential realism which asserts that theoretical terms refer. Churchland confesses that 'I do not believe that the terms of "mature" science must typically refer to real things' (Churchland 1982: 227). In short, in response to anti-realist good punches, realists like Churchland develop an unorthodox realism culminating in eliminative materialism, while those like Hooker develop an evolutionary naturalistic realism.

Scientific realism emerging for the next bout in the championship fight is, according to Hooker, something like the following. The external world subsists independently of our cognitive capacities. We interact with that world and represent it to ourselves in our scientific theories. The anti-realism of constructive empiricism is in no way opposed to this. The realist, however, maintains that the observable and unobservable features of a theory are on equal footing ontologically and epistemologically. In Churchland's terminology, since our observations are theory-laden, 'our observational ontology is rendered exactly as dubious as our non-observational ontology' (Churchland 1982: 227). In other words, contrary to constructive empiricism which is selectively non-sceptical about observable entities, the realist holds that 'the global excellence of a theory is the ultimate measure of truth and ontology at all levels of cognition' from the observable to the unobservable (Churchland 1982: 226). Our ontological commitments do not divide according to the constructive empiricist's arbitrary division between the observable and unobservable. Rather, empirical adequacy is merely one component in determining our ontological commitments. Furthermore, the constructive empiricist's sharp divide between the epistemic and pragmatic virtues of a theory is equally arbitrary. The theory-ladenness of the facts plays a central role in this realist position. Since the facts are theory-laden and since we have no neutral language in which the facts can be presented in a theory-independent way, clearly a debate will emerge concerning the correct or the best way of articulating the facts. Churchland sees no way of addressing this issue within constructive empiricism's division between epistemic and pragmatic virtues. The only way to rationally decide on theory-laden facts is to accept those articulated in the most simple, coherent, unified theory with the greatest explanatory power, i.e. to give epistemic weight to van Fraassen's pragmatic criteria. Moreover, a holistic evolutionary account of the development of our cognitive capacities would exclude the constructive empiricist's schizoid division into purely epistemic ones on the one hand and anthropomorphic pragmatic ones on the other. The holism of our intellectual capacities, which range from our fallible perceptual abilities to our fallible abilities to theorize, prevails. In evolutionary naturalist realism, EN realism for short, both of these fallible ranges of capacities evolved in idiosyncratic ecological conditions and both mutually complement each other.

EN realism is attempting to furnish 'a complete naturalistic account of the species *Homo Sapiens* in its full evolutionary setting' (Hooker 1987: 150). In this setting, science is a social endeavour linked to a vast range of life-goals extending over individual, national or species interests. Hence, contrary to constructive empiricism with its focus on the single, scientific, epistemic goal of empirical adequacy, EN realism includes numerous goals for science, such as relief from ignorance, survival, security, self-expression, technological mastery and power. Moreover, even though these are interconnected in a complex manner, they are strictly on par with each other. Constructive empiricism has lost sight of this evolutionary context and hence it furnishes a very limited and oversimplified epistemic aim for science. This failure leads it in turn to postulate a totally inadequate account of the structure of actual science and of its epistemic acceptance.

According to EN realism, a scientific theory has both 'internal' and 'external' global characteristics (Hooker 1987: 111–12). The former includes a theoretical-world-view which (a) provides us with the appropriate language to be used in describing the world, (b) specifies what is and what is not observable and the conditions of observability, (c) constructs instruments for measuring and specifies the degree of reliability of these measurements and (d) specifies what is causally, statistically or accidentally connected. Among the external global characteristics are the theoretical factors which influence the choice of area to be investigated empirically and the theoretical work which is required for the characterization of the putative related variables. They also include the theories presupposed in the development of specific experimental procedures and in the processing of experimental data. Finally, they include a mathematical analysis of these data which computes the relevant quantities in question. Clearly, the external global characteristics include a range of auxiliary theories other than the theory in question. This range extends from theories of physics on the one hand to psychological theories on the other. The epistemic acceptance of a theory is relative to both these internal and external global characteristics and cannot be adequately conveyed by the constructive empiricist's simplistic notion of an isomorphism between empirical substructures and the observable data. On the contrary, the epistemic acceptance of a theory is a complex issue involving decision-making problems at numerous levels. These levels may include (a) that of applied theory, such as the theory of instrumentation focused on specific situations, (b) that of general theory where the general principles are organized and developed, (c) that of background theories which are normally not questioned, (d) that of mathematical models with their idealizations etc. and (e) that of systematic ontology wherein the fundamental entities of the world are made explicit. To reduce this complex decision-making process to a logical isomorphism, as suggested by constructive empiricism, is to utterly misrepresent the actual situation of epistemic acceptance.

CAUSAL HOLISM AND THE AIMS OF SCIENCE

It is now time to switch from Hausman's metaphor of the boxing ring, where one contender only can emerge victorious, to the more traditional metaphor exploited by philosophers as divergent as Plato and Marx, namely, a dialogue. In this dialogical setting scientific realism is the thesis and constructive empiricism is the antithesis. Rather than one of these emerging as the current champion, what is required is a novel synthesis which, by integrating the respective merits of each, will transcend the conflicts between them. In this chapter we propose to introduce such a synthesis, which we call causal holism, and to outline how this synthesis can furnish a challenging framework within which a fruitful philosophy of economics may be constructed. Before we spell out the details of this novel synthesis, a few preliminary remarks about the choice of name may be in order. Holism is chosen because the atomistic approach to language, which was symptomatic of much of logical positivism and other logical atomistic accounts, such as that of the early Wittgenstein, is rejected. At the level of scientific language we adopt a specific holistic view in which theory is indispensable to the accurate description of reality both physical and social. Thus causal holists agree with numerous realists and constructive empiricists that scientific description is theory-laden. Moreover, like constructive empiricists, they break all links between theory and scientific explanation. The explanatory dimension of science, which is very extensive indeed, is rich in extraneous narrative demanded by the specific contextual situatedness of our explanatory endeavours. Scientific explanation is unequivocally located in the non-epistemic dimension of science. However, contrary to constructive empiricism, causal holism insists that furnishing accurate descriptions of the real observable causes in operation in both the physical and social worlds is integral to science at the epistemic level. In other words, pure science constructs models which furnish accurate descriptions of both observable events and observable causes in the physical and social worlds. Thus causal holists maintain that the discovery and description of real observable causes pertains to pure science and that this is independent of the quest for scientific explanation which is located, à la constructive empiricism, in applied science. In short, contrary to constructive empiricism, causality is unequivocally relocated in the epistemic dimension of science while, contrary to scientific realism, explanation is located in pragmatics. The quest for causes and the quest for explanations are distinct: the latter, depending on the contextual narrative, may or may not depend on the former, but the former is completely independent of the latter. Finally, contrary to scientific realism, our knowledge of causes is limited to what is in principle observable. In short, the causal holist rejects any transcendental realist theory of causality on the one hand and any empiricist theory reducing causality to correlations on the other. In causal holism the focus is on observable causes.

We now proceed to spell out the details of causal holism by, first, examining its conception of the aims of science. We then consider its reinterpretation of the constructive empiricist's notion of empirical adequacy in terms of descriptive adequacy and continue by developing its account of scientific explanation. Finally, before deploying causal holism as a framework for re-examing McCloskey's rhetorical approach, we reconsider the quest for unification and its possible ontological ramifications, thereby further differentiating causal holism from scientific realism.

According to constructive empiricism the aim of science is the construction of theories which are empirically adequate, whereas evolutionary naturalistic realism relocates this issue in an evolutionary context of a multiplicity of aims all on equal par. The position of the EN realist is, prima facie, more plausible. Different individuals can and do have very different ends or aims for engaging in scientific activity and various organizations or institutions have various interests in cultivating this kind of activity. The constructive empiricist, however, fully accepts the latter. Thus van Fraassen explicitly distinguishes between the aim of an activity, say chess, and the motives, ends or intentions for playing it, which can vary from player to player (van Fraassen 1980: 8). The aim of chess is to checkmate one's opponent: this determines what counts as success in playing that game. Similarly, the aim of science is what is to count as success in that enterprise, which may be pursued by individuals or encouraged by government or private sector institutions for any number of motives or ends. In this fashion, the constructive empiricist differentiates between the aim of science and other ends or interests of either individuals engaged in that activity or those institutions cultivating it.

The causal holist has a certain sympathy with this manner of differentiating between the EN realist's multiplicity of aims. There is a clear consensus on the aim of chess and this can be distinguished from the other ends of the individual players. Scientific activity, however, is rather complex in comparison with a game like chess. It is more like the activity of maintaining a ship at sea than playing chess in that it entails a multiplicity of aims, i.e. what counts as success is a multiple-criteria, rather than a single criterion, affair. Moreover, some of these criteria can change over time and a constellation of subsidiary aims may be linked to these principal aims. According to causal holism, the central aims of science include, first, the accurate description of the entities and events in the actual world and of their developments through history and, second, furnishing satisfactory explanations of some of these events. In view of the manner in which science is actually developing in our contemporary western society, either of these primary aims may be in the process of being subsumed under others, such as prediction and technological control. The latter are clearly central to accounts of science as divergent as EN realism and Habermasian critical theory. To the extent that these latter philosophies are diagnostically perceptive, they indicate that the social world of science is itself a contingent one and that its boundaries are not eternally fixed by some eternally fixed class of epistemic aims. In causal holism the subsidiary aims of science are numerous and these can vary dramatically from science to science. For those sciences in which laboratory experimentation plays a significant part, Hooker's external global characteristics indicate some of these. In non-laboratory sciences, such as archaeology or geology, the development of specific techniques, such as the periodization of artefacts or deposits, are included in their subsidiary aims. In sciences which are largely influenced by mathematics, the explication of empirical concepts in mathematically tractable ways, the discovery/construction of equations linking these and deriving solutions for them are also subsidiary aims.

Some of the distinctive features of causal holism become apparent in its approach to the primary aims of economics. In this connection the causal holist distinguishes between pure and applied economics. The primary aim of furnishing accurate descriptions falls within the perimeters of pure economics, while the other primary aim, i.e. furnishing appropriate explanations of specific economic events, falls within the boundaries of applied economics. In connection with the former aim the causal holist unequivocally accepts the contemporary truism that economic description is theory-laden. There is no theory-neutral language available in which economics can describe the social world once and for all in terms of some kind of eternally fixed set of purely descriptive terms. Rather, economic theory plays an indispensable role in our appropriate descriptions of the social world. The causal holist is working under the shadow of Quine's holism as outlined in Chapter 3 above. Moreover, the causal holist fully endorses the EN realists' sophisticated account of the diversified roles of various theories in scientific activity. In view of this combination, it immediately follows that no economic observation statement taken in isolation can mirror image any portion of the real world. As we saw in Chapter 3, our factual economic statements come before the bar of experience holistically and not atomistically. Thus the causal holist sees no way of avoiding the Duhem–Quine underdetermination thesis in its weak formulation. In particular, the causal holist fully endorses the constructive empiricist's position that the so-called empirical substructures of an economic theory or model are theory-laden and this thesis applies to our descriptions of economic systems, institutions, agents and their actions. When engaged in such descriptions one is presupposing some conceptual framework or other, be it that of some specific economic theory or that of common sense. All economic descriptions are theory-laden.

CAUSAL HOLISM AND DESCRIPTIVE ADEQUACY

Like scientific realists and constructive empiricists, causal holists agree that there is a natural and a social world and that we are attempting to describe these worlds as accurately as is possible for us fallible humans. Moreover, consonant with Aristotelian realists, we access the external world through our senses; consonant with Quine's holism, this access is theory-laden; and consonant with van Fraassen's constructive empiricism, the physical sciences extend the observational boundaries of our fallible senses. In causal holism our descriptive knowledge, our observational access to the world and our theoretical activity are inextricably linked. The causal holist's central picture of human observation is that of inputs from the external world being received by fallible sensory beings and these sensory inputs being processed through changing, theory-laden codes, thereby producing factual descriptions at the output level. In this fashion, empirical adequacy, understood as descriptive adequacy, is a central aim in the construction of any empirical theory, including economics.

The causal holist's conception of empirical adequacy, however, is not identical to that of constructive empiricism. To mark this difference we use the phrase 'descriptive adequacy'. Like constructive empiricism, a descriptively adequate theory encompasses the theory-laden descriptions of observational entities and events of the physical and social world but, contrary to constructive empiricism, it also encompasses the description of the observable causes among these events. In answer to the question 'what does a descriptively adequate theory describe?' the causal holist answers: contingent entities and events, contingent regularities among these events and contingent causes of events. The primary aim of any pure science is thereby extended to include accurate descriptions of the observable causes which are actually operational in the world. In other words, to readapt J.L. Mackie's famous phrase, causes are part of the cement of the actual observable world and hence, contrary to van Fraassen, science aims to describe these observable features of the real world. However, contrary to either Lawsonian or essentialist scientific realism, the epistemic aim of science does not extend to any theory-laden description of unobservable structures of intransitive objects or unobservable essences. The epistemic focus is on what is observable-in-principle. In the causal holist perspective, just as entities, like water, cats or trees, are observable to us so are causal events, like this acid burning that piece of wood or a specific earthquake causing the vibration of a specific building. In short, pure science is concerned with the construction of descriptively adequate theories and this includes furnishing descriptions of contingent causes which obtain in the observable world.

The rationale for the causal holist claim that some causes are actual and observable can be summed up in the following steps. First, the concept of cause is shown to be both a vague and a useful one. Second, we argue that causes are in principle as observable as entities, such as water, which are deemed to be observable by constructive empiricists. This latter thesis is established by demonstrating that the term 'cause' is learned in the same way as any other observational term. Finally, we argue that constructive empiricists' legitimate objections to the conceptual framework in which scientific realists embed the concept of cause does not justify the constructive empiricist's suspension of judgement on actual observable causes. In connection with the first step, van Fraassen correctly maintains that any vague predicate is useful provided it has clear cases and clear counter-cases (van Fraassen 1980: 16). For instance, the predicate 'observable' is absolutely central to constructive empiricism but van Fraassen holds that it is vague. Looking through a telescope at the moons of Jupiter or looking with the unaided eye at a cat are clear examples of observation. Deducing Pythagoras' theorem from Euclidean axioms is a clear example of non-observation. The notion of causality, like that of observability, is also both vague and useful. 'Drinking a sufficient quantity of arsenic causes death' is a clear example of a causal relationship, while 'taking out an insurance policy does not cause the insured person to live longer' is a clear counter-instance. Hence, on the constructive empiricist's criteria for a viable but vague concept, the notion of cause fulfils these criteria.

In connection with the second step, the causal holist maintains that, in view of the constructive empiricist's contention that entities like water are observable, causes are equally observable. According to constructive empiricism, water exists in the actual world, water is observable but our characterizations of water presuppose corrigible, theory-laden conceptions. How does one learn such observational terms? According to causal holism, first, one is shown clear instances, such as the water in a river or a spring, and clear counter-instances, such as petrol or iodine. Such ostensive exemplars, however, are not sufficient. One must also learn to use the term 'water' in, what Putnam calls, stereotypical generalizations, such as 'water is a liquid' or 'it is less dense than mercury'. Second, as Putnam has taught us, propositions expressing stereotypical characteristics are not analytic truths. Rather, stereotypes hold for the most part and their correct usage presupposes that there are exceptions or borderline cases. Third, these stereotypical characteristics are in turn interconnected in a theoretical network to other relevant predicates, such as 'water is a chemical compound rather than an element' or 'it is compounded of hydrogen and oxygen'. This theoretical network is a specific, fallible, holistic system. Its fallibility and corrigibility are evident from the fact that, for instance, the Greek scientists of Aristotle's time had a different holistic theoretical network to ours. For instance, according to these Greek scientists, being an element was a stereotypical characteristic of water. Nevertheless, even though its ostensive exemplars, its stereotypical characteristics or its theoretical network are open to correction, according to constructive empiricists, water is an observable entity.

According to causal holism, the same is true of the term cause. It is learned in exactly the same manner as the term water. Clear instances and counter-instances of causal connections are presented. Also, stereotypical characteristics of causal connections are learned, such as a cause precedes its effect, or if a cause is present and no other countervailing factors are operational, its effect will occur. These in turn are embedded in some relevant theoretical network such as nomic universals, causal necessity, counter-factual conditionals and causal laws. As in the case of water, either the exemplars or stereotypes are subject to change in light of the progress of our knowledge. Finally, radical changes in the theoretical network in which the term cause is embedded are also possible. These changes, however, are not sufficient to establish the non-reality of causes. The constructive empiricist allows for such changes in the case of water and the observable term 'cause' is on a similar footing. Hence van Fraassen's telling critique of scientific realists' theoretical network, in which they embed scientific causal claims, does not legitimate his conclusion that causal connections, over and above regular sequences of events, fall within the constructive empiricist's suspension of judgement. In other words, despite our legitimate critique of the Aristotelian conceptual framework in which Greek scientists of that time embedded the term 'water', constructive empiricists do not conclude that water is neither real nor observable. Similarly, the constructive empiricist's penetrating critique of the realists' conceptual framework in which they embed the term 'cause' does not suffice to establish that causes are neither real nor observable. Rather, we have shown that some causal connections are as observable as water and the other observable entities acknowledged by constructive empiricism. Hence descriptive adequacy includes both the description of observable events and entities of the actual world and the description of observable causes of that world.

Economics, as a descriptive science, falls within the range of application of causal holism. Despite the fact that economic systems are not natural in the way, say, an astronomical system is natural, and despite the fact that economic actions have a hermeneutical dimension, a central task for economics is to accurately describe economic actions, their institutional and social settings, and the manner in which these institutional and social settings have changed in historical time. To this descriptive end, economists construct economic models in the expectation that these will be vindicated as descriptively adequate. As far as the causal holist can tell, there is no other scientific way of describing the contingent economic world and its history. In particular, causal holists attempt to discover the contingent observational causes in operation in actual economies and have no objection to a Millean emphasis on a plurality of causal factors. This recourse to causes, however, is neither within a Lawsonian realist perspective of unobservable structures nor a constructive empiricist reduction of causes to Humean regularities.

Any descriptively adequate economic model is confined to empirical investigations into contingent causal chains which are in principle observable and, since Lawsonian causal mechanisms are non-empirical, these fall outside the scope of the causal holist notion of descriptive adequacy. This rejection of the Lawsonian realist notion of economic causality, however, does not imply that causal holists must therefore opt for a Humean regularity account of economic causality. Limiting the choice between either the Lawsonian realist conception on the one hand and a Humean regularity approach on the other fails to acknowledge that a viable middle ground is available. Causal holism furnishes this middle ground. A descriptively adequate economic theory furnishes accurate descriptions of the contingent and observable causal chains operational in real economies.

Let us now address how causal holism differs from the constructive empiricist's explication of empirical adequacy which, as we saw in the last chapter, is characterized by an isomorphism between the theory-laden substructures of a model and the observable data. As we already noted, van Fraassen distinguishes between observing and observing that. Clearly, the latter is theory-laden but the former, we presume, is not. Moreover, in view of this distinction, one could reasonably argue that the observable phenomena of science are not theory-laden. Indeed, van Frassen explicitly endorses this conclusion. He says 'I regard what is observable as a theory-independent question' (van Fraassen 1980: 57). This, however, is patently wrong. According to van Fraassen the observable phenomena of physics are the results of laboratory measurements and as, for instance, the EN realist points out, these are theory-laden. The measurements of the laboratory sciences are as theory-infected as the empirical substructures. Contrary to van Fraassen's distinction between observing and observing that and contrary to Lawson's realist account of abstraction discussed in Chapter 5, the causal holist maintains that our observational access to the world is not direct. The laboratory measurements, which in large sections of the physical sciences constitute the highest court of appeal, are underdetermined by, as it were, the raw data of experience. There is no question of one-to-one correspondence between these measurement results and that data. As van Fraassen himself notes, his account of empirical adequacy is an idealization. According to causal holism, it is not an epistemically helpful one. The logical notion of isomorphism fails to grasp the rich complexity of empirical or descriptive adequacy which results from its embeddedness in 'historical' time, rather than the 'logical' time of isomorphisms.

As we have already emphasized, the observable phenomena are theory-laden: scientists do not access the external world directly or immediately. In line with Quine's holism, any scientific observable phenomenon is a product of inputs from the environment received through our fallible sensory organs or their extensions and a fallible linguistic framework subject to a variety of learning-feedback mechanisms. Although observable phenomena clearly do not mirror image the constitutents of the world, they constitute the highest court of appeal for the scientific community. These observable phenomena are located in historical time and the concept of descriptive adequacy must be sensitive to this location. Initially we will illustrate this location in historical time by reference to the defunct phlogiston theory and its replacement by atomic theory. Dephlogisticated air supporting burning was an observable phenomenon as articulated in phlogiston theory. However, when phlogiston theory was replaced by atomic theory, the observable entity, phlogiston, was rejected, while the observable entity, dephlogisticated air, was reconstrued as oxygen. In this revolutionary change the observable phenomena of phlogiston theory were translated, not in a one-to-one but in a one-to-many way, into the observable phenomena of atomic physics. Since there is no theory-neutral way common to both theories for expressing the observable phenomena, the causal holist uses some principle of charitable translation, as outlined by Churchland or others (Churchland 1979) for relating the observable phenomena according to phlogiston theory to some of the observational phenomena of atomic physics. Thus the causal holist gives due credit to (a) the role of rejected theory in the observable phenomena as reported in the history of science, (b) a complex, historical one-to-many relationship, meditated by charitable translation, between the observable phenomena of successive theories and (c) the role of contemporary theories in the observable phenomena as articulated by the contemporary scientific community. Indeed, the latter extends to the EN realist's account of the multifarious roles of various theories in the measurement results of contemporary science. Finally, the descriptive inadequacy of phlogiston theory was exposed by atomic theory. The former lacked the resources necessary for the accurate description of hosts of observable phenomena which were drawn to humanity's attention for the first time in its history by the construction of atomic theory.

The constructive empiricist's idealized notion of a logical isomorphism, by abstracting from the rich complexities of historical time, such as the historically located charitable translations between the observable phenomena of successive theories, fails to acknowledge the sophisticated intricacy of descriptive adequacy. According to causal holism, the observable phenomena, though located in historical time and consequently subject to the kinds of alterations indicated by the 'phlogiston' example, constitute the highest court of appeal in science. The causal holist's basic picture of the decision-making process on descriptive adequacy is as follows. Like Kuhnian normal scientists, we have a rich reservoir of descriptive knowledge available. This knowledge is conveyed in currently acceptable theories. Scientists construct models of specific domains in light of these 'consensus' theories. At this stage the picture, as it were, bifurcates, depending on whether or not the science in question extends the boundaries of the observable by the invention of theory-laden, observational-experimental procedures. In the former, the novel experimental results, furnished by unanticipated extensions of the boundaries of the observable, constitute a new testing ground for the descriptive adequacy of the model. The outcome may be a vindication of the model based on the 'consensus' theories, a partial change in some of the consensus theories or, with the aid of scientific imagination, a new theory is constructed which

effects a revolutionary change and thereby establishes the descriptive inadequacy of the 'consensus' position. With the success of the new theory, the
scientist claims descriptive adequacy for it. Finally, this decision is arrived at
in a specific historical setting and charitable translation, combined with many
of the EN realist's internal and external global characteristics, is indispensable
to this epistemic decision-making process.

In sciences like economics, where the extension of the boundaries of the
observable does not occur in the above dramatic way, one must seek other
ways of evaluating their descriptive adequacy. Once again economists will
construct models of specific domains in light of their 'consensus' theories.
These models will specify or suggest some possible observational domains
hitherto not fully researched. These domains are investigated by more fine
grained observations or empirical investigations into the full range of existing
economies or a more detailed examination of those recorded in history. For
instance, the causal holist has no objection to the development of a rich
reservoir of econometric or other techniques for investigating causal relationships. These techniques should contribute to the empirical investigation
into the descriptive adequacy or otherwise of specific economic models.
Moreover, like constructive empiricists, causal holists fully acknowledge that
the construction/discovery and refinement of such techniques is no mean
achievement. The possible outcomes of these empirical investigations will be
much the same as in the case of those specialized sciences which extend the
boundaries of the observable. In other words, rather than extending the
boundaries of the observable, economists engage in more fine-grained or
more extensive empirical investigations. However, before making any commitment to the descriptive adequacy of a new model, the descriptions of both
models are compared by a process of mutual charitable translation. The
epistemic decision on descriptive adequacy is pivoted on which model is
judged to furnish the most accurate and comprehensive descriptions.

In summary, causal holists accept much of the constructive empiricist's
critique of scientific realism. In particular, they, like constructive empiricists,
distinguish between pure and applied economics and maintain that the
construction of descriptively adequate theories is a primary aim of the former.
Unlike the constructive empiricist, however, the causal holist argues that
some contingent economic causes are real and observable and consequently
their descriptions must be included within the scope of pure economics.
Finally, in view of its claim that our observational access to the economic
world is theory-laden, the causal holist rejects the constructive empiricist's
explication of empirical adequacy in terms of the logical notion of an
isomorphism. Any explication of this notion must be located in the richness
and contingency of historical time which acknowledges diachronic, one-to-
many, relationships between the descriptive propositions of successive economic theories. In this connection the epistemic decision on descriptive
adequacy depends on an evaluation of the descriptive resources of the

competing economic models which in turn presupposes charitable translation and, as we shall see later, this evaluation is not independent of epistemic ontological considerations, though these considerations are much more complex than those adduced by realists.

Finally, in view of its unequivocal endorsement of Quine's holism at the level of meaning, causal holism *ipso facto* endorses a Caldwellian critical pluralism. Its specific critical pluralism, however, is particularly robust. The central focus is on the deployment and extension of the complex range of decision-making procedures located in historical time used to ascertain the descriptive adequacy of an economic theory. These epistemic procedures, ranging from charitable translation to those of the EN realist noted earlier, make any emergent pluralism robust in that they constantly challenge economists to rationally decide between competing economic models or frameworks. Pluralism will emerge only after rigorous empirical investigations fail to establish the descriptive adequacy of one of a range of competing economic frameworks. At any given time rival economic theories may be vying for descriptive adequacy and, while fully acknowledging that this decision-making process is intricate, causal holists persistently pursue the implementation of that process. Pluralism concretely comes into play here only when economists are fully satisfied that each rival position is descriptively adequate. Thus this pluralism fully endorses the fullest possible investigations into the descriptive adequacy of rival economic theories.

CAUSAL HOLISM AND EXPLANATION

In connection with the intriguing issue of economic explanation, the causal holist endorses the constructive empiricist's analysis of the context-dependency of why-questions. An economic explanation is an answer to a specific why-question in a specific context which includes or presupposes specific contrasts, and the explanation is rendered economic by virtue of the choice of salient factors from an economic theory rather than from some other domain, such as politics, religion or metaphysics. Hence, like constructive empiricism, the activity of economic explanation is very much a question of the subsequent and derivative use of an economic theory which is held to be descriptively adequate on grounds totally independent of its explanatory contexts. Explanations are frequently furnished in intricate non-scientific contexts which may require a host of rhetorical techniques, while discovering economic causes is an integral part of the construction of a descriptively adequate economic theory and is thereby independent of the contextual dimension of economic explanation. Contrary to constructive empiricism, depending on the contexts in question, some economic explanations will be causal, i.e. will make explicit reference to some part of the causal economic network which produced the effect, while others may not.

With the crucial qualification whereby the discovery and description of actual observable economic causes is relocated in the epistemic domain of descriptive adequacy, the causal holist accepts the constructive empiricist's contextual account of the economic explanation of specific events and happenings. Because of the vast number of different contexts and the variety of factors at play in them, economic explanation is a much more diffuse and involved affair than the already intricate, pure economic activity of discovering and describing the actual economic causal webs which obtain in the real world. Economic explanation pertains to the application of economics in diverse contexts and the manner of its application is largely determined by specific contextual factors which may have nothing to do with the actual causal structures of various economic events. Hence, in accordance with constructive empiricism, causal holists hold that an economic explanation is an answer to a specific why-question which occurs in a specific context and that this central activity pertains to applied, rather than pure, economics. Successful economic explanations, though clearly a central activity of economists, has no role to play in the more fundamental ascertainment of the descriptive adequacy of an economic theory in the epistemic domain of pure economics. In other words, scientific explanation is a central aim of economics but it pertains to applied, rather than to pure economics. The causal holist locates the description of contingent observable causes in pure economics and the context-laden task of economic explanation in applied economics. This division may appear arbitrary: why should economic causes be distinct from economic explanations? The principal reason is that economic explanations include divergent non-epistemic narratives required by their location in specific, pragmatic contexts, whereas economic causes, as described in pure economics, are independent of these non-epistemic explanatory narratives. Certainly, some explanatory narratives will include some causes already identified in pure economics. In such cases the economic explanation is causal. However, because of the diversity of explanatory contexts, not all economic explanations are causal. Many economic explanations include narratives which transcend the boundaries of the causal relationships identified in pure economics. The accurate description of observable economic causes pertains to the epistemic dimension of this scientific discipline and this activity is independent of the multifarious narrative contexts presupposed in the non-epistemic activity of economic explanation.

Moreover, like the constructive empiricist, the causal holist acknowledges that the normal use of the expression 'scientific explanation' is not limited to answers to why-questions related to specific events or happenings. Scientists also sincerely maintain that their theories explain, as when a physicist maintains that Newtonian theory explains the tides or that the kinetic theory of gases explains Boyle's law. As we saw in the last chapter, the constructive empiricist acknowledges these additional usages. In the case where Newton's theory is said to explain the tides, this is reconstrued to read something like the following. Relative to the background theory of Newtonian physics, the gravitational attraction of the moon is the relevant fact which explains the motion of the tides. The causal holist has no objection to this kind of approach: when one claims that a theory, rather than a specific event, explains another specific event, like the tides, one is claiming that the theory in question has the epistemic resources to specify a relevant part of the actual causal network. Thus causal holists go further than constructive empiricists in their interpretation of such claims. The theory in question has the resources to identify a significant observable node in the causal chain and thereby the causal holist reads the claim as being a proxy for a specific causal explanation. With these crucial qualifications, causal holism endorses the constructive empiricist approach to scientific explanation. Clearly this endorsement implies that causal holism rejects the Lawsonian realist account of explanation which is central to Lawson's economic methodology.

CAUSAL HOLISM, UNIFICATION AND ONTOLOGY

Let us now focus on the constructive empiricist's claim that a theory can explain a law. As we saw in the last chapter, this claim is read as follows. The theory is sufficiently unified in that it has the conceptual resources within it to 'derive' the law in question, or the law can be rewritten in such a way that it is embedded in the theory. Hence such a theory is more unified than another which lacks the required resources for embedding the law. In this view one may reasonably conclude that, according to constructive empiricism, the epistemic aim of science is the construction of a unified theory which is empirically adequate. In other words, the test for the success of pure science includes unification and, as we saw in the last chapter, Mäki maintains that unification, for a substantial group of realists, has an ontological reductionist dimension to it. This reductionism is evident in radical scientific realists' belief that the basic entities of their theory, which are frequently theoretical or unobservable, refer to the fundamental entities of the actual world. Moreover, while EN realists espouse a less radical position, they, also display ontological reductionist tendencies. This is evident from their egalitarian holism in which the observational or empirical dimension is on equal par with the theoretical or rational dimension both epistemologically and ontologically. Thus unification plays an indispensable role in prescribing the ontology of the EN realist's theoretical world-view. Both the ontological, non-observational categories of the unified theory and its observational categories are fallible, both are epistemically on par and both are the best we have. In either case such realists give an epistemic answer as to why unification is integral to the aim of pure science whereas constructive empiricists, in so far as they maintain that unification is merely a pragmatic and not an epistemic virtue, leave us at a loss as to why pure science, puts such a premium on it. In constructive empiricism there is no epistemic reason for the pursuit of unification, whereas in realism the reason is epistemic.

The causal holist certainly concedes that unification, in some sense, is a central ideal guiding some theoretical work in contemporary physics. Whether or not this ideal is too idealistic, there is without doubt no consensus on how it is to be attained. Indeed, there is no consensus whether or not it is attainable within the confines of contemporary physics. The diverging views of Hawking and Penrose are engaging illustrations of this lack of consensus. Moreover, according to Nancy Cartwright's challenging account, the cost of the limited unification which has been achieved to date in physics is at a very high price, namely, descriptive inadequacy (Cartwright 1983). The manner in which fundamental physics has achieved unification is such that its fundamental laws are false! Even if one does not concur with this provocative conclusion, the EN realist's account of the internal and external global characteristics shows that the unification thus far achieved is not a simple reduction as understood by numerous philosophers, in that other theories play an indispensable role in its actual accomplishment. Consequently, the process of unification is much more complex than a simple reduction to one and only one theoretical framework. In view of the many factors, ranging from *ceteris paribus* conditions to the role of other theories in the actual processes of unification in physics, the causal holist has reasonable reservations about its reductionist connotations as understood in much of philosophy of science.

Moreover, the causal holist, contrary to the EN realist, is not an egalitarian holist. EN realism is basically a juxtaposition of the dualistic systems of rationalism and empiricism with a principle of equality between them, while causal holism synthesizes theoretical activity, scientific description and observation in its notion of descriptive adequacy. Rather than theory and observation leading separate lives, as in the dualistic holism of EN realism, the causal holist accepts the Aristotelian realist thesis that we access the external world through our senses but integrates theoretical activity to this means of access. Hence the primacy is given to descriptive adequacy in which theoretical activity is integrated in historical time, through a variety of feedback mechanisms and other means, to our observational capacities. In particular, in connection with the ontology of a unified theory the causal holist is certainly non-egalitarian. With respect to the ontological dimensions of any scientific theory, the causal holist insists on the following distinctions. First, like most realists, there is ontology in the sense of what is real whether we can know it or not. In the case of the physical sciences we believe there is a world out there, external to us, a world which we did not invent. Our epistemic ideal is to know as much as possible about that world. In addition to the physical environment, the social sciences, including economics, also engage a constructed world, where intentional actions have unanticipated consequences. As with the physical sciences, the epistemic ideal is to know as much as possible about this social world. Second, we have model ontology in the sense of what our scientific models say there is. In this connection it is useful to adopt Geach's distinction, borrowed from Frege, between objects

172

in the sense of what the existential quantifier and the other ontological apparatus of modern logic say exists and a proper subset of such objects, namely, *actual* objects in the sense of those which either initiate or undergo change (Geach 1969). For instance, the number seventeen is a non-actual object: our mathematical theories say that numbers exist but these neither initiate nor undergo change. We can use Quine's phrase and say that mathematics is ontologically committed to numbers as non-actual objects (Quine 1960). However, as Quine also points out, it is possible to defeat such an ontological commitment. If we succeed in the foundations of mathematics in translating our discourse about numbers into statements about classes, for instance, then mathematics is no longer committed to numbers as distinct objects. Of course, in such an eventuality, the mathematician is ontologically committed to classes. Unlike mathematics, modern chemistry is ontologically committed to say, hydrogen as an actual entity. Hydrogen is part of the model ontology of modern science but hydrogen, unlike the number seventeen, is an actual entity in that, for instance, it enters into chemical reactions and so forth. According to causal holism, the model ontology of empirical sciences, both physical and social, primarily concerns actual entities or objects and relations between these.

Finally, causal holists focus on what they call the model's epistemic ontology. This is a subset of the set of the actual objects in the model ontology. In accepting a theory as descriptively adequate, the causal holist is maintaining that what the theory says about observable actual entities has a high probability of being true. The level of justifiable belief in terms of high probabilities of being true is limited to the model's epistemic ontology. In this approach, as we already noted, an actual observable entity of a theory which is believed to be descriptively adequate, but which subsequently is found to be otherwise, may be rejected. Phlogiston theory was the example used. Phlogiston was an observable actual entity which subsequent science rejected, while the observable actual entity 'dephlogisticated air' was charitably reconstrued as oxygen within modern atomic theory. In such revolutionary changes the causal holist requires a principle of charitable translation whereby the highly probable descriptive statements in the rejected theory are translated, in a one-to-many fashion, into highly probable descriptive statements about some of the epistemic ontological entities of the new theory. Thus even the observable members of the model's epistemic ontology are not eternally fixed. Some of these may have to be rejected or charitably reconstrued in light of the progress of science. Scientific realists, from Lawson to Mäki, fail to identify these crucial ontological distinctions.

With respect to the unobservable actual entities of the model ontology, the causal holist's view is largely one of scepticism. Certainly, like the constructive empiricist, the theory says these entities exist and such statements are either true or false. Moreover, the physical sciences can extend the boundaries of the observable and some of the current unobservable entities will be relocated within the new observable boundaries. However, in so far as others will remain unobservable, in view of the Quinean thesis that a plurality of descriptively adequate theories is possible, the causal holist suspends judgement on these. In other words, the unification of science may be accomplished in a plurality of ways and the causal holist has no procedure for rationally deciding between the different, unobservable, ontological entities postulated by these theories, all of which are deemed to be descriptively adequate. The upshot is that, unlike EN realism, the model ontology of any science actively engaged in the pursuit of unification cannot be read in an egalitarian metaphysical way. In the context of a unified scientific theory, it is necessary, first, to distinguish between the various ontological categories noted above, second, the various ways – only some few of which were mentioned – in which they can change or be abandoned, and finally, to recognize that Quine's pluralism forces us to suspend judgement on the unobservable-in-principle entities of any unified theory.

Clearly, the causal holist gives a very different account of unificatory reduction to that of Mäki's radical scientific realist. As we saw in the last chapter, such realists draw a sharp distinction between common sense and science, especially their respective ontologies. Mäki suggests that radical scientific realists give priority to the ontology of science rather than that of common sense. In causal holism, however, the divide between common sense and science is not sharp: science is merely a more codified version of common sense or, if one prefers, common sense is merely a less codified version of science. Indeed, much of contemporary common sense is influenced by past scientific theory. More generally, the absence of a sharp divide results from Quine's holism as outlined in Chapter 3, especially from the thesis that the meanings of words are located in sentences which in turn are located in conceptual frameworks. In this holist approach both common-sense and scientific descriptions are, in a broad sense, theory-laden. In particular, contrary to Mäki's radical scientific realist, the causal holist does not give precedence to the ontology of science as opposed to that of common sense. As we have just seen, causal holists are much more discriminating. They differentiate between the actual and non-actual model ontology of any conceptual scheme, be it that of common sense or that of science. Furthermore, they differentiate the epistemic ontology from within the actual model ontology, thereby allowing a suspension of judgement on the unobservable actual entities of the model ontology. Like Mäki's radical realist, the causal holist fully acknowledges that the rational economist, in rejecting one theory and epistemically accepting another, is *ipso facto* engaging in a theoretical redescription of the domain in question. However, contrary to Mäki's radical realist suggestion, this theoretical redescription is not necessarily accompanied by ontological reduction. Certainly, the priority is given to the epistemic ontology of the best model and, as we have already noted, this may effect a change in some epistemic actual entities, but the economist who subscribes to causal holism will suspend judgement on the unobservable-in-principle entities of the best economic model's actual ontology. The issue is not between the ontology of common sense and that of economic theory. Rather, it is a question of suspending judgement on what is unobservable in principle in one's best economic model and of deciding on that model's epistemic ontology.

This causal holist approach to epistemic ontology may be further clarified by contrasting it to Mäki's clarification of an essentialist realist account of the neoclassical theory of the firm. As we already noted, according to the essentialist scientific realist's reading of neoclassical theory, the common-sense account of the business firm is false. In this reading, neoclassical theory itself furnishes us with the true essence of the firm. Causal holists, however, would make no such claim. They would not maintain that at rock bottom or in essence business firms are maximizers. A causal holist gives priority to the question as to whether or not neoclassical theory is descriptively adequate. Let us suppose that a group of economists totally immersed in neoclassical theory has no doubts about its descriptive adequacy. Such a group, if committed to causal holism, would maintain that what neoclassical theory says about business firms is empirically well-corroborated and thereby has a high probability of being true. This group, however, would make no claim whatsoever about the essence of the business firm. Moreover, at the onto-logical level, in view of the causal holist's approach to the concept of observable, the business firm is as observable as any other social institution or natural kind object. In other words, the business firm belongs to the epistemic ontology of neoclassical economics, and neoclassical economics specifies, in Putnam's terminology, its principal stereotypical characteristics. Despite this, causal holists are keenly aware that any stereotypical character-istic is not an essential one and that the future of economics may well force them to change a whole range of these characteristics. In such an eventuality the business firm would still be observable. It is just that the neoclassical economist would be wrong about its stereotypes. In short, in causal holism, contrary to Mäki's account of essentialist realism, the emphasis is on a specific subsection of the model's ontology, namely, the model's epistemic ontology. Moreover, the economists' descriptions of the entities of the model's epi-stemic ontology are fallible and corrigible. There is no claim to articulate the essences, hidden or otherwise. The causal holist is satisfied with Putnam-type, corrigible stereotypes.

We have thus far not questioned the assumption that unification is central to economics. We will now adumbrate how causal holism challenges this assumption. To this end, it is useful to consider the extensive range of disciplines which currently operate under the umbrella of science. As we saw in Chapter 4, Lawson favours naturalism in which the physical and human sciences share a common method characterized by transcendental realism. The causal holist is a much weaker naturalist than Lawson. If one follows

Quine (1960) in giving a very abstract, general account of the method of science, namely, coherence, simplicity, a taste for tradition and the bar of experience, this characterization applies across the spectrum of the sciences and, to that extent, the causal holist accepts naturalism. However, this weak naturalism does not preclude the causal holist from maintaining that the term science is a Wittgensteinian, multiple-criteria, family resemblance concept. The resemblances between the various sciences are akin to the resemblances between an extended family where no one characteristic is shared by all. Thus as one moves across the methodological spectrum of the sciences from quantum physics to economics or psychology, one finds a variety of emphases and changes, with some features predominant among some disciplines while playing little or no role in others. In this Wittgensteinian approach, advocated by the causal holist, just because unification plays a significant role in parts of physics, it does not follow that it must play an equal role in all the other sciences. In particular, the fact that a sector of theoretical physics pursues unification does not imply that economics must also engage in a similar pursuit in the name of mature science.

In this Wittgensteinian perspective it is possible that physics, which is frequently presented as the paradigm or exemplar of science, may be a rather unique member of that family with a wide range of distinctive features. When we look at scientific disciplines, like botany, geology, oceanography or field zoology, to mention but a few, the unification which accompanies the centrality of some mathematical models of contemporary physics does indeed appear to be unique to a limited range of sciences. Furthermore, the history of physics suggests that it obtained vast tracts of information in statics, dynamics, electricity, magnetism, optics, sound and so on before it attempted any scientific unification and that this division of labour played an indispensable role in the emergence of its various unificatory attempts. Moreover, prescriptive, metaphysical unificatory systems, as Woo (1990), for instance, suggests, have not served the interests of science. Such prescriptive systems decide in advance of sufficient empirical investigations the direction of the ontological reduction by making too hasty a commitment to certain entities as basic or essential. In the human sciences metaphysical behaviourism is a clear example of such a metaphysical unificatory system. Physicalism, which asserts that all the sciences must be reduced to physics, is also psychologically a very influential metaphysical unificatory system. It plays a significant part in the not uncommon belief which, contrary to the Wittgensteinian approach advocated above, gives privileged status to physics over and above the other sciences. According to causal holism, physicalism amounts to one member of the family of science unjustifiably dominating and dictating to the others. More precisely, in view of the actual practice of unification in theoretical physics itself, as outlined by EN realism and Cartwright, for instance, the pursuit of physicalism is rather idealistic. The unification of contemporary physics is strewn with *ceteris paribus* qualifications, *ad hoc* adjustments, the use of other theories and so on and thereby it fails to approximate to the pure metaphysical reduction assumed by many physicalists. Having recourse to physicalism as a means of conferring a privileged status on physics and thereby on the quest for unification is not a legitimate move within causal holism.

Rather, economics belongs to a family of scientific disciplines which is primarily concerned with the construction of models which are descriptively adequate to current and past economic activity, structures and institutions. In view of the fact that unification is not a central preoccupation in many mature sciences, there is no onus on economics to pursue, in the name of mature science, a rigorous policy of unification. Indeed, in view of the actual manner in which unification is achieved in physics, a rigorous policy of unification may be too idealistic. Be that as it may, since economic time is historical, rather than logico-mathematical, there is a grave danger that a single-minded quest for unification, through the use of mathematical models, could conceal from view the rich diversity of economic conditions which contributed to the birth, development or demise of sundry contingent economic institutions and structures dispersed across the history of divergent human cultures and civilizations. If this were to happen, these mathematico-economic models would be descriptively inadequate to that range. Moreover, the quest for unification runs the risk of economic models being read in a metaphysical reductionist way, i.e. as expressing the fundamentals or essentials of the economic order, without recourse to the ontological refinements and scrutiny specified by causal holism. In causal holism the epistemic focus is on observable events and observable causes. In this context, what is deemed essential from the point of view of one economic problematic may be accidental or irrelevant for another problematic. In this way there is no temptation to read an economic theory in a metaphysical reductionist fashion. Finally, in view of the manner which the physical sciences pursued a prudent division of labour which, de facto at least, suspended the quest for unification until sufficiently rich reservoirs of information were accumulated in prima facie divergent domains, a similar strategy for economics is not irrational, especially in view of the prima facie diversity of economic structures and institutions which have appeared and disappeared in the history of civilization.

CAUSAL HOLISM AND RHETORIC:
MODELS AND METAPHORS

We have outlined some of the principal themes of causal holism and maintained that it furnishes a more sophisticated methodological framework for the philosophy of economics than either scientific realism or constructive empiricism. In the causal holist approach the focus is on the construction of a variety of economic models which enable us to accurately describe, in a theory-laden fashion, economic events, actions, structures and institutions in historical time. However, according to economic rhetoricians, it is precisely this central concern with scientific models which undermines the causal holist's defence of economic methodology. As we saw in Chapter 3, numerous authors explicate theoretical models in terms of emphatic and resonant metaphors. Economic rhetoricians fully endorse this explication and use it to vindicate their analysis. In this connection McCloskey sums up his position in the heading 'Models are Nonornamental Metaphors' (1985: 74). While maintaining that economic notions like the 'invisible hand' are metaphorical, he also maintains that, for instance, marginal productivity theory and the representation of markets by supply and demand curves are equally metaphorical. Indeed, he insists that 'each step in economic reasoning... is metaphoric' (McCloskey 1985: 75). One may feel that McCloskey's own penchant for rhetoric, especially hyperbolic language, is at work here. Of course all scientists on some occasion or other use figurative or metaphorical language and economists are no exceptions. Obviously these figurative usages do not penetrate to the core of their scientific work, especially their mathematical models. The latter are clearly immune from such peripheral, metaphorical influences. Contrary to such a pervasive common-sense assumption, McCloskey's thesis is that, notwithstanding the fact that numerous methodologists, philosophers and economists fail to recognize the indispensable role of metaphor in mathematical models, in so far as any science uses such models, it is *ipso facto* appealing to nonornamental metaphors. Metaphor extends to both the peripheral usage of figurative language and to the use of mathematical models in all of the sciences, including economics.

McCloskey's thesis can be butressed by the following considerations. As we saw in Chapter 3, theoretical models are indispensable cognitive tools which are ultimately metaphorical in nature. For instance, the wave theory of light was founded on the metaphor that light is a wave. Without this initial metaphor, the scientific exploitation of the domain of optics in terms of the mathematical model connecting, for example, speed of light with frequency and wavelength would not have materialized. In numerous instances theoretical models play an indispensable role in the construction of mathematical models and the former are, at root, nonornamental metaphors. In other words, many mathematical models are embedded in theoretical models or the latter constitute an integral part of the historical background to the former. In view of their background location, which can often be lost in the text book presentation of mathematical models, it is not surprising that many economists fail to recognize that their models have an indispensable metaphorical dimension. In this perspective McCloskey's thesis that rhetoric is in no way opposed to, and indeed may enhance, the quantification of economics becomes plausible. Mathematical models are refinements of theoretical models which are essentially metaphorical in character.

Contrary to the pervasive, common-sense assumption noted above, there is no hyperbole in McCloskey's claim that each step in economic reasoning is metaphoric. Indeed, the major conclusions of causal holism could be used to substantiate McCloskey's claim. First, causal holists argue that all economic description is theory-laden. In other words, economic descriptions and theoretical models are inextricably linked and, since the latter are metaphorical, so too are the former. Second, causal claims, according to causal holists, are inextricably linked to theoretical models and *ipso facto* to metaphors. Finally, the context dependency of economic explanation allows for an even more extensive use of metaphor. In short, through the vehicle of theoretical models, metaphor becomes all-pervasive in economic reasoning. McCloskey is drawing our attention to this indispensable and extensive role of metaphor in economics and to the fact that this centrality is neither acknowledged nor accepted by modernist philosophies. Moreover, he sees no option but to reject economic methodology as characterized by modernism. This total rejection, however, does not entail the abandonment of rationality. The post-modernist rationality to be used in the evaluation of pure and applied economics is that of the home of metaphor, namely, literature: 'what is successful in economic metaphor is what is successful in poetry, and the success is analysable in similar terms' (McCloskey 1985: 78). The suggestion is that the rationality of any discipline using theoretical-mathematical models is that of literature. In this fashion, McCloskey assimilates rhetoric to poetry.

This latter assimilation, however, is itself not persuasive. Just because metaphor is indispensable to rhetoric and poetry, this does not imply that it plays the same role in both. In this regard Aristotle was much more perceptive and persuasive than McCloskey. As we outlined in Chapter 2, metaphor in Aristotelian tragic poetry is located in the triad of poiesis-mimesis-catharsis while in Aristotelian rhetoric it is located in the triad of rhetoric-proof-persuasion. If Aristotle were alive today, in all probability he would argue that the language-game of tragic poetry is not to be confused with that of rhetoric and consequently the rationality of literature is not all-pervasive. Moreover, causal holists suggest that, if one cultivates a perceptive eye for detail, one will see that there are different language-games, ranging from the sciences at one end of the spectrum to poetry and literature at the other, and that there is no question of reducing the ranges of rational criteria at one end to those at the other. McCloskey articulates the belief that 'science advances by healthy conversation, not adherence to a methodology' (1985: 174), but fails to note that there are vast varieties of conversations and that some of these, including the classically recognized domains of rhetoric, presuppose methodology, although not in the simplistic sense of modernism. In particular, though McCloskey is emphatic about the metaphor that scientific models are metaphoric, the latter metaphor is not resonant: it conceals numerous differences between the manner in which the sciences deploy and develop models and the subtle, intricate network of uses of metaphors in poetry. Before addressing these differences, it may be useful to briefly summarize the causal holist's conception of metaphor and to specify the limited similarities between models and metaphors as acknowledged by causal holists.

Like McCloskey, we accept that some metaphors are nonornamental in that they serve genuine cognitive interests. For argument sake, let us accept Black's interactive theory of metaphor – clearly McCloskey is sympathetic to this analysis. According to the interactive approach, a metaphor, like 'man is a wolf', has a principal and subsidiary subject, 'man' being the principal subject and 'wolf' the subsidiary one. The 'system of associated commonplaces' of the secondary subject is freely evoked by an effective metaphor. A person hearing the metaphor can construct new implications about the primary subject in light of the associated commonplaces of the secondary subject. Indeed, the metaphor is none the less effective even when the commonplaces of the secondary subject are known falsehoods or merely partial truths. By exploiting these associated commonplaces, a powerful metaphor can restructure and radically alter our initial understanding of the primary subject. We reconceptualize the primary subject through supressing some of its original stereotypes and simultaneously inventing novel ones in light of the associated commonplaces of the metaphoric predication. Finally and centrally, in Black's interaction theory, metaphorical predication is distinct from the predication of a simile or analogy (Black 1962). A weak metaphor can be explicated in terms of the latter but powerful metaphors cannot be so explicated. As Black himself clearly perceived, if this were not so, then the interaction theory of metaphor would be redundant: any powerful metaphor could be eliminated and replaced by a literal simile or analogy. The logic of metaphorical predication is not to be confused with the logic of analogical predication. In short, a powerful metaphor has the capacity to bring two separate domains into a cognitive relationship which, prior to its invention, could neither be anticipated nor predicted and which subsequently cannot be paraphrased away. The primary subject is reconceptualized in a new way.

In Wittgensteinian terminology an interactive metaphor changes the usage of the primary term in a radical way and hence alters its sense. According to causal holism, this is also true of some theoretical models in science. The Bohr and subsequent models of the atom, for instance, effected a cognitive relationship between domains which prior to the construction of these models were inconceivable and which subsequently could not be paraphrased into the conceptual resources of the older, pre-Bohr theories. Clearly, an interactive metaphor and a novel theoretical model have this highly significant characteristic in common: both effect a change in the meanings of terms, in the Wittgensteinian sense of meaning. Indeed, this common characteristic is the basis of the metaphorical construal of theoretical models and especially their alignment, *à la* McCloskey, to poetic metaphors. This latter alignment, however, cannot be sustained. It is a source of dissonance rather than resonance. It fails to acknowledge the numerous differences between models and metaphors.

This conclusion is defended in the context of the causal holist's approach to language. Like Quine, causal holists hold that terms are centrally used in sentences and that sentences are embedded in systems of sentences. Let us briefly focus on an interaction metaphor as used in poetry. As McCloskey readily admits, a poem is not written in the same way as a scientific report, a scientific text or a scientific theory. A poetic interactive metaphor, in Black's most apt phrase, *evokes* the system of commonplaces associated with the secondary subject. This subtle delicate metaphorical evocation effected by the pen and the imagination of the poet is quite different from the explicit, *analogical–empirical* deployment of a theoretical model by the pen and laboratory of the physicist. The latter is clearly evident in the wave model of light. By analogy to sound waves, physicists postulate that light waves have frequencies, amplitudes, wavelengths, velocities in different media, and so forth. They then proceed to empirically verify these analogical predictions. This analogical exploitation of the primary domain is a distinctive feature of theoretical models in comparison with interactive metaphors. As we have just seen, and as Black clearly points out, an interactive metaphor is not an analogy. The copula of the interactive metaphor is not explicated in terms of the analogies of a simile. If it were, the whole rationale for the interactive view of metaphors, which is central to McCloskey's position, would collapse. However, some pertinent usages of theoretical models, especially in the kind of measurements mentioned above, function as analogies. An extensive range of theoretical models have their own specific analogical subtlety which is not to be confused with the metaphorical subtlety of poetry.

There are other differences between the use of metaphor in poetry and the scientific use of theoretical or mathematical models. For instance, in some poetry there is a significant oscillation between sense and sound and the choice of an evocative metaphor can facilitate this oscillation. Such oscillations have no role in theoretical models. Furthermore, metaphors in poetry may express or evoke different moods. In particular, an interaction metaphor of a poem may infuse the feelings attached to the secondary subject into a primary one. Such transferences of feelings or moods and the variety thereof play no role in the empirical exploitation of scientific models. Finally, poets like novelists may ignore reality and construct an imaginary fictitious world. To begin to understand such literature requires the acknowledgement of fiction as fiction. Clearly, the criteria for the evaluation of such a poem is far from those adumbrated by causal holists for the evaluation of a theoretical model where the epistemic concern is with descriptive adequacy to the actual world. In short, scientific imagination, as articulated in its models, is constrained by descriptive adequacy whereas literary imagination is not similarly constrained. In subsuming economics within the ambit of literary criticism, McCloskey is failing to acknowledge these significant differences.

We fully acknowledge that some theoretical models, like some metaphors, effect a radical change in sense. What was previously accepted as a category mistake may, through either a powerful metaphor or theoretical model, become reasonable and even a commonplace. This change in sense gives rise to the issue of reference. Philosophers of literature are certainly concerned with this issue. In particular, they are concerned with the reference of metaphors or, if one prefers, what metaphorical sentences say about reality. Clearly, McCloskey is correct in assuming that the standard interpretation of modernist philosophy is neither sufficiently perceptive nor adept at answer- - ing this challenging question. The causal holist is also concerned with issues of reference, especially the question of the reference of scientific terms, or what different scientific sentences say about reality. When we examine the question of what a scientific sentence says about reality, the causal holist has recourse to the distinctions between the various ontological categories discussed above. The principal preoccupation is with the model's epistemic ontology and its empirical investigation. These categories, however, have no role to play in any philosophical elucidation of the referential role of metaphor in a literary work such as a poem or a play. Even a peripheral reading of Ricoeur's *Rule of Metaphor* (1986) suffices to show this. Our task here is not to furnish a philosophy of literature. Rather, we wish to show that the question of reference in scientific models is quite distinct from that of literature, a point which McCloskey fails to perceive in his reduction of the former to the latter. This is a crucial difference between scientific models and poetic metaphors. Clearly, literary works can illuminate in a distinctive fashion the human condition. Such works display possible worlds, rich in human significance and open to a variety of interpretations. These literary displays may be imaginative, challenging, provocative, compelling or illuminating. Furthermore, literary displays may create, arouse or evoke certain moods or emotions. Their referential role, however, is not that of the theoretical model with its primary focus on its epistemic ontology and its descriptive adequacy. McCloskey replaces modernism's colonial expansionist aspirations, which reduced everything to reason as characterized by science, by another post-modern colonial expansionist philosophy, namely, the reduction of everything to literary rationality. What is required is a Wittgensteinian recognition of the multiplicity and rich diversity of language-games or, in McCloskey's terminology, ranges of conversations. In short, poetry and literature, while genuinely cognitive, do not pursue the hunt for reason along the same lines as empirical sciences which, at the ontological level, are primarily concerned with their models' epistemic ontology. Scientific models, when viewed from the ontological perspective of descriptive adequacy, do not, contrary to McCloskey, function as literary metaphors.

Our critique of McCloskey may be summarized as follows. When a novel theoretical model becomes accepted, at the Wittgensteinian level of sense as usage, it effects a new sense which, prior to its construction, could not be antecedently predicted and which cannot be paraphrased into the language of the older models. At this level, models, like metaphors, are indispensable, cognitive tools. However, the experimental logic of scientific models is that of analogy and not of powerful interactive metaphors. For instance, by analogy to the parent situation of sound waves, the predicates 'wavelength', 'amplitude', 'frequency' and so on are applied to light and these are empirically, i.e. experimentally, investigated. This analogical exploitation of parent situations differentiates scientific models from powerful metaphors, at least those which fall within the scope of Black's nonornamental, interactive theory. Moreover, poetic metaphors serve a host of aesthetic, fictional and psychological functions which are not served by scientific models. Finally, and most significantly, at the level of ontology or reference, theoretical models distinguish between the actual and non-actual entities postulated by the model. In particular, at the level of actual objects, it distinguishes between the model's epistemic ontology and its unobservable, purely theoretical entities. Ontological commitments are confined to the former and are suspended in the case of the latter. This ontological differentiation simply does not arise or apply in the case of powerful literary metaphors. Hence the weight of evidence unambiguously corroborates the causal holist's conclusion that models are not literary metaphors.

In short, just as Orwell's pigs point out that all animals are equal but some are more equal than others, similarly, if one wants to hold that all discourses are metaphorical, we point out that some are more metaphorical than others. Causal holists would thus introduce a product differentiation between metaphor in rhetoric, metaphor in poetics and metaphor in science. The latter is called a scientific model to highlight its different analogical and ontological functions to that of metaphor in poetry. These scientific models have their own specific epistemic dimension which is totally ignored by McCloskey's unjustified assimilation of models to powerful metaphors.

8

FROM FRIEDMAN TO KALDOR
A causal holist critique of the methodology
of neoclassical economics

In the previous chapter we outlined how causal holism transcends the debate
between scientific realism and constructive empiricism. We also specified how
it distances itself from the economic rhetorician's reduction of economic
models to nonornamental metaphors. In this chapter we propose to further
articulate the causal holist methodological framework by re-engaging the
methodological writings of Friedman and Kaldor. We focus on these writings
for many reasons. Clearly, the coherence of the present narrative forces these
upon us: as we have seen Mäki uses Friedman to articulate his version of
realism, while Lawson uses Kaldor for his articulation of transcendental
realism. Moreover, Friedman's famous piece from 1953 is a sophisticated
methodological defence of neoclassical economics, while Kaldor's writings
consist of a devastating critique of the latter type of economics. By seriously
engaging these methodological writings, the novel contribution of causal
holism to the contemporary debate in the methodology of economics
becomes more apparent. Finally, it should be noted that our focus on
Friedman's 1953 piece in no way takes away from the excellent analysis of
Friedman's contribution furnished by de Marchi and Hirsch which focuses
on Friedman's own practice of economics. This analysis is to be welcomed.
Our critique of Friedman's methodological piece merely complements the
latter monumental analysis. Our central purpose is to clarify and further
delineate the manner in which causal holism, as a methodological framework,
is dissatisfied with Friedman's methodological defence of neoclassical economics and simultaneously the manner in which it reorientates the general
methodological evaluation of neoclassical theory. This reorientation is con-
solidated by its reinterpretation of Kaldor's methodological contributions.

THE CAUSAL HOLIST REVISITS FRIEDMAN

As we saw in Chapter 5, Friedman fairs rather badly in a realist setting. While
in Lawson's opinion Friedman's position is erroneous and confused, in
Mäki's eyes it is ambiguous, obscure and inconsistent. Certainly, we agreed
with Mäki that Friedman speaks to an extensive range of philosophers of

science. Indeed, we briefly suggested the possibility that Friedman's basic tenet, what Mäki calls the F thesis, i.e. the central criterion of theory choice in economics concerns its predictive capacities rather than the realism of its assumptions, is a specific methodological principle which is not inferred from any preferred philosophy of science such as Popperianism or scientific realism or whatever. Clearly, Friedman's primary problematic is quite specific in that it is unambiguously focused on the maximization hypothesis and his basic query is with the rational decision-making process on the acceptability or otherwise of that hypothesis as part of the systematic knowledge of positive economics. In particular, he is concerned with whether or not it can be tested by the 'realism of its assumptions'.

According to Friedman, much of the criticism of neoclassical economics 'is based almost entirely on supposedly directly perceived discrepancies between the 'assumptions' and the 'real world' (Friedman 1953: 31). He cites recent criticisms of the maximization-of-returns hypothesis as a clear example of what he has in mind. These criticisms are based on the grounds that business people do not behave as the theory 'assumes' they do. The Hall and Hitch work and other sociological questionnaires or interviews with business people clearly showed that, according to their own accounts of the factors affecting their decision making, they are not maximizers. This sociological evidence suggests that the basic assumption of neoclassical economics does not hold. Friedman, however, maintains that such questionnaire results are 'almost entirely useless as a means of *testing* the validity of economic hypotheses' (ibid.: 31). In short, as an economist, Friedman wishes to defend orthodox, i.e. neoclassical economics from the force of such sociological surveys and other criticisms based on its perceived unrealistic assumptions. Through a close examination of Friedman's piece we demonstrate that his case, which is not derived or directly deduced from any 'school' of philosophy, such as philosophical instrumentalism or Popperian falsificationism, is, contrary to Mäki's realist reading, neither obscure nor inconsistent. Rather, it is a sophisticated, low-level, two-pronged piece of reasoning with a threefold argument by analogy constructed along the first prong, while the web of arguments along the second prong concern his analysis of the roles of assumptions in economics. Despite its sophistication and coherence, as causal holists we find that his case does not establish his conclusion beyond reasonable doubt. Indeed, the causal holist maintains that a prima facie case exists against Friedman's conclusion and that this must be explored, not by philosophers of economics, but by economists themselves.

Friedman uses three analogues in arguing for 'the impossibility of testing a theory by its assumptions' (Friedman 1953: 17–18), namely, the motion of a falling body in Newtonian mechanics, the density of leaves on a tree and an expert billiard player. The first analogy is a specific case of the application of mathematical models discussed in Chapter 3. The second is designed to be an analogue of numerous hypotheses in the social sciences and the third is an analogue involving human behaviour. A casual reading may suggest that the three analogies are superfluous. The first one would appear to suffice. A closer reading, however, shows that substantive different points are being made about so-called assumptions by means of the different analogies and that these substantive differences are crucial to Friedman's case.

In the first analogue – the Newtonian, mathematical model – Friedman contrasts the fall of a compact ball to that of a feather and correctly concludes that this mathematical model states that, under a wide range of circumstances, bodies falling in the atmosphere behave *as if* they were falling in a vacuum. In the language of economics this statement would be phrased as follows: the model assumes a vacuum. However, he quickly adds that this hypothesis can readily be rephrased without any mention of a vacuum as follows: 'under a wide range of circumstances the distance a body falls in a given time is given by the equation $s = 1/2 \, g \, t^2$' (Friedman 1953: 17–18). Moreover, he correctly adds that when the hypothesis is thus rephrased, an important empirical task is to specify the circumstances under which the Newtonain equation applies. He also adds that the so-called assumption *in this specific case*, i.e. a vacuum, actually identifies some of these conditions. For instance, it specifies that the existence of air pressure or the shape of a body have no appreciable effect on the distance a body falls in a given time. In other words, the so-called vacuum assumption of this Newtonian model (unlike the assumptions of the other analogues) is merely a convenient way of specifying some of the conditions under which the model applies. Moreover, Friedman is quite explicit and emphatic about the centrality of the specification of these conditions. He says: 'such a specification is not one thing and the hypothesis another. The specification is itself an essential part of the hypothesis, and it is a part that is peculiarly likely to be revised and extended as experience accumulates' (ibid.: 17–18).

If one were to focus solely on this Newtonian analogue, Friedman is making a very interesting, original suggestion, namely, Newtonian physicists should refrain from any recourse to the misleading language surrounding the notion of the realism of its vacuum assumption. Alternatively, they should focus on the significant problem of specifying the circumstances or conditions under which this model may be applied. Similarly, in the case of neoclassical economics the question is not whether or not its so-called assumptions are realistic. Rather, one should specify and evaluate the circumstances or conditions under which it applies. One possibility is that the conditions of its applicability may be such that neoclassical theory is applicable in some cases but not in others. In the latter eventuality, i.e. in the circumstances in which it does not apply, it is clearly, in the language of the causal holist, descriptively inadequate. Indeed, this conclusion follows from Friedman's analysis of the motion of a feather in his deployment of his first analogue. The circumstances under which this elementary Newtonian model holds are such that it does not furnish a descriptively adequate description of the motion of a feather. Similarly, those who criticize the neoclassical maximization hypothesis as having unrealistic assumptions are really saying that the conditions of its applicability are such that it does not supply a descriptively adequate description of certain economic events. Hence Friedman's first analogue does *not* demonstrate the impossibility of testing the maximization hypothesis by the realism of its assumptions. On the contrary, it gives a very specific explication to the rather vague notion of realism of assumptions in terms of a specification of the conditions of the applicability of that hypothesis. This explication clearly legitimates empirical testing in terms of an empirical investigation into the conditions of the applicability of that hypothesis.

In our opinion Friedman recognized this and consequently introduced and developed the second analogue, namely, 'the hypothesis that the leaves on a tree are positioned as if each leaf deliberately sought to maximize the amount of sunlight it receives' (Friedman 1953: 19). Indeed, according to Friedman this is a 'constructed' example which is 'an analogue of many hypotheses in the social sciences' (ibid.). Moreover, unlike the previous example, Friedman explicitly points out that its assumptions 'play no part' in specifying the conditions or circumstances under which the hypothesis applies (ibid.: 20). Friedman is thus using the second analogy in a distinct way from the Newtonian one. His thesis may be summed up as follows. The neoclassical maximization hypothesis is analogous to both the Newtonian model and to the leaves-on-a-tree model in that falling stones behave as if they were falling in a vacuum, the leaves are positioned as if each leaf acted in a deliberate fashion and entrepreneurs behave as if they were maximizing returns. Second, the neoclassical hypothesis is disanalogous to the Newtonian model in that the assumptions of the latter specify some of its empirical conditions of applicability, whereas this is not true of the neoclassical hypothesis. However, in this respect the neoclassical hypothesis is analogous to the contrived leaves-on-a-tree model: its assumptions are completely irrelevant to specifying any empirical investigation into the position of leaves on trees. In other words, the neoclassical hypothesis is more analogous to the leaves-on-a-tree model than to the Newtonian model. Third, since the assumptions do not specify the conditions of its applicability, unlike the Newtonian analogue, their lack of realism cannot be explicated or reinterpreted in terms of the conditions of its applicability. Unlike the Newtonian analogue, the vague notion of 'realism of assumptions' cannot be given a precise explication in terms of a specification of the conditions of applicability. The leaves-on-the-tree analogue highlights this truth. Consequently, in Friedman's eyes, the latter analogue is quite distinct from the Newtonian one and is indispensable to his case. In this respect Friedman is quite sophisticated and is certainly not inconsistent, at least on these grounds.

The third analogue, namely, the expert billiard player executes his shots as if he knew the relevant application of the complicated mathematics governing the motions of billiard balls, is, we are told, 'largely parallel' to the second. Despite its lack of realism, our confidence in this hypothesis is derived from the belief that, unless a billiard player is in some way capable of reaching the same result as the expert mathematical physicist, he would not in fact be an expert billiard player. With this final example we are, in Friedman's terminology, 'only a short step' from the neoclassical maximization hypothesis. In this behavioural comparison we are even closer than the previous analogue to the situation which pertains in neoclassical economics. Just as the billiard player does not make the specific mathematical calculations, businessmen do not solve the appropriate equations. Nevertheless, both behave as if they knew the appropriate mathematics. As we move from the Newtonian analogue to that of the expert billiard player, the positive analogy, i.e. the range of similarities between the latter and the neoclassical maximization hypothesis, increases, while its negative analogy, i.e. the range of dissimilarities, diminishes.

In our opinion, the expert billiard player analogue brings into focus Friedman's specific defence of the neoclassical maximization hypothesis, namely, what Maurice Lagueux and other methodologists call a 'survival' argument (Lagueux 1991). Unless the behaviour of a billiard player in some fashion or other approximates to the behaviour of a mathematically proficient expert calculating the appropriate angles, forces and so forth, such a person would not be an expert billiard player: he would not survive as a superstar of billiards. Similarly, 'unless the behaviour of business men in some way or other approximates to behaviour consistent with the maximization of returns, it seems unlikely that they would remain in business for long' (Friedman 1953: 22). Alternatively, as Friedman himself also puts it, the maximization hypothesis 'summarizes appropriately the conditions for survival' (ibid.).

Although each of the three arguments by analogy shows that firms behave as if they were maximizers, the third argument has the distinctive component of a survival one. It is this distinctive element which ultimately underwrites Friedman's methodological defence of the maximization hypothesis: if firms do not behave in accordance with its perscriptions, the market will force them to the wall. This defence has nothing to do with instrumentalism, scientific realism or Popperianism as general methodologies of science. Rather, Friedman is making his case by a series of sophisticated arguments by analogy. By working closely with his text, the outcome is that Friedman's argument for the impossibility of testing the maximization hypothesis by its assumptions has the form of a survival argument. Moreover, contrary to Mäki, there is no inconsistency in this argument. On the contrary, it is, as the above analysis shows, a very sophisticated piece of analogical reasoning. Indeed, this piece of analogical reasoning is in turn conjoined to another sophisticated network of considerations which constitute the second prong of Friedman's case.

We now address this prong. In section four of his paper, which is devoted to the significance and role of 'assumptions', Friedman notes three possible distinct roles. First, assumptions 'are sometimes a convenient way of specifying the conditions under which the theory is expected to be valid' – a topic which we have already addressed and one on which Friedman also feels no necessity to say anything further. Second, assumptions may 'sometimes facilitate an indirect test of an hypothesis' (Friedman 1953: 23). Prima facie this role undermines Friedman's strong thesis of 'the impossibility of testing a theory by its assumptions' (ibid.: 17–18). This prima facie case is butressed by the fact, readily conceded by Friedman, that there are different ways of axiomatizing the same empirical theory, so that what is an axiom in one formulation is a theorem in another and vice versa. This possibility, in Friedman's own words, 'implies the possibility of interchanging "implications" and "assumptions" in the substantive hypothesis' (ibid.: 27). Thus in the axiomatization where the assumptions are theorems or consequences, if these assumptions do not correspond to the observable facts then, following Popper, the theory is in difficulty. But this amounts to testing a theory by the realism of its assumptions: in Friedman's terminology it consists of the investigation of 'the directly perceived discrepancies between the "assumptions" and the "real world"' (ibid.: 31).

On this reading it is very difficult to see how Friedman could call this kind of testing indirect. Logically, the situation is as follows. Axioms Ai combined with assumptions Pa are shown to be logically equivalent to Axioms Bj combined with assumptions Pb, such that Pa ≠ Pb. When we take the latter formulation, assumptions Pa are among the consequences of the theory relative to the axiomatization Bj. If assumptions Pa are found to obtain in the observable world then they are realistic and, if not, they are unrealistic. This testing is clearly not incompatible with Friedman's own F thesis as enunciated by Mäki, namely, the only way of testing neoclassical economics is by investigating its consequences: in this case the assumptions are among the latter. Furthermore, in the Popperian account of science, such testing is direct, yet Friedman explicitly limits the role of assumptions to indirect testing. One may legitimately enquire about Friedman's criterion for the indirect testing of an assumption. Clearly, it cannot be related to the plurality of axiomatizations of economics since, as we have just seen, such an analysis immediately leads us into direct testing. Fortunately, it is possible to give a conclusive answer to the latter enquiry. Friedman furnishes an unequivocal example of what he has in mind by indirect testing. The example concerns the behaviour of an oligopoly (Friedman 1953: 27). If we *assume* the maximization hypothesis, M, combined with the presence of an oligopoly, O, and certain initial conditions, Ci, we can predict a basing-point pricing system, B. Logically M + O + Ci imply B. In this case the primary purpose is to predict market behaviour. Friedman now says that *if we adopt a new purpose*, namely, to decide what cases to prosecute under certain antitrust laws, we now *assume* a basing-point pricing system, i.e. B. In this new purpose area, B + O imply a conspiracy to restrain trade, CRT. What was for the *first purpose* an implication is for the *second purpose* an assumption and vice versa. Friedman's point about indirect testing is that 'in the absence of other evidence', confirmation of B + O, by the presence of letters, memoranda and the like required to prove CRT, would 'give us greater confidence than we would otherwise have' in M. 'It is much harder to say how much greater confidence it justifies' but it does give us some (ibid.: 28).

The logic of this example is clearly not that of the multiple axiomatizations of a domain. Also, the example furnishes a coherent criterion for indirect testing which is very plausible indeed. Furthermore, this kind of indirect testing does not invalidate his thesis that it is impossible to test a theory by its assumptions, since such indirect testing on its own would not be sufficient for those advocating the realism of assumptions. Its evidence would be too weak. In this Friedman is, in our opinion, correct. Once again there is no question of a glaring inconsistency in Friedman defending the indirect testing of an assumption and holding that it is impossible to test a theory by its assumptions. On the contrary, given his own understanding of indirect testing, he is perfectly consistent.

We now turn to the third possible role which Friedman assigns to assumptions, namely, 'they are often an economical mode of describing or presenting a theory' (ibid.: 23) and we shall see how he uses this role to expose, what he perceives to be, a range of difficulties in the case of his opponents. In Friedman's view any hypothesis consists of two parts. i.e. an 'abstract model simpler than the "real world" containing only the forces that the hypothesis asserts to be important' and 'a set of rules' linking the entities in the model to observable phenomena (ibid.: 24). The two parts are radically different. The abstract model is an 'algebra' or 'logic' which is consistent and complete, while the rules 'cannot possibly be abstract and complete' (ibid.: 25). The example guiding Friedman's division is Euclidean geometry. He correctly points out that this system is a logically consistent, abstract model with its entities precisely defined. These entities, however, are clearly unrealistic: there is, for instance, no such thing in the physical world as a Euclidean point or straight line.

Moreover, what are called the crucial assumptions of a theory are attempts 'to state the key elements of the abstract model' (Friedman 1953: 26). More precisely, assumptions may be relevant to the rigorous articulation of the abstract model but they are not used in articulating the rules linking the model to the observable world. In Friedman's terminology, one should sharply distinguish between considerations of 'analytical relevance', which are focused on the abstract model, on the one hand and 'descriptive accuracy' on the other (ibid.: 33). Basic assumptions may be concerned with the former but never with the latter: they may play an analytical role only. In the context of this distinction between 'analytical relevance' and 'descriptive accuracy', Friedman uses his thesis that the crucial assumptions are sometimes pertinent to the former but not to the latter to highlight a 'basic confusion' in the argument of those advocating the evaluation of the maximization hypothesis by the realism of its assumptions. The advocates of realistic assumptions, in failing to distinguish between 'analytical relevancy' and 'descriptive accuracy', are erroneously assuming that crucial assumptions are relevant to the latter when in fact they are merely used in articulating the former. They confuse considerations pertaining to the articulation of the abstract model with considerations pertaining to the application of the model to observable reality.

This basic confusion in turn may result in a subsequent misunderstanding of the role of 'ideal types' in economic theory on the part of those advocating realistic assumptions. This misunderstanding is expressed in the claim that ideal types are 'strictly descriptive categories intended to correspond directly and fully to entities in the real world independently of the purpose for which the model is being used' (ibid.: 34). Prima facie this misunderstanding is merely another reformation of the basic confusion. However, on closer analysis this is not the case. Indeed, Friedman supplies this close analysis by commenting on Marshall's use of two 'ideal' types of firms, namely, atomistically competitive firms and monopolistic ones. Rejecting the basic confusion between analytic relevancy and descriptive accuracy, Friedman states that these ideal types are not intended to be descriptive and adds 'they are designed to isolate the features that are crucial for a particular problem' (ibid.: 36). This addition is significant: without it the subsequent misunderstanding is merely another way of verbalizing the basic confusion. Friedman, moreover, is quite explicit about its significance. He claims:

> Everything depends on the problem; there is no inconsistency in regarding the same firm as if it were a perfect competitor for one problem and a monopolist for another, just as there is none in regarding the same chalk mark as a Euclidean line for one problem, a Euclidean surface for another and a Euclidean solid for a third.
>
> (Friedman 1953: 36)

In other words in the domain of economics the interpretation of ideal types across a range of problems is *not* invariant. In general, ideal type A for problematic P1 can be predicated of firm, Fi, and ideal type B, such that B is contained in the class of not A, can be predicated of the same firm, Fi, for problematic P2. Those advocating the realism of assumptions fail to appreciate this fact. They require or implicitly assume that the same ideal type should be used for all problematics.

However, if we grant this to Friedman then there is no reason why the same logic should not apply to the ideal type used in the neoclassical maximization hypothesis which, for short, we shall call maximizer, M. Ideal type M can be predicated of firm, Fi, for problematic P3 and ideal type N, such that N is contained in the class of not M, can be predicated of the same

191

firm, Fi, for problematic P4. Thus the logic of Friedman's argument here is that the maximization hypothesis has not universal application: the proposition that for all economic problematics all firms are maximizers is not true. From a causal holist perspective, if Friedman's analysis is empirically vindicated, neoclassical idealizations are descriptively inadequate in some problematics and hence an alternative theory is required. One can easily imagine that numerous critics of neoclassical economics, on the grounds that its assumptions are unrealistic, would be satisfied to accept this as a reasonable reformulation of their opposition.

Let us now return to Friedman's location of assumptions in the analytical part of science, which appears to be straightforward, at least in his Euclidean exemplar. According to causal holism, Friedman's distinction between the analytical and the descriptive dimensions of a model, if interpreted in an absolute manner, smacks of the syntactical approach to science which, à la constructive empiricism, is not justifiable. Friedman, however, prevaricates about this distinction. In a very brief discussion of what he calls a 'striking illustration' of the basic confusion between analytical relevance and descriptive accuracy, he briefly refers to a more sophisticated relationship between scientific facts and theory which runs counter to his standard positivist division into analytic and descriptive elements. Briefly, but emphatically, he denies the possibility of neatly separating a theory from the facts. 'Known facts cannot be set on one side; a theory to apply "closely to reality", on the other. A theory is the way we perceive "facts", and we cannot perceive "facts" without a theory' (Friedman 1953: 34).

This view that facts are theory-laden is one which, as we have seen, is absolutely central to causal holism. Moreover, what Friedman correctly sees as a basic confusion relative to his syntactical analysis of scientific theory, is, in this causal holist view, not a confusion at all. Following Quine and van Fraassen, one cannot neatly divide any scientific language into distinct analytical and descriptive dimensions: our scientific language in general and economic language in particular is a complex holistic web or network in which the Friedmanite analytic-descriptive dichotomy does not hold. In the causal holist approach this specific Friedmanite argument to the effect that those who demand more realistic assumptions in economics are basically confused does not stand up to critical scrutiny.

Friedman is not content to let his case rest. He attempts to buttress it by introducing two additional objections to his opponents. The first infers that those advocating realistic assumptions are at a total loss to specify acceptable criteria of degrees of realism, other than testing by prediction. Friedman correctly points out that if one were demanding a completely 'realistic' account of, say, the wheat market one would have to include not only the conditions directly contributing to supply and demand but also a whole host of other conditions ranging from the chemistry of the soil to the kind of coins used. Thus he concludes that no reasonable person would accept such an extreme of realism as a proper objective. In other words, it is a question of degrees of realism and the crucial question is 'what is the criterion by which to judge whether a particular departure from realism is or is not acceptable?' (Friedman 1953: 32). There is only one way of making such a judgement, i.e. formulate the appropriate hypothesis about the relevant departure and test it by means of its predictions.

In response to this, the realistic assumption theorists want to say that of course all assumptions are unrealistic but some are more unrealistic than others. Friedman has no objection to this reply. Rather, his point is a Wittgensteinian one, namely, would these same theorists specify the criterion of an acceptable degree of realism other than the deductive testing of the appropriate hypothesis? Friedman suspects that they are at a loss to supply the appropriate criterion. However, in causal holism all is not lost for realistic assumption theorists. They could elaborate the following schematic case. In the first place, the concept of 'realistic' is, a 'multiple-criteria', and not a 'single-criterion', one with no one criterion being absolutely necessary. In this connection it is crucially important to distinguish between this Wittgensteinian type, multiple-criteria characterization of the concept of unrealistic and a Mäki-type disjunctive characterization as outlined in Chapter 5. If one of its disjunctive criteria obtains, a disjunctive concept is applicable. A multiple-criteria concept is not so liberal. Its application is a question of weightings attached to each individual criterion and, second, a range of these criteria, rather than one criterion, should be satisfied or exemplified. Moreover, the criteria will change over the history of a discipline and from one discipline to another. For instance, much of what is deemed realistic in Newtonian physics would be deemed unrealistic in Aristotelian physics and, similarly, some of what is deemed realistic in quantum physics could be deemed unrealistic in either Newtonian physics or contemporary geology. Thus the criteria of realistic are developed in the context of what Popperian's call background knowledge or what EN realists call external global characteristics.

In the specific case of neoclassical economics the maximization hypothesis claims that both firms and consumers are maximizers. The criteria for the realisticness of the assumptions of this hypothesis are developed in the context of contemporary background knowledge, ranging from the observable behaviour of firms and consumers, through our best available knowledge of human information processing, to contemporary philosophical psychology which focuses on the richness of human action. The hypothesis could be shown to be unrealistic, if the weight of evidence from our best theories about human actions, to the manner in which human information is processed, to an analysis of the verbalized intentions of producers and consumers converge on the conclusion that firms and consumers do not meet the conditions of maximization. However, if this range of evidence does not converge, then the issue of its unrealisticness is an open question.

The inclusion of verbalized intentions into the range of criteria for the application of the concept of realistic brings us to Friedman's final reservation. This reservation focuses on the economist's sense of autonomy. As we already noted, the use of sociological questionnaires as a means of *testing* the validity of economic hypotheses is, in Friedman's opinion, 'almost entirely useless' (1953: 31, footnote 22). In many ways Friedman is re-echoing the history of economics as an endeavour to secure its own distinctive autonomy from psychology on the one hand and sociology on the other and, as a practising economist, he is loath to surrender this hard won autonomy. Those arguing for the lack of realism in the assumptions of neoclassical economics, however, while recognizing a relative autonomy for economics, would, in Woo's terminology, allow some interface between economics and neighbouring disciplines (Woo 1990). In some circumstances questionnaires could be appropriate. According to causal holists, the rejection of an economic theory on such grounds alone, however, would, in Kaldor's terminology, be too 'monist'. Other grounds would also be required. In short, the causal holist holds, à *la* Woo, for some interfacing between economics and relevant neighbourhood disciplines without surrendering the entire burden of economic evaluation to the neighbourhood regions. In this relative autonomous region it is possible that some economic hypotheses are more realistic than others.

We may sum up as follows. In his second prong Friedman attempts to expose a range of difficulties in the position of those advocating the realism of assumptions as a criterion for the evaluation of neoclassical economics. While his arguments here are complex and challenging, they are far from foolproof. Perhaps Friedman himself recognized this for he admits that he has less confidence in them than in the analogical arguments adduced in the first prong. With this admission we briefly turn to the causal holist's attitude towards Friedman's survival argument which has already been identified as the distinctive feature of the first prong of his case. The reader will recall that, according to causal holism, a central aim of economics as a pure science is the construction of models which are descriptively adequate to economic events, actions, institutions and structures as these unfold in historical time. In particular, when firms collapse the causal holist will attempt to uncover the contingent causal chains which result in these specific collapses and, where relevant, contingent causal trends. In this causal holist context, analogical arguments based on limited similarities between business firms and billiard players are no substitute for a thorough empirical investigation into the collapse of firms over both the short and the long run. In connection with neoclassical economics' relevance to the collapse of firms, the causal holist's central general question is whether or not neoclassical theory furnishes, in its models, accurate economic descriptions of all the observable causes of these collapses? This is an epistemic question concerning its descriptive adequacy which is pursued by pure economists. Causal holists tell us that this question is central to the issue of the descriptive adequacy of neoclassical economics but, as philosophers of science, clearly they cannot answer it. The answer is obtained in pure economic empirical research. The above Friedmanite analogy, however, is of no help in this regard.

The causal holist also draws our attention to a central specific question, i.e. what in Friedman's opinion, is the precise empirical contribution of the neoclassical maximization hypothesis to the accurate description of these collapses? Certainly, Friedman's analogy to billiard players fails to specify in a precise manner the empirical role of this hypothesis in the collapse of firms. Taken on this empirical level, Friedman's survival argument could be a claim to the effect that the absence of the pursuit of the maximization of returns is the only causal trend actually in operation in the collapse of firms in the contemporary economic world. This question, however, cannot be settled by analogy to billiard players or to the density of leaves on a tree. Once again it is a matter for empirical investigation.

Friedman's survival argument could also be interpreted as specifying a necessary condition for the survival of business firms. Just as biology has demonstrated that oxygen is a necessary condition for life, neoclassical economics demonstrates that maximization of returns is necessary for survival in the contemporary economic world. If this necessary condition is not fulfilled by any firm, the market will force it to the wall. According to causal holism, the specification of necessary conditions for the survival of firms in the contemporary world is also an empirical task and any empirical hypothesis in this regard must be open to a rigorous empirical investigation. The maximization hypothesis could be such a necessary condition. The question, however, is not about logical possibilities nor indeed about plausibility. The issue is whether or not this is shown by empirical investigation. The maximization hypothesis, understood as an appropriate summary of the necessary conditions for the survival of a firm, must be fully investigated in an empirical way. Analogical arguments adduced by Friedman are no surrogates for this economic evaluation.

Friedman's survival argument could also be read in a prescriptive way. This prescriptive reading would ultimately have recourse to the prescriptive dimension inherent in the concept of rationality. On this reading, Friedman is maintaining that any firm acting contrary to the assumptions of the neoclassical economics is acting irrationally and that the consequences of such irrational behaviour will inevitably lead to its demise. Maximization is thus a necessary condition of the prescriptive notion of rational behaviour. While acknowledging that the issue of rationality is very complex and beyond the scope of the present work, causal holists welcome all scientific investigation into the manner in which rational economic decisions are actually formed and executed. However, they distinguish between the concept of rationality as actually used in economic decision making and its execution on the one hand and the logico-prescriptive accounts of what rationality should be, as formulated by a priorist game theorists and others. Economics as a science is certainly concerned with descriptively adequate descriptions of the former. In connection with the latter, some of this work may produce useful explications of the way the concept of rationality is actually used by economic agents and thereby be utilized in the construction of empirically adequate descriptions of economic rational decision making. Such explications, however, have to prove their empirical worth when so used. Moreover, as Quine pointed out (Quine 1960), there is always more than one way of explicating a term and hence explications should not be construed as conveying the essential characteristics of any term in its pre-explicative state. If Friedman's survival argument is read in a prescriptive way then clearly maximization is a necessary condition of the concept of rationality as explicated by neo-classical economics. This does not imply that it is a necessary condition of the concept of rationality as used in actual decision making. Any such claim has to be established by empirical investigation and not by a priorist game theorists or other a priorist approaches. In short, causal holists, by putting the focus on descriptive adequacy, throw a sceptical eye on any Friedmanite attempt to defend the maximization hypothesis on the grounds of a survival argument by analogy to billiard players or other analogues. The epistemic focus in on descriptive adequacy and, as we have pointed out time and again, this is a matter of persistent and thorough empirical investigation.

CAUSAL HOLISM AND KALDOR'S CRITIQUE OF EQUILIBRIUM THEORY

Causal holism furnishes the philosophy of economics with a challenging methodological framework which synergizes the advantages of both constructive empiricism and scientific realism. As we have already seen, in this novel framework economics is located within the family of scientific disciplines without recourse to any strong version of naturalism. The principal epistemic task of the pure economist is the construction of models which are empirically adequate to contemporary economic actions, structures, systems and institutions on the one hand, and to the history of these institutions, systems and structures on the other. Causal holists, with their focus on the construction of descriptively adequate models, are at liberty to investigate all aspects of the contemporary economic world and how it relates to other domains in its full richness and complexity. Moreover, they are also concerned with describing past economic systems and the webs of historical relationships between these. The focus is clearly on descriptive adequacy. The economic models aim at furnishing theory-laden descriptions which accurately characterize the events, the tendencies and the contingent network of causes in operation in any economic domain, including any interactions between economic and non-economic institutions, such as those of law or politics. The causal holist, however, is at pains to point out the indispensability of economic theory for this process of description. Just as the

196

description of the physical world proves to be a very challenging task demanding the reconstruction of our theoretical frameworks, the accurate description of the economic world and its history is equally challenging.

Theoretical models occupy the centre stage in causal holism and descriptive adequacy takes precedence over other virtues, such as simplicity or unification. In connection with the ontological ramifications of any economic model, one must distinguish between actual and non-actual objects of the model's overall ontology on the one hand, and between the model's overall ontology and the model's epistemic ontology on the other. In this fashion, the causal holist does not automatically read the basic ontological categories of the model's general ontology as *ipso facto* referring to the essential or basic structures of an actual economy. Finally, economic explanation is an additional derivative task which is located in specific contexts and these contexts crucially impinge on the explanatory activities by specifying, often tacitly, the appropriate relevancy requirements. An economic explanation is an answer to a specific why-question in a specific context and the explanation is economic, rather than, say, political, in so far as the salient explanatory factor is chosen from an economic, rather than a political or some other, model. Thus economic explanation pertains to applied, rather than to pure, science. In order to further elucidate the ramifications of causal holism for the philosophy of economics, we will, *à la* Lawson, articulate it through a discussion of Kaldor's methodological concerns.

As we have already seem Kaldor was one of the major figures in the Cambridge critique of orthodox economics in the postwar period. Moreover, his contribution was on an altogether broader front than many of his Cambridge colleagues. This followed from his view that there is not 'a single, overwhelming objection to orthodox economic theory: there are a number of different points that are distinct though interrelated' (Kaldor 1975: 347–8). In this regard he considered some of his Cambridge colleagues as 'monists', in that they believed that their exposure of the logical flaws in the theory of marginal productivity was 'alone sufficient to pull the rug from under the neoclassical value theory' (ibid.: 348). Kaldor felt that both the 'monist' approach was too narrow and that even the contested terrain of marginal productivity theory was not necessarily the most important issue to address. For Kaldor there were 'other things to object to that in some ways are even more misleading than the application of marginal productivity theory to the division between wages and profits, which has been the main subject of discussion' (ibid.: 348).

According to Kaldor,. scientific theorists ought to begin their theory construction with a summary of the known facts in the domain of investigation. In the case of economics, since the required summary is normally presented in a statistical fashion, the economic theorist starts with a 'stylized' view of the facts. These stylized facts are statistical, but not universal, generalizations about empirical regularities. Kaldor himself furnishes a number of examples, e.g. that the UK productivity rate in the postwar period has been less than that of comparable industrial economies. The economist then proceeds to construct an economic theory on what Kaldor calls the 'as if' method. While Kaldor does not spell out the full details of this method, it is reasonable to reconstruct his position as follows. First, economists abstract or develop higher-level hypotheses consistent with these stylized facts and, on this basis, proceed to construct an economic theory. Second, they attempt to systematically organize the theory which, according to the logical ideal, takes the form of an axiomatic system. Finally, the constructed theory is inductively tested. In this connection Lawson correctly notes that Kaldor argued that the second step must be subordinate to the third, i.e. that the inductive testing is more important than the process of axiomatization.

The causal holist has no objection to this Kaldorian approach. The central aim of any pure science is the construction of a descriptively adequate theory, i.e. a theory which is true about the observable events and happenings in the relevant domain. In the particular case of economics this would entail the construction of economic models and clearly Kaldor's stylized facts consti-tute an excellent starting point. Based on these stylized facts, the economist must construct a model of the relevant portion of the economic world under consideration. In causal holism the emphasis is on models of the domain under investigation and not on the pure axiomatic system. The scientific action is at the level of these models. Hence causal holists would welcome Kaldor's subordination of deduction or the formalization of economics to induction. In particular, they would agree with Kaldor's distinction between an empirical scientific theory and a purely mathematical, axiomatic system (Kaldor 1972: 1239). The latter, according to causal holism, is not an empirical science. On the contrary, it pertains to logic or pure mathematics. Formal axiomatic systems must be interpreted in some domain, and thereby furnish a model, to become an empirical science. This is of central importance to causal holism and this is very much the attitude of Kaldor. Finally, when the model is constructed, the pure economist must, by means of empirical investigation, ascertain whether or not the descriptions of the economic world supplied by the model are true. If they are not then the theory is descriptively inadequate. In our opinion this is the principal charge brought by Kaldor against neoclassical economics.

The target of Kaldor's critique was what he termed 'equilibrium eco-nomics'. More specifically, the notion of equilibrium which he had in mind was 'the general economic equilibrium originally formulated by Walras, and developed, with ever-increasing elegance, exactness, and logical precision by the mathematical economists of our own generation' (Kaldor 1972: 1237). His criticism of this mode of theorizing was both devastating and unambiguous. It was, he argued, 'barren and irrelevant as an apparatus of thought to deal with the manner of operation of economic forces, or as an instrument for non-trivial prediction concerning the effects of economic changes' (ibid.: 1237).

He went further and argued that, such was the powerful influence exerted by equilibrium economics, it 'had become a major obstacle to the development of economics as a science' (ibid.: 1237).

Kaldor's conception of 'economics as a science' is fundamental to his critique of equilibrium economics. For him science is 'a body of theorems based on assumptions that are empirically derived (from observations) and which embody hypotheses that are capable of verification both in regard to the assumptions and the predictions' (ibid.: 1237). Based on this characterization of science, Kaldor subjects equilibrium economics to a relentless critique. Not only is there no attempt in general at verifying the realism of the assumptions used in equilibrium theory, but these assumptions, though purporting to represent a scientific theory, are either unverifiable – such as producers maximizing their profits or consumers their utility – or are directly contradicted by observation. According to Kaldor, instances of the latter are represented by the use of such constructs as perfect competition, perfect divisibility, linear-homogeneous and continuously differentiable production functions, impersonal market relations, exclusive role of prices in information transmission and perfect knowledge of all relevant prices by economic agents along with perfect foresight. In addition there is the requirement of a constant and unchanging set of products and similar conditions for production processes, none of which, according to Kaldor, are operationally defined (Kaldor 1972: 1238). As he noted, 'no attempt is made to show how these axiomatic concepts are to be defined or recognised in relation to empirical material' (ibid.: 1238). Neither was there in general any investigation of whether the resulting theory of equilibrium prices had 'any explanatory power or relevance in relation to actual prices' (ibid.: 1238). The pervasive theme of Kaldor's methodological critique of orthodox equilibrium theory is the patent descriptive inadequacy of this theory and consequently its inability to engage the reality of the complexities of the economic system of the developed market economies. His overall conclusion, which reflected the intensity of his rejection of equilibrium theorizing, was that 'without a major act of demolition – without destroying the basic conceptual framework – it is impossible to make any real progress' (ibid.: 1240).

Kaldor's radical concern with the issue of the descriptive inadequacy of orthodox equilibrium theory is contained in his analysis of a number of key areas, which formed the basis of his substantive critique of equilibrium economics. Analysis of these areas appeared in various degrees of elaboration in most of Kaldor's major postwar methodological writings (Kaldor 1972, 1975, 1985), but they are most systematically outlined in his 1983 Okun Lectures (Kaldor 1985). As presented in the Okun Lectures, Kaldor identified three substantive areas which he addressed in considerable detail. The first was the issue of how markets work and why their mode of operation precluded a pure price system of market clearing; the second was how prices were formed and how competition operated in the context of 'the quasi-competitive or quasi-monopolistic markets that embrace a very large part of a modern industrial economy' (ibid.: 12). The final issue, which represented for Kaldor 'an outline of an alternative approach to orthodox equilibrium theory', examined the implications for economics of re-incorporating the powerful influences of increasing returns.

In the process of endeavouring to formulate this 'alternative approach' centred on increasing returns to scale, Kaldor articulates some of his most fundamental objections to equilibrium economics as it developed in the postwar period. He contrasts developments in the postwar period with the 'great innovative period of the 1930s'. The postwar period has been characterized by an explosive growth in mathematical economics but, for Kaldor, this has resulted in imposing an increasingly restrictive intellectual perspective on economics, rather than leading to an expanded set of scientific insights into the evolving complexity of advanced economic systems. The colonization of economics by mathematics in this period is, for Kaldor, akin to the creation, borrowing Heisenberg's expression, of a 'mathematical crystal', with its connotations of the perfectibility of a logical system 'which cannot be farther improved or perfected' (Kaldor 1985: 60). General equilibrium had, according to Kaldor, achieved this state of becoming a 'mathematical crystal' by the early 1950s. Such was the fascination of the economic profession with the neo-Walrasian framework that 'economic theorists' views of reality became increasingly distorted, so as to come closer to the theoretical image rather than the other way round' (ibid.: 60).

Kaldor invoked Marshall's well-known misgivings about the use of mathematics in economics to counterbalance the influence exercised by the neo-Walrasian paradigm on orthodox economics. But he also invoked the larger Marshallian framework, based on an evolutionary paradigm, to buttress his critique of orthodox equilibrium economics. In this context Kaldor's concept of time is of paramount importance to understand his intellectual commitment to increasing returns as the basis of his 'alternative approach'. Time for Kaldor was to be conceived of as 'a continuing and irreversible process'. In short, the proper concept of time was real historical time with its corollary of the need to engage the influence of the specificity of context and circumstance. This was a fundamental proposition which Kaldor shared with other members of the Cambridge School, particularly Joan Robinson (1974, 1977). Kaldor further argued that it 'was impossible to assume the constancy of anything over time'. But while everything was in a continuous process of change, the forces 'that make for change are endogenous not exogenous to the system' (Kaldor 1985: 61). The only real exogenous factor was whatever existed at a given moment of time, the legacy of an unchangeable past. This historical legacy would determine future events in a manner that varied inversely with the distance of the future from the present. Therefore the capacity to predict an uncertain future becomes progressively less with respect to the more distant, as compared to the more immediate, future. For

Kaldor, the concept of equilibrium and, in particular, the notion of long-run equilibrium, represented an utter rejection of this line of analysis. Since equilibrium requires that the operation of economic forces are explained by the interaction of a given set of exogenously given variables with the endogenous variables to be determined, the concept of time underlying equilibrium implies that the exogenous factors must be 'independent of history in their most important characteristics' if their stability is to be assured (Kaldor 1985: 62). Kaldor argued that continuous growth 'can only be thought of within this intellectual framework as a steady state' where everything changes at proportionate rates, 'though what the proportions are, or what the growth rate is, is itself the outcome of economic forces, as in von Neumann's celebrated growth model' (ibid.: 62). But Kaldor pointed out that 'the two really important things Neumann's model was not capable of dealing with is continuous change in knowledge and the existence of non-linearities in productive activities, in other words, increasing returns' (ibid.: 63). Therefore Kaldor's intellectual commitment to increasing returns must be linked within the larger framework of his ideas to a critique of time as embodied in the concept of equilibrium. This conceptual critique was buttressed by the evidence that at 'the empirical level, nobody doubts that in any economic activity which involves the processing or transformation of basic materials – in other words, in industry – increasing returns dominate' (Kaldor 1972: 1242). Similarly, with respect to his analysis of the working of markets and the formation of prices and implications of their performance for the competitive process, his main concern was the need to delineate a more empirically accurate description of their structure and operations. In short, orthodox economics is extensively descriptively inadequate.

We agree with Lawson that transcendental realism is a much better approach to economic methodology than current orthodox approaches, including philosophical instrumentalism. The methodological approach of the transcendental realist, as opposed to the philosophical instrumentalist, is accurately summed up by Lawson into three stages. The first involves the identification of some empirical phenomena of interest. As we have already seen, causal holists have no objection to such a starting point. Indeed, they would point out that the identification of such phenomena presupposes some conceptual scheme or other. Presumably the realist would have no objection to this caveat, since it is a consequence of the rejection of the dual-language approach which permeated the orthodox logical positivist approach, including instrumentalism, to methodology. Thus Kaldor's stylized facts are located among others in the conceptual scheme of statistics.

The second step noted by Lawson includes the construction of a model which entails the empirical phenomena noted in the first step. Once again the causal holist has no objection to this, on condition that one clearly separates the task of pure economics, namely, the construction of a model which is descriptively adequate, and the contextualized task of applied economics which furnishes explanations of particular economic events or facts. In short, as we have already seen, model construction and model testing is not to be confused with the contextualized task of scientific explanation. Thus the causal holist rejects the transcendental realist analysis of economic explanation, while retaining the centrality of economic models. The third stage, which is normally rejected by instrumentalists, entails the subjection of the entities postulated at the modelling stage to further continuous scrutiny. Taken at face value, causal holists fully endorse this stage. In their view there is a socio-economic world and their aim is to discover as much as they possibly can about that world. To this end they construct models and continuously probe the observational entities and mechanisms postulated by these models in the hope of discovering more observable knowledge about the world. The only constraint they impose on whether or not they will believe in the actual entities postulated by the model is that these entities must be observable in principle. As we have already seen, the causal holist emphasizes the model's epistemic ontology. Like scientific realists, causal holists maintain that observable events in both the physical and economic worlds can be hidden from us and an effective economic model can reveal these hidden events and mechanisms, whereas a descriptively inadequate one will conceal some of these mechanisms. In the same vein Kaldor maintains that equilibrium economics gives 'a misleading "paradigm" ... of the world as it is: it gives a misleading impression of the ... manner of operation of economic forces' (1975: 347). Moreover, Kaldor points out that science is 'a body of theorems based on assumptions that are empirically derived and which embody hypotheses that are capable of verification both in regard to assumptions and the predictions' (Kaldor 1972: 1238). Clearly, Kaldor is concerned with limiting his commitment to what is in principle observable – a guiding principle of causal holism.

If an economic model were to postulate an entity or mechanism which is in principle unobservable or non-empirical, causal holists would adopt the following attitude. Unlike philosophical instrumentalists, they would acknowledge that the model literally says there is such a mechanism. Moreover, contrary to the instrumentalist, they would argue that these propositions describing the unobservable mechanisms are either true or false. Finally, they would argue that we cannot know whether these descriptions of unobservable mechanisms are true or false. There is always a plurality of incompatible but descriptively adequate models which postulate different unobservable mechanisms. Since these models are by assumption each descriptively adequate, i.e. each is giving accurate descriptions of what is observable, there is no way of knowing which descriptions of the unobservable mechanisms postulated by the theory are true.

Transcendental realists, however, are operating with a different picture. In their view the observable economic world is the product of hidden generative structures and mechanisms which are non-empirical. These hidden non-empirical mechanisms have the power or capacity to act in certain ways by virtue of certain enduring intrinsic structures. In the observable world, however, the actualization of these powers and tendencies may be effected by all kinds of concrete factors and thus may be present without being manifest in the observable world. These generative non-empirical mechanisms have to be inferred from the empirical evidence. According to Lawson, Kaldor obscured this realist dimension by arguing for the superiority of induction over deduction. Rather, in Lawsonian realism the inference to the generative hidden structures is neither deductive nor inductive. In the philosophical literature it is called abduction or retroduction. Clearly, this distinct kind of inference is of central importance to many realists, especially Lawsonian ones.

The causal holist, like Kaldor, has no recourse to this kind of inference. Causal holism, like Lawsonian realism, involves a strong commitment to identifying hidden real economic structures and mechanisms. The economic world is a mesh of structures which result from the intended and unintended actions of human agents and much of this complex world may be hidden from our eyes. We have to discover these hidden mechanisms. To this end we construct models and, by means of both induction and deduction, we empirically probe these models to the limits of what is observable. The aim, like that of the realist, is to obtain knowledge of the real structures and to expose what is hidden. The hidden, however, which we can reveal, is limited to what is in principle observable.

A central weakness of transcendental realism is acknowledged by Lawson when he says that 'retroduction by itself may well lead to a plurality of hypotheses of possible causal mechanisms' (Lawson 1989a: 69). In other words, there is a plurality of models each compatible with the empirical evidence, but each of these models gives conflicting accounts of the real, but non-observable, generative mechanisms. Causal holists see no way of deciding on this incompatibility. Their attitude is that each of those theories is at best descriptively adequate. However, if the hidden mechanisms are observable in principle, then the attitude is that they can be detected in the empirical world. In this case the attitude of the causal holist is identical to that of the realist, namely, the reality of any positive structure or mechanism must itself be subject to empirical scrutiny. In this case the empirical scrutiny takes the form of inductive investigation, which again would explain Kaldor's emphasis on induction rather than deduction. However, there is no question of some special retroductive inference to unobservable causes. Thus causal holism retains the empirical advantages of transcendental realism without the realist preoccupation with abduction or retroduction and without the equation of unobservable entities postulated by a descriptively adequate theory with hidden, non-empirical structures. To sum up, the fact that Kaldor gives priority to induction rather than deduction, that he is centrally preoccupied with observation, that he exposes the descriptive inadequacy of equilibrium economics by a non-monist critique and does not explicitly engage in abductive inferences reinforces a causal holist interpretation of his methodological contribution. In short, Kaldor's non-monist critique concretely demonstrates how the causal holist notion of descriptive adequacy is to be deployed in pure economics.

In this chapter we have navigated through the challenging seas of the methodological writings of two highly esteemed economists of this century. This navigation serves the purpose of further delineating the methodological map of causal holism, especially its contribution to pure economists in their endeavours in constructing and evaluating economic models. By putting the focus on descriptive adequacy and observable causes, the causal holist reconstructs economic methodology which transcends the Kuhnian–Popperian debate on the one hand and the scientific realist-constructive empiricist debate on the other.

9

CAUSAL HOLISM
Beyond rhetoric and realism

In the foregoing narrative economic rhetoric was introduced as a post-modern response to the deficiencies of the positivist and Popperian legacies in the domain of economic methodology. We also traced how contemporary realism, emerged in the latter half of this century to fill the lacuna left by twentieth-century positivism, while simultaneously responding to the contemporary relativist tendencies identified in the work of Feyerabend and Kuhn. With this methodological background in place, the challenging manner in which Lawson and Mäki exploit their respective interpretations of realism in the philosophy of economics was outlined. The narrative then progressed onto the constructive empiricist critique of scientific realism and to the manner in which constructive empiricism could be deployed in contemporary philosophy of economics. However, we rejected each of these three approaches as inadequate philosophies of economics. Neither economic rhetoric nor scientific realism nor constructive empiricism gives an adequate account of such critical issues as the role of theory in economics or the epistemic/ontological dimensions of economic model building, especially the epistemic issue of the descriptive adequacy of economic theory. In our opinion, an alternative novel methodological framework is required to remedy these deficiencies. This alternative framework we have termed causal holism. By reinterpreting Quine's holism and by extending the ongoing debate between scientific realists and constructive empiricists, causal holism emerged as a challenging methodological framework for economics.

By way of conclusion we will further discuss some of the major points of difference between causal holism and rhetoric on the one hand and between the former and the scientific realists conception of economics on the other. While both causal holists and economic rhetoricians value economic models, the former disagrees with the latter's thesis that economic models are nonornamental metaphors. The causal holist focuses on an economic model in the semantical, as opposed to the syntactical, sense of that term. A semantical economic model presupposes an already existing economic theory which furnishes the conceptual resources, principles and presuppositions for the construction of specific models. These models are constructed and used when economists are attempting to resolve some problem about an economic event, action, agent, institution, tendency, structure or resource *et al.* in the real social world. In this approach economic models are very close to Black's theoretical models discussed in Chapter 3.

Mathematical economic models also presuppose an economic theory and the causal holist has no objection in principle to the work of pure economic theorists, as illustrated in the work of Hahn, Debreu or Arrow, who construct and investigate the implications of such models. This, however, is a subsidiary aim of pure economic theory within the causal holist framework. Fundamentally, any economic model, be it mathematical or not, is a model of an actual economy or some constituent part of such an economy. Any economic model must be investigated by the wide range of inductive, i.e. empirical, procedures available to economists with a view to ascertaining its descriptive adequacy. Thus mathematical economic models, like any other model, must be subjected to all the existing rigours of our inductive procedures, culminating in an evaluation of their descriptive adequacy. If this inductive testing is either ignored or not given due recognition, economics ceases to be an empirical science. Moreover, if an extensive range of models, mathematical or otherwise, constructed in the light of the same economic theory is found to be descriptively inadequate, this reflects on the economic theory which governed the construction of that range. This is precisely what Kaldor did in his devastating non-monist critique of neoclassical theory. He argued that, since neoclassical theory failed to furnish descriptively accurate models of various aspects of actual economies, neoclassical theory should be rejected as descriptively inadequate. In our opinion, the actual realization of this central epistemic aim is either completely ignored or not duly recognized by economic rhetoricians and a major reason for this failure lies in the economic rhetoricians unjustified assimilation of economic models to nonornamental metaphors.

Despite this crucial difference, causal holists fully agree with Klamer's thesis that economics, in describing human economic interactions, is concerned with a human world where perfect certainty does not obtain. We also concur with Klamer that economists in using models do many things other than asserting propositions or making projections. In this connection causal holists draw on Searle's distinction between 'a speaker's utterance meaning' and 'sentence meaning' (Searle 1980: 93). For instance, where an economist utters the sentence 'firms are maximizers' or states the basic axioms of neoclassical theory, her or his utterance meaning can range from irony to indirect speech acts. The economic rhetorician correctly draws our attention to this wide range of things which can be and actually are done in uttering economic sentences.

However, unlike economic rhetoricians, causal holists also draw our attention to the semantical aspect of the economist's utterances, which Searle calls 'sentence meaning'. The latter concerns the literal meaning of the sentence uttered, as distinct from what the economist does or intends to do by uttering it. The uttered proposition "firms are maximizers" has a literal meaning closely related to its truth conditions and this is independent of an economist's utterance meaning. Literally, many of the propositions of a semantical economic model are theory-laden descriptions which are true or false and economists, by means of a wide range of inductive procedures, investigate the descriptive adequacy of these models. However, by assimilating economic models to metaphors, economic rhetoricians fail to recognize this crucial distinction between the literal and the metaphorical. Causal holists, unlike economic rhetoricians, acknowledge both the utterance and the sentence meanings of the statements in economic models and thereby give a more comprehensive account of actual economic activity than economic rhetoric.

There is much more to actual economic activity than that acknowledged by economic rhetoricians. Causal holism, by taking on board recent developments in the philosophy of science on the one hand and developments in the archaeology and genealogy of human institutions as explored by Foucault on the other, draws together in one methodological framework this extended spectrum of economic activity. This spectrum ranges from inductive investigations into the descriptive adequacy of an economic theory to a non-epistemic contextual analysis of what economists do in furnishing economic explanations. Rhetoricians maintain that their philosophy of economics is a philosophy grounded in what economists actually do. Causal holism, however, is better than rhetoric on that count, in that it draws our attention to a much wider range of economic activities than those acknowledged by rhetoricians. Moreover, it supplies a richer and more sophisticated methodological framework for this economic practice than the rhetorical frameworks developed to date.

Let us now turn our attention to the manner in which causal holism differs from scientific realism, especially Lawson's critical realism. As we already indicated, causal holism, like Lawsonian realism, is unequivocally committed to the thesis that the philosophy of science is centrally relevant to the methodology of economics. Unlike Lawsonian realism, which has its origins in contemporary realist developments in philosophy of science, especially Bhaskar's transcendental realism, causal holism has its origins in Quine's holism and van Fraassen's constructive empiricism. These divergent philosophical lineage's are significant. As we already noted, Lawson, following Bhaskar, sees philosophy as distinct from science. Philosophy, 'by the use of "pure reason" but not by the use of pure reason alone' (Bhaskar 1979: 7), poses the Kantian transcendental-type question about the conditions of the possibility of specific contingent scientific practices. The philosophical transcendental answer necessitates a world of structured intransitive objects. In this transcendental approach, philosophy, given its association with pure reason, is distinct and separate from scientific knowledge which, in Bhaskar–

Lawson terminology, is 'transitive', i.e. fallible, and subject to radical change in historical time. This division we called Lawson's dualism of philosophy and science. By the use of distinct philosophical reasoning about contingent scientific practices, philosophy tells us that intransitive structured objects are necessary, whereas our scientific rational endeavours always culminate in transitive, fallible knowledge, where pure or a priori philosophical reasoning has no part.

This kind of dualism has a long and distinguished lineage but, as Bhaskar clearly perceives (Bhaskar 1979: 6), this dualistic picture of a priori pure reasoning of philosophy and fallible reasoning of contingent science is not shared by Quine. In Quine's picture, the philosopher and scientist are both mariners on board the ship of knowledge and both share the same bag of rational fallible tools (Quine 1960: 3). In this Quinean picture, shared by causal holism, the transitivity or fallibility of scientific knowledge extends to philosophy. The Bhaskar–Lawson conception of philosophical reasoning does not apply in Quine's picture. It is beyond the scope of this work to pursue these central differences further. This issue is extensively discussed in O'Gorman (1989). For our present purposes it is sufficient to note that causal holism, under the shadow of Quine, does not share the Bhaskar–Lawson dualistic picture of a priori philosophical truths and of fallible a posteriori scientific knowledge. The philosopher has no such privileged status in causal holism. The difference between the philosopher and scientist is not a difference in kinds of activities. Rather, the difference is a pragmatic one based on a conventional division of labour on board the ship of fallible knowledge. In this way causal holism, like economic rhetoric, is centrally a post-modernist or post-Enlightenment philosophy of economics. Finally, it may be worth noting that in a very recent article (Lawson 1994d: 20) Lawson modifies his philosophical transcendentalism, in allowing its results to be 'fallible and corrigible'.

Aside from participating in divergent pictures of the philosophy–science nexus, causal holism differs from Lawsonian realism on a number of other substantive issues, especially the role of theory in economics, economic explanation, and economic causality. We will now address these methodological differences. The causal holist's analysis of economic theory is very much influenced by Quine's holism. As Quine so aptly puts it 'Analyse theory-building how we will, we must start in the middle' (Quine 1960: 4). Any economist describing economic actions, events, institutions, resources, structures or tendencies, is already caught in the middle of some economic theory or other, ranging from neoclassical to Marxist. There is no theory-neutral position from which economists may view and thereby describe an actual economy. In Quine's phrase 'There is no such cosmic exile' (Quine 1960: 275). Thus economists use the conceptual resources of a shared theory to construct a semantical economic model of some observable aspect of an actual economy and, in addition, they must both deploy and develop the inductive methodological resources of that theory to ascertain the descriptive adequacy of the constructed model. The epistemic focus is on semantical models which furnish us with theory-laden descriptions of some observable aspect of an economy, and on the shared economic theory which guided the construction of the economic model, influenced the choice of issues to be tested and identified the specific range of inductive procedures used in that testing. If a wide range of economic models is judged to be descriptively inadequate, economists are rationally compelled to re-examine their shared underlying theory. In this re-examination, economists will use the full resources of their expertise and scientific imagination. The outcome of their deliberations may lead to either a major transformation of the shared theory or its replacement by a novel theory. As we already indicated, Kaldor's critique of neoclassical economics exemplifies this causal holist methodology.

In this way the evaluation of the descriptive adequacy of an economic theory is much the same as that in any other science. In this connection, however, it should be noted that causal holism approaches the general issue of the application of scientific methodology to economic methodology in a different way to the Lawsonian realist. By arguing that the concept of science is a Wittgensteinian family resemblance one, causal holists maintain that economics, without sharing all of the central characteristics of the physical sciences, is none the less an authentic scientific endeavour. In particular, like Lawsonian realists, causal holists acknowledge an indispensable hermeneutical dimension to economic actions. This hermeneutical dimension implies that if and when an economic theory is assimilated by economic agents, it becomes an indispensable component of their actions in that these economic agents use the conceptual resources of their assimilated economic theory in identifying their own economic actions. In particular, the causal holist, in giving accurate descriptions of the economic actions of agents in communities separated from us by either long distances of time or space, have to endeavour to discover the assimilated economic theories native to the agents in those distant cultures. Imposing the descriptive language of neoclassical economics on such agents is failing to acknowledge this hermeneutical dimension. Moreover, causal holism, while taking on board Quine's holism and extending it to this central hermeneutical dimension, does not share Quine's behaviouristic tendencies. In other words, causal holists read Quine's holism through the eyes of the later Wittigenstein where behaviouristic concepts have no privileged role. The descriptive focus is on human action, embedded in language-games or forms of life, with little probability of reducing these actions to behaviour.

However, the descriptive task of the causal holist does not stop at economic actions. As any social scientist readily acknowledges, economic actions can have both unforeseen and unintended consequences. Furthermore, economic actions do not occur in a socio-economic vacuum. They are embedded in a web of socio-economic structures, institutions, dynamic mechanisms and tendencies. The accurate description of these socio-economic realities, and the manner of their alterations in historical time, is not limited to the conceptual resources of the internalized theory of the economic agents acting in those socio-economic settings. The causal holist, by recourse to the normal range of inductive practices used by economic historians combined with the archaeological and genealogical analyses so ably pioneered by Foucault, will investigate the constitution, *modus operandi* and patterns of change of these socio-economic realities. Once again the central focus will be on the accurate description of these socio-economic realities and the manner in which they change in historical time. In this connection the causal holist is not optimistic that neoclassical theory has the required inductive resources for this descriptive task and, if this is so, it must be deemed to be descriptively inadequate.

In causal holism one of the central challenges to the science of economics is the construction of a theory which will be adequate to this extensive range of descriptive tasks. This is an ongoing challenge and the causal holist suggests that Foucault's archaeological genealogical contributions, could make a significant contribution to economic practice. Be that as it may, clearly, causal holists share with both transcendental realists and economic rhetoricians the thesis that economics is not primarily a predictive discipline. Friedman's methodological defence of neoclassical theory, by putting the methodological spotlight on the predictive testing of economic theories, fails to appreciate their indispensable descriptive role.

However, contrary to Lawsonian realism, causal holism shifts the focus of theoretical assessment away from economic explanation in terms of non-empirical structures and mechanisms and onto the descriptive adequacy of an economic theory. The Lawsonian critical realist is committed to the scientific realist picture of economic explanation in terms of deep, non-empirical structures or mechanisms which generate the observable economic phenomena. The causal holist, under the shadow of van Fraassen's constructive empiricism, does not share this alluring transcendental realist picture. The causal holist approach to economic explanation is centrally rooted in what economists do rather than in what they say they are doing. It is alleged that Einstein once advised philosophers to look at what physicists do rather than on what they say they are doing. Certainly, Wittgenstein draws our attention to the dangers of taking language seriously when so to speak it is 'on holidays'. Many economists undoubtedly speak of theory construction and theory evaluation in terms of furnishing satisfactory explanations. They also speak of explaining specific economic events and happenings. The causal holist looks at what economists do when they speak in these ways. When economists speak of theory construction–evaluation in terms of explanation they are actually talking about their economic activities of theory and model construction and their evaluation of the descriptive adequacy of these constructions. At the other end of the spectrum, when economists speak of explaining specific events they are actually answering specific why-questions posed in specific contexts. These two kinds of activities are distinct. The former concerns the epistemic relationship between an economic theory or model and the real social world of economic transactions. The latter is specifically narrative-laden in that diverse, rich narrative contexts crucially influence the choice of salient explanatory factors. In order to clearly identify these different kinds of economic activity, both of which are referred to by the term 'explanation' as normally used, we call the former epistemic activities and the latter non-epistemic. The activity of furnishing explanations of specific economic events falls into this non-epistemic domain. The actual explanatory activities of economists, however, range over much more than narrative-laden explanations of specific events. For instance, economists may explain why they introduced some idealization or other into a model, why they choose to use linear equations in some econometric model, or how they derived a particular solution to some equation. These also are explanations which have nothing to do with the causal webs operating in the real socio-economic world and nothing to do with the epistemic evaluation of a model as descriptively adequate. These kinds of economic explanatory activities are thereby also located in the non-epistemic domain. Unlike causal holists, Lawsonian realists fail to address this vast range of varieties of economic explanations and fail to appreciate the implications of the various non-epistemic ways these economic explanations are context-laden.

Clearly, the causal holist approach to economic explanation is under the shadows of constructive empiricism. However, unlike constructive empiricism, causal holists maintain that there are real observable causal webs in operation in actual economies and in the transformation of economic systems in real historical time. Moreover, like Lawsonian realists, these causal webs are not reducible to individual economic agents. Causal holism emphatically rejects both methodological individualism and metaphysical reductionist individualism. Where causal holists differ from Lawsonian realists is that the causal webs which can be discovered by economists are not non-empirical. Rather, in causal holism the economically knowable causal structures are in principle empirical or observable. Indeed, a central epistemic task of economic theory is the construction both of the appropriate range of inductive procedures for the discovery of observable causal webs and of the conceptual resources for the accurate description of these same webs. Frequently these causal webs are hidden, but this concealment does not imply that they are non-empirical. The causal webs which may be discovered and described by economists are contingent, subject to change and empirical.

In particular, there is no question of theoretical economics furnishing approximately true descriptions of non-empirical generative structures, powers or mechanisms. The causal holist objection to Lawsonian realism is not that of the later Putnam's internal realism. The internal realist holds that:

211

in a way, it should have been realised a long time ago that the talk of powers in 'modern' philosophy was problematical, for such talk is a hang-over from medieval philosophy, not something that belongs in its own right to the new picture.

(Putnam 1987: 23)

A world governed by scientific laws is one thing, 'a medieval (or an Aristotelian) world governed by Substantial Forms which manifest themselves as "tendencies" rather than as exceptionless laws is something else' (ibid.: 24). Contrary to internal realists, causal holists do not maintain that the concepts of capacities and powers should be rejected as empty residues of an outdated philosophy. Rather, our objection is to the Lawsonian realist thesis that the structured entities which possess these powers are claimed to be non-empirical. If one postulates non-empirical entities, how can economists go on to furnish theoretical descriptions of these and know that their descriptions are correct or approximately true? Quine has taught us that it is not beyond the ingenuity of economists to construct a range of incompatible economic theories such that each one is compatible with the empirical evidence. Given this pluralism, causal holists do not see any rational way of deciding which non-empirical referents they should choose nor which theoretical descriptions are true of these non-empirical entities. Rather, by the imaginative extension and the creative application of their inductive resources for discovering causes and simultaneously by improving the conceptual or descriptive resources of their theoretical frameworks, causal holists pursue the identification and description of (the hidden or otherwise) causal webs operational in real historical time. These causal webs, however, are not non-empirical: economic knowledge is limited to the boundaries of the observable.

In this connection it should be noted that the concept of the observable has been radically reconstructed in contemporary holistic approaches to the philosophy of science. Among the factors that have affected this reconstruction is the thesis that scientific description is theory-laden, that the concept of the observable is a vague but useful predicate and that science extends the boundaries of the observable. This reconstruction liberates the causal holist from the shackles of both the traditional empiricist and the logical positivist reductionist explications of the observable. In particular, it enabled us to argue that the philosophical difficulties – and there are many – raised by philosophers in their conflicting analyses of causality – do not imply that economists should abandon the search for observable causal webs. The observable causes discovered and described by economists are contingent and subject to change in historical time.

Finally, contrary to Lawsonian realists, there is no question of a special kind of inference to non-empirical structures or mechanisms. This separate kind of scientific inference, which is distinct from induction on the one hand

212

and the philosophical transcendental argument on the other, is called abduction and Lawson associates this abductive inference with the use of analogy and metaphor. Of course causal holists fully acknowledge the role of economic imagination in the construction or reshaping of both economic theory and economic models. In particular, they see analogy as a central inductive tool. For causal holists analogy plays many roles ranging from the construction of specific economic models to inductive arguments based on similarities between different systems. Moreover, causal holists, under the influence of the later Wittgenstein, totally reject any empiricist building block conception of economic language on the one hand or any Aristotelian Thomistic abstractionist account on the other. Economic language, like the rest of our natural languages, is a humanly-constructed holistic web with a long and a complex history. Thus our sophisticated linguistic capacities in general and our analogical capacities in particular, clearly allow the Lawsonian realist the possibility of economic theories postulating non-empirical entities. In causal holism, however, Quinean considerations prevent us from extending our scientific knowledge to these entities.

Furthermore, causal holists acknowledge that the process of inference to the best explanation (Lipton 1991) is a valuable inductive process. For instance, if we see shoe prints in the snow the best explanation is that a human being, rather than a monkey wearing shoes, passed by. However, if the scientific realist wishes to explicate the notion of abductive inference in terms of an inference to the best explanation and thereby argue that the non-empirical entities postulated by our mature, best confirmed economic theory is the best explanation of the observable economic facts and observable tendencies, the causal holist refuses to take this final step. According to causal holism, abductive inferences understood as inferences to the best explanation are limited to the domain of the observable. The principal reason for this limitation is the same as that used against the transcendental realist's use of non-empirical mechanisms. Quine teaches us that there is a multiplicity of such explanations, each compatible with the empirical evidence and hence we have no rational way of choosing between these. In other words, when the process of inference to the best explanation is extended to postulated non-empirical entities, there is no one best explanation. There are many best explanations with no rational way of deciding between them. In causal holism economists can discover the hidden causal webs operating through economic systems and their transformations without recourse to the additional realist strategy of non-empirical mechanisms and specific abductive inferences to these mechanisms.

To conclude, causal holism is a sophisticated economic methodology which is centrally committed to the empirical evaluation of economic theories. It reconstructs the methodological framework of economics by acknowledging that economic explanation and theory are irrevocably separated and by linking the latter to economic description. Thus the construction of economic models which furnish accurate theory-laden descriptions of the economic world is firmly located in the epistemic dimension of that science. Moreover, the causal holist reconstruction also requires the acknowledgement of another separation, namely, that of causality from explanation. The former, along with theory and description, is located in the epistemic dimension, while explanation is relocated in the non-epistemic domain. Finally, this reconstruction is achieved without recourse to any demands for either unification or ontological reduction. By emphasizing economic models, especially their descriptive adequacy and changing epistemic ontologies, causal holism takes us beyond both rhetoric and realism in its reconstruction of economic methodology thereby opening a new agenda for future methodological research.

BIBLIOGRAPHY

Ahonen, G. (1989) 'On the empirical content of Keynes' *General Theory'*, *Ricerche Economiche* 43: 256–67.

—— (1990) 'Commentary on Hands' "Second thoughts on 'Second thoughts'" on the Lakatosian progress of *The General Theory'*, *Review of Political Economy* 2: 94–101.

Archibald, G.C. (1979) 'Method and appraisal in economics', *Philosophy of the Social Sciences* 9: 304–15.

Aristotle (1954) *The Rhetoric and the Poetics of Aristotle*, with introduction and notes by F. Solmsen, New York: Random House.

Backhouse, R.E. (1985) *A History of Modern Economic Analysis*, Oxford: Basil Blackwell.

—— (1992) 'The constructivist critique of economic methodology', *Methodus* 4(1): 65–82.

Beed, C. (1991) 'Philosophy of science and contemporary economics: an overview', *Journal of Post Keynesian Economics* 13(4): 459–94.

Bell, D. and Kristol, I. (1981) *The Crisis in Economic Theory*, New York: Basic Books.

Bhaskar, R. (1975) *A Realist Theory of Science*, (2nd edn 1978, Harvester Press) Leeds: Leeds Books.

—— (1979) *The Possibility of Naturalism*, Brighton: Harvester Press.

Black, M. (1962) *Models and Metaphors*, Ithaca: Cornell University Press.

Blaug, M. (1975) 'Kuhn versus Lakatos, on paradigms versus research programmes in the history of economics', *History of Political Economy* 7: 399–433.

—— (1976) 'Kuhn versus Lakatos on paradigms versus research programmes in the history of economics', in S. Latsis (ed.) *Method and Appraisal in Economics*, Cambridge: Cambridge University Press.

—— (1980a) *The Methodology of Economics*, (2nd edn 1992) Cambridge: Cambridge University Press.

—— (1980b) *A Methodological Appraisal of Marxian Economics*, Amsterdam: North-Holland.

—— (1984) 'Comment on Hutchison: our methodological crisis', in P. Wiles and G. Routh (eds) *Economics in Disarray*, Oxford: Basil Blackwell.

—— (1990) 'Reply to Hands', *Review of Political Economy* 2: 102–4.

—— (1991) 'Second thoughts on the Keynesian revolution', *History of Political Economy* 23: 171–92.

Boland, L. (1977) 'Testability in economic science', *South African Journal of Economics* 45: 93–105.

—— (1979) 'A critique of Friedman's critics', *Journal of Economic Literature* 17: 503–22.

—— (1982) *The Foundations of Economic Method*, London: Allen & Unwin.

—— (1985a) *A Methodology for a New Microeconomics*, London: Allen & Unwin.

—— (1985b) 'Reflections on Blaug's *Methodology of Economics*: suggestions for a revised edition', *Eastern Economic Journal* 11: 450–4.

Boylan, T.A. and O'Gorman, P.F. (1991a) 'Economic theory and explanation: a constructive empiricist perspective', *Methodus* 3(1): 53–7.

—— and —— (1991b) 'Explanation, ontology and reductionism in economics: a constructive empiricist perspective', *Methodus* 3(2): 107–10.

—— and —— (1991c) 'The critique of equilibrium theory in economic methodology: a constructive empiricist perspective', *International Studies in the Philosophy of Science* 5(2): 131–42.

—— and —— (1992) 'Constructive empiricism: a reconstruction of economic methodology', *The Journal of Interdisciplinary Economics* 4(2): 145–60.

Bridgman, P. (1927) *The Logic of Modern Physics*, New York: Macmillan.

—— (1938) 'Operational analysis', *Philosophy of Science* 5: 114–31.

Bronfenbrenner, M. (1971) 'The "structure of scientific revolution" in economic thought', *History of Political Economy* 3: 136–51.

Cairnes, J.E. (1857) *The Character and Logical Method of Political Economy*, (2nd edn 1875) London: Longman.

Caldwell, B.J. (1981) 'Book review: Blaug's *The Methodology of Economics*', *Southern Economic Journal* 48: 242–5.

—— (1982) *Beyond Positivism: Economic Methodology in the Twentieth Century*, London: George Allen & Unwin.

—— (1984a) *Appraisal and Criticism in Economics*, Boston: Allen & Unwin.

—— (1984b) 'Some problems with falsification in Economics', *Philosophy of the Social Sciences* 14: 489–95.

—— (1985) 'Some reflections on *Beyond Positivism*', *Journal of Economic Issues* 19: 187–94.

—— (1986) 'Towards a broader conception of criticism', *History of Political Economy* 18: 675–81.

—— (1988a) 'Developments in economic methodology with implications for political science', *Politics* 8(2): 43–8.

—— (1988b) 'The case for pluralism', in N. de Marchi (ed.) *The Popperian Legacy in Economics*, Cambridge: Cambridge University Press.

—— (1989) 'The trend of methodological thinking', *Ricerche Economiche* 43(1–2): 8–20.

—— (1990) 'Does methodology matter? How should it be practiced?', *Finnish Economic Papers*, 3(1): 64–71.

—— (1991) 'Clarifying Popper', *Journal of Economic Literature* 24: 1–33.

—— and Coats, A.W. (1984) 'The rhetoric of economists: a comment on McCloskey', *Journal of Economic Literature* 22: 575–8.

Cartwright, N. (1983) *How the Laws of Physics Lie*, Oxford: Clarendon Press.

—— (1989) *Nature's Capacities and their Measurement*, Oxford: Clarendon Press.

Charemza, W.W. and Deadman, D.F. (1992) *New Directions in Econometric Practice*, Aldershot: Edward Elgar.

Choi, Y.B. (1991) 'An Interview with Arjo Klamer', *Methodus* 3(1): 131–8.

Churchland, P.M. (1979) *Realism and the Plasticity of Mind*, Cambridge: Cambridge University Press.

—— (1982) 'The anti-realist epistemology of van Fraassen's *The Scientific Image*', *Pacific Philosophical Quarterly*, 63: 226–35.

—— and Hooker, C.A. (eds) (1985) *Images of Science: Essays on Realism and Empiricism*, Chicago: University of Chicago Press.

Coats, A.W. (1967) 'Sociological aspects of British economic thought (ca. 1880–1930)', *Journal of Political Economy* 75: 706–29.

—— (1969) 'Is there a "structure of scientific revolutions" in economics?', *Kyklos* 22: 289–96.

—— (1977) 'The current "crisis" in economics in historical perspective', *Nebraska Journal of Economics* 16: 3–16.

—— (1980) 'The culture and the economists: some reflections on Anglo-American differences', *History of Political Economy* 12: 588–609.

—— (ed.) (1981) *Economists in Government: An International Comparative Study*, Durham: Duke University Press.

—— (1982) 'The methodology of economics: some recent contributions', *Kyklos* 35: 310–21.

—— (1984) 'The sociology of knowledge and the history of economics', *Research in the History of Economic Thought and Methodology* 2: 211–34.

—— (1986a) 'Economic methodology: theory, practice and the current state of economics', *Kyklos* 39: 109–15.

—— (1986b) 'Review of Whitley', *History of Political Economy* 18: 68–86.

Coddington, A. (1975) 'The rationale of general equilibrium economics', *Economic Inquiry* 13: 539–58.

Cross, R. (1982) 'The Duhem–Quine thesis, Lakatos and the appraisal of theories in macroeconomics', *Economic Journal* 92: 320–40.

—— (1984) 'Monetarism and Duhem's thesis', in P. Wiles and G. Routh (eds) *Economics in Disarray*, Oxford: Basil Blackwell.

Dagum, C. (1986) 'Economic models, system and structure, philosophy of science and Lakatos' methodology of scientific research programmes', *Rivista Internazionale di Scienze Economiche e Commercialli* 33: 859–86.

Darnell, A.C. and Evans, J.L. (1990) *The Limits of Econometrics*, Aldershot: Edward Elgar.

Davidson, D. (1980) *Actions and Events*, Oxford: Clarendon Press.

de Marchi, N. (ed.) (1988) *The Popperian Legacy in Economics*, Cambridge: Cambridge University Press.

—— (ed.) (1992) *Post-Popperian Methodology: Recovering Practice*, Boston: Kluwer.

—— and Blaug, M. (eds) (1991) *Appraising Economic Theories: Studies in the Methodology of Research Progress*, Aldershot: Edward Elgar.

Dilthey, W. (1976) *Selected Writings*, trans. H.P. Rickman, Cambridge: Cambridge University Press.

Dolan, E.G. (ed.) (1976) *The Foundations of Modern Austrian Economics*, Kansas City: Sheed and Ward.

Duhem, P. (1977) *The Aim and Structure of Physical Theory*, trans. P.P. Wiener, (original edition 1914), New York: Atheneum.

Earl, P. (ed.) (1988) *Psychological Economics*, Boston: Kluwer Academic.

Elster, J. (1983a) *Explaining Technical Change: A Case Study in the Philosophy of Science*, Cambridge: Cambridge University Press.

—— (1983b) *Sour Grapes: Studies in the Subversion of Rationality*, Cambridge: Cambridge University Press.

Enfield, P. (1991) 'Realism, empiricism and scientific revolutions', *Philosophy of Science*, 58(3): 468–85.

Feyerabend, P. (1978) *Science in a Free Society*, London: New Left Books.

—— (1980) *Against Method*, London: Verso.

—— (1981) *Realism, Rationalism and Scientific Method; Philosophical Papers, Vol. I*, Cambridge: Cambridge University Press.

Fisher, R. (1986) *The Logic of Economic Discovery: Neoclassical Economics and the Marginal Revolution*, New York: New York University Press.

217

BIBLIOGRAPHY

Foucault, M. (1967) *Madness and Civilization*, trans. R. Howard, London: Tavistock Publications.

—— (1974) *The Archaeology of Knowledge*, trans. A.M. Sheridan Smith, London: Tavistock Publications.

Friedman, M. (1953) 'The methodology of positive economics', in M. Friedman *Essays in Positive Economics*, Chicago: University of Chicago Press.

Fulton, G. (1984) 'Research programmes in economics', *History of Political Economy* 16: 187–206.

Gadamer, H.G. (1975) *Truth and Method*, trans. G. Barden and J. Cumming, New York: Seabury Press.

—— (1976) *Philosophical Hermeneutics*, trans. D.E. Linge, Berkeley: University of California Press.

Garfinkel, A. (1981) *Forms of Explanation*, New Haven: Yale University Press.

Geach, P. (1969) *God and the Soul*, London: Routledge and Kegan Paul.

Gerrard, B. (1990) 'On matters methodological in economics', *Journal of Economic Surveys* 4,2: 197–223.

Gilad, B. and Kaish, S. (eds) (1986) *Handbook of Behavioural Economics*, Greenwich CT: JAI Press.

Gillies, D. (1993) *Philosophy of Science in the Twentieth Century*, Oxford: Basil Blackwell.

Glass, J.C. and Johnson, W. (1988) 'Metaphysics, MSRP and economics', *British Journal for the Philosophy of Science* 39: 313–29.

—— (1989) *Economics: Progression, Stagnation or Degeneration*, Hemel Hempstead: Harvester Wheatsheaf.

Gonce, R.A. (1972) 'Frank Knight on social control and the scope and method of economics', *Southern Economic Journal* 38: 547–58.

Granger, C.W.J. (ed.) (1990) *Modelling Economic Series: Readings in Econometric Methodology*, Oxford: Oxford University Press.

Habermas, J. (1979) *Communication and the Evolution of Society*, trans. T. McCarthy, London: Heinemann.

—— (1981) *Knowledge and Human Interests*, trans. J.J. Shapiro, London: Heinemann.

Hacking, I. (1975) *Why Does Language Matter to Philosophy?* Cambridge: Cambridge University Press.

Hall, R.L. and Hitch, C.J. (1939) 'Price theory and business behaviour', *Oxford Economic Papers* 2: 12–45.

Hands, D. Wade, (1985a) 'Karl Popper and economic methodology', *Economics and Philosophy* 1: 83–99.

—— (1985b) 'Second thoughts on Lakatos', *History of Political Economy* 17(1): 1–16.

—— (1985c) 'The structuralist view of economic theories: a review essay', *Economics and Philosophy* 1(1): 303–35.

—— (1990a) 'Thirteen theses on progress in economic methodology', *Finnish Economic Papers* 3(1): 72–5.

—— (1990b) 'Second thoughts on "second thoughts": reconsidering the Lakatosian progress of *The General Theory*', *Review of Political Economy* 2: 69–81.

—— (1991) 'The problem of excess content: economics, novelty and a long Popperian tale', in N. de Marchi and M. Blaug (eds) *Appraising Economic Theories; Studies in the Methodology of Research Programmes*, Aldershot: Edward Elgar.

—— (1992) 'Falsification, situational analysis and scientific research programs: the Popperian tradition in economic methodology', in N. de Marchi (ed.) *Post-Popperian Methodology: Recovering Practice*, Boston: Kluwer.

Harré, R. (1967) *An Introduction to the Logic of the Sciences*, London: Macmillan.

—— (1970) *The Principles of Scientific Thinking*, London: Macmillan.

—— and Madden, E.H. (1975) *Causal Powers*, Oxford: Basil Blackwell.

—— and Secord, P.F. (1972) *The Explanation of Social Behaviour*, Oxford: Basil Blackwell.

Hausman, D.M. (1982) 'Constructive empiricism contested', *Pacific Philosophical Quarterly* 63: 21–8.

—— (ed.) (1984) *The Philosophy of Economics: An Anthology*, Cambridge: Cambridge University Press.

—— (1985) 'Is falsification unpractised or unpractisable?' *Philosophy of the Social Sciences* 15: 313–19.

—— (1989) 'Economic methodology in a nutshell', *Journal of Economic Perspectives*, 3(2): 115–27.

—— (1992) *The Inexact and Separate Science of Economics*, Cambridge: Cambridge University Press.

Hempel, C. (1965) *Aspects of Scientific Explanation*, New York: Macmillan.

—— (1966) *Philosophy of Natural Science*, Englewood Cliffs NJ: Prentice Hall.

Henderson, W., Dudley-Evans, T. and Backhouse, R. (eds) (1992) *Economics and Language*, London: Routledge.

Hendry, D. (1980) 'Econometrics: Alchemy or science?', *Economica* 47: 387–406.

Hesse, M. (1963) *Models and Analogies in Science*, London: Sheed and Ward.

—— (1970) 'Quine and a New Empiricism' in *Knowledge and Necessity*, foreword by G.N.A. Vesey, Royal Institute of Philosophy Lectures, 3: 191–209, London: Macmillan.

—— (1974) *The Structure of Scientific Inference*, London: Macmillan.

Hicks, J.R. (1976) '"Revolutions" in economics', in S. Latsis (ed.) *Method and Appraisal in Economics*, Cambridge: Cambridge University Press.

Hirsch, A. and de Marchi, N. (1990) *Milton Friedman: Economics in Theory and Practice*, Ann Arbor: The University of Michigan Press.

Hodgson, G. (1988) *Economics and Institutions: A Manifesto for a Modern Institutional Economics*, Philadelphia: University of Philadelphia Press.

Hogarth, R. and Reder, M. (eds.) (1987) *Rational Choice: The Contrast between Economics and Psychology*, Chicago: University of Chicago Press.

Hooker, C.A. (1987) *A Realistic Theory of Science*, Albany: State University of New York Press.

Hutchison, T.W. (1938) *The Significance and basic Postulates of Economic Theory*, London: Macmillan.

—— (1941) 'The significance and basic postulates of economic theory: a reply to Professor Knight', *Journal of Political Economy* 49: 732–50.

—— (1964) *'Positive' Economics and Policy Objectives*, London: Allen & Unwin.

—— (1968) *Economics and Economic Policy in Britain, 1946–1966*, London: Allen & Unwin.

—— (1976) 'On the history and philosophy of science and economics', in S. Latsis (ed.) *Method and Appraisal in Economics*, Cambridge: Cambridge University Press.

—— (1977) *Knowledge and Ignorance in Economics*, Oxford: Basil Blackwell.

—— (1978) *On Revolution and Progress in Economic Knowledge*, Cambridge: Cambridge University Press.

—— (1981) *The Politics and Philosophy of Economics: Marxians, Keynesians, and Austrians*, Oxford: Basil Blackwell.

Jalladeau, J. (1978) 'Research program versus paradigm in the development of economics', *Journal of Economic Issues* 12: 583608.

Jones, E. (1977) 'Positive economics or what?', *The Economic Record* 53: 350–63.

Kaldor, N. (1966) 'Marginal productivity and the macro-economic theories of distribution comment on Samuelson and Modigliani', *Review of Economic Studies* 33(4): 309–19.

—— (1972) 'The irrelevance of equilibrium economics', *Economic Journal* 82(4): 1237–55.

—— (1975) 'What is wrong with economic theory?', *Quarterly Journal of Economics* 89(3): 347–57.

—— (1978) *Further Essays on Economic Theory*, London: Duckworth.

—— (1984) *Causes of Growth and Stagnation in the World Economy*, Mattioli Lectures.

—— (1985) *Economics without Equilibrium*, Cardiff: University College Cardiff Press.

Keynes, J.N. (1891) *The Scope and Method of Political Economy*, London: Macmillan.

Kirzner, I. (ed.) (1986) *Subjectivism, Intelligibility and Economic Understanding*, New York: New York University Press.

Kitcher, P. and Salmon, W. (eds) (1989) *Scientific Explanation*, Minnesota Studies in the Philosophy of Science 13, Minneapolis: University of Minnesota Press.

Klamer, A. (1984a) 'Levels of discourse in new classical economics', *History of Political Economy* 16(2): 263–90.

—— (1984b) *Conversations with Economists*, Totowa NJ: Rowman and Allanhold.

—— (1987) 'As if economists and their subjects were rational', in J.S. Nelson, A. Megill and D.N. McCloskey (eds.) *The Rhetoric of the Human Sciences*, Madison: University of Wisconsin Press.

—— (1988) 'Economics as discourse', in N. de Marchi (ed.) *The Popperian Legacy in Economics*, Cambridge: Cambridge University Press.

—— (1991) 'In interview with Y.B. Choi', *Methodus*, 3(1): 131–8.

—— McCloskey, D.N. and Solow, R.M. (1988) *The Consequences of Economic Rhetoric*, Cambridge: Cambridge University Press.

Klant, J. (1984) *The Rules of the Game: The Logical Structure of Economic Theories*, trans. I. Swart, Cambridge: Cambridge University Press.

Klappholz, K. and Agassi, J. (1959) 'Methodological prescriptions in economics', *Economica* NS 26: 60–74.

Knight, F. (1935) *The Ethics of Competition and Other Essays*, New York and London: Harper and Brothers.

—— (1940) 'What is "truth" in economics', *Journal of Political Economy*, 48: 1–32.

—— (1941) 'The significance and basic postulates of economic theory: a rejoinder', *Journal of Political Economy* 49: 750–3.

Knorr-Cetina, K. (1981) *The Manufacture of Knowledge: An Essay on the Constructivist and the Contextual Nature of Science*, Oxford: Pergamon Press.

—— (1982) 'The constructivist program in the sociology of science: retreats or advances?', *Social Studies of Sciences* 12: 311–30.

Knowles, D. (ed.) (1990) *Explanation and its Limits*, Cambridge: Cambridge University Press.

Koertge, N. (1974) 'On Popper's Philosophy of Social Science', in K.F. Schaffner and R.S. Cohen (eds) *Philosophy of Science Association* 1972, Dordrecht: Reidel.

Kolakowski, L. (1972) *Positivist Philosophy: From Hume to the Vienna Circle*, Harmondsworth, Middlesex: Penguin Books.

Koopmans, T. (1957) *Three Essays on the State of Economic Science*, New York: McGraw-Hill.

Kripke, S.K. (1980) *Naming and Necessity*, Oxford: Blackwell.

Kuhn, T.S. (1962) *The Structure of Scientific Revolutions*, (2nd edn. 1970), Chicago: University of Chicago Press.

—— (1977) *The Essential Tension*, Chicago: University of Chicago Press.

Kunin, L. and Weaver, F.S. (1971) 'On the structure of scientific revolutions in economics', *History of Political Economy* 3: 391–7.

Lagueux, M. (1991) 'Rationality and mechanisms in economics', paper read at *9th*

International Congress of Logic, Methodology and Philosophy of Science, University of Uppsala, Sweden.

Lakatos, I. (1970) 'Falsification and the methodology of scientific research programmes', in I. Lakatos and A. Musgrave (eds) *Criticism and the Growth of Knowledge*, Cambridge: Cambridge University Press.

Langlois, R. (ed.) (1986) *Economics as a Process*, Cambridge: Cambridge University Press.

Latsis, S. (1972) 'Situational determinism in economics', *British Journal for the Philosophy of Science* 23: 207–45.

—— (1976) *Method and Appraisal in Economics*, Cambridge: Cambridge University Press.

Laudan, L. (1990) *Science and Relativism*, Chicago: University of Chicago Press.

Lavoie, D. (ed.) (1990) *Economics and Hermeneutics*, London: Routledge.

Lawson, T. (1985) 'Uncertainty and Economic Analysis', *Economic Journal* 95: 909–27.

—— (1989a) 'Abstraction, tendencies and stylised facts: a realist approach to economic analysis', *Cambridge Journal of Economics* 13: 59–78.

—— (1989b) 'Realism and instrumentalism in the development of econometrics', *Oxford Economic Papers* 14: 236–58.

—— (1992a) 'Realism, closed systems and Friedman', *Research in the History of Economic Thought and Methodology*, 10: 149–69.

—— (1992b) 'Realism, closed systems and expectations', mimeo, Faculty of Economics and Politics, University of Cambridge.

—— (1992c) 'Realism and Hayek: A Case of Continuous Transformation', revised version of paper presented at a Conference on *The Economics of E.A. Hayek*, at Sant' Arcangelo di Romagna Forli, Italy, 2–4 July 1992.

—— (1994a) 'Realism, philosophical', in G. Hodgson, M. Tool and W.J. Samuels (eds) *Handbook of Evolutionary and Institutional Economics*, Aldershot: Edward Elgar.

—— (1994b) 'Methodology', in G. Hodgson, M. Tool and W.J. Samuels (eds) *Handbook of Evolutionary and Institutional Economics*, Aldershot: Edward Elgar.

—— (1994c) 'Econometrics, the limits of', in G. Hodgson, M. Tool and W.J. Samuels (eds) *Handbook of Evolutionary and Institutional Economics*, Aldershot: Edward Elgar.

—— (1994d) 'A Realist Theory for Economics' in R. Backhouse (ed.), *New Directions in Economic Methodology*, London: Routledge.

Leamer, E. (1983) 'Let's take the con out of econometrics', *American Economic Review* 23: 31–43.

Lester, R. (1946) 'Shortcomings of marginal analysis for wage-employment problems', *American Economic Review* 36: 62–82.

—— (1947) 'Marginalism, minimum wages and labour markets', *American Economic Review* 37: 135–48.

Leijonhufvud, A. (1976) 'Schools, "revolutions", and research programmes in economic theory', in S. Latsis (ed.) *Method and Appraisal in Economics*, Cambridge: Cambridge University Press.

Leplin, J. (ed.) (1984) *Scientific Realism*, Berkeley: University of California Press.

—— (1988) 'Is essentialism unscientific?', *Philosophy of Science* 55(4): 493–510.

Lewis, D. (1973) *Counterfactuals*, Cambridge, Mass: Harvard University Press.

Lipton, P. (1991) *Inference to the Best Explanation*, London: Routledge.

Machlup, F. (1946) 'Marginal analysis and empirical research', *American Economic Review* 36: 519–54.

—— (1947) 'Rejoinder to an antimarginalist', *American Economic Review* 37: 148–54.

—— (1955) 'The problem of verification in economics', *Southern Economic Journal* 22: 1–21.

—— (1964) 'Professor Samuelson on theory and realism', *American Economic Review* 54: 733–6.

McCloskey, D.N. (1983) 'The Rhetoric of Economics', *Journal of Economic Literature* 21: 481–517.

—— (1984) 'Reply to Caldwell and Coats', *Journal of Economic Literature* 22: 579–80.

—— (1985) *The Rhetoric of Economics*, Madison: University of Wisconsin Press.

—— (1987) *The Writing of Economics*, New York: Macmillan.

—— (1988) 'Two replies and a dialogue on the rhetoric of economics: Mäki, Rappaport, Rosenberg', *Economics and Philosophy*, 1: 150–66.

—— (1990) *If You're So Smart: The Narrative of Economic Expertise*, Chicago: University of Chicago Press.

Mackay, A. (1980) *Arrow's Theorem: The Paradox of Social Choice: A Case Study in the Philosophy of Economics*, New Haven: Yale University Press.

Mackie, J.L. (1980) *The Cement of the Universe*, Oxford: Clarendon Press.

McMichael, A. (1985) 'van Fraassen's Instrumentalism', *British Journal for the Philosophy of Science* 36: 257–72.

McMullin, E. (ed.) (1988) *Construction and Constraint*, Notre Dame: University of Notre Dame Press.

Maddock, R. (1984) 'Rational expectations macrotheory: a Lakatosian case study in programme adjustment', *History of Political Economy* 16(2): 291–309.

Mäki, U. (1986) 'Rhetoric at the expense of coherence: a reinterpretation of Milton Friedman's methodology', *Research in the History of Economic Thought and Methodology* 4: 127–43.

—— (1988a) 'How to combine rhetoric and realism in the methodology of economics', *Economics and Philosophy* 4(1): 89–109.

—— (1988b) 'Realism, economics and rhetoric: A rejoinder to McCloskey', *Economics and Philosophy* 4(1): 167–9.

—— (1989) 'On the problem of realism in economics', *Ricerche Economiche* 43: 176–98.

—— (1990a) 'Mengerian economics in realist perspective', *History of Political Economy* 22: 289–310.

—— (1990b) 'Scientific realism and Austrian explanation', *Review of Political Economy* 2: 310–44.

—— (1990c) 'Methodology of economics: complaints and guidelines' *Finnish Economic Papers*, 3(1): 77–84.

—— (1992) 'Friedman and realism', *Research in the History of Economic Thought and Methodology* 10: 1–36.

—— (1993) 'Two philosophies of the rhetoric of economics', in W. Henderson, T. Dudley-Evans and R. Backhouse (eds) *Economics and Language*, London: Routledge.

Margolis, J. (1991) *The Truth about Relativism*, Oxford: Basil Blackwell.

Melitz, J. (1965) 'Friedman and Machlup on the significance of testing economic assumptions', *Journal of Political Economy* 73: 37–60.

Mirowski, P. (1989a) *More Heat than Light*, Cambridge: Cambridge University Press.

—— (1989b) 'How not to do things with metaphors: Paul Samuelson and the science of neoclassical economics', *Studies in the History and Philosophy of Science* 20: 175–91.

—— (1992) 'Three vignettes on the state of economic rhetoric', in N. de Marchi (ed.) *Post-Popperian Methodology of Economics: Recovering Practice*, Boston: Kluwer.

Nagel, E. (1961) *The Structure of Science*, London: Routledge and Kegan Paul.

Nelson, A. (1986) 'New individualist foundations for economics', *Nous* 20: 469–90.

Newton-Smith, W.H. (1981) *The Rationality of Science*, London: Routledge and Kegan Paul.

O'Driscoll, R. and Rizzo, M. (1985) *The Economics of Time and Ignorance*, Oxford: Basil Blackwell.

O'Gorman, P.F. (1989) *Rationality and Relativity, The Quest for Objective Knowledge*, Aldershot: Avebury Press.

Ortony, A. (ed.) (1980) *Metaphor and Thought*, Cambridge: Cambridge University Press.

Papandreou, A. G. (1958) *Economics as a Science*, Chicago: Lippencott.

Passmore, J. (1967) 'Logical Positivism' in *The Encyclopaedia of Philosophy* 5: 52–7, London and New York: The Macmillan Company and The Free Press.

—— (1968) *A Hundred Years of Philosophy*, Harmondsworth, Middlesex: Penguin Books.

Popper, K. (1945) *The Open Society and its Enemies*, 2 vols, London: Routledge and Kegan Paul.

—— (1957) *The Poverty of Historicism*, London: Routledge and Kegan Paul.

—— (1963) *Conjectures and Refutations*, London: Routledge and Kegan Paul.

—— (1976a) *Unended Quest: An Intellectual Biography*, London: Fontana.

—— (1976b) 'The Logic of the Social Sciences', in T. Adorno *et al.* (eds) *The Positivist Dispute in German Sociology*, New York: Harper & Row.

—— (1983a) *Realism and the Aim of Science*, vol. 1 of The postscript to the *Logic of Scientific Discovery*, W.W. Bartley III (ed.), Totowa, NJ: Rowman and Littlefield.

—— (1983b) 'The Rationality Principle', in D. Miller (ed.) *A Pocket Popper*, Oxford: Fontana Paperbacks.

Putnam, H. (1975a) *Mathematics Matter and Method: Philosophical Papers, Vol. 1*, Cambridge: Cambridge University Press.

—— (1975b) *Mind Language and Reality: Philosophical Papers, Vol. II*, Cambridge: Cambridge University Press.

—— (1978) *Meaning and the Moral Sciences*, London: Routledge and Kegan Paul.

—— (1981) *Reason, Truth and History*, Cambridge: Cambridge University Press.

—— (1987) *The Many Faces of Realism*, La Salle: Open Court.

Quine, W.V.O. (1953) *From a Logical Point of View*, New York: Harper and Rowe.

—— (1960) *Word and Object*, Cambridge, Mass: MIT Press.

—— (1969) *Ontological Relativity and Other Essays*, New York: Columbia University Press.

—— (1981) *Theories and Things*, Cambridge, Mass: Harvard University Press.

Rappaport, S. (1988a) 'Economic methodology: rhetoric and epistemology', *Economics and Philosophy* 4(1): 110–28.

—— (1988b) 'Argument, truth and economic methodology: a rejoinder to McCloskey', *Economics and Philosophy* 4(1): 170–2.

Redman, D.A. (1991) *Economics and the Philosophy of Science*, Oxford: Oxford University Press.

Ricoeur, P. (1983), *Hermeneutics and the Human Sciences* trans. J.B. Thompson, Cambridge: Cambridge University Press.

—— (1986) *The Rule of Metaphor*, London: Routledge and Kegan Paul.

Rizzo, M. (1982) 'Mises and Lakatos: a reformulation of Austrian methodology', in I Kirzner (ed.) *Method, Process and Austrian Economics: Essays in Honour of Ludwig von Mises*, Lexington, MA: D.C. Heath.

Robbins, L. (1935) 2nd edn (1st edn 1932) *An Essay on the Nature and Significance of Economic Science*, London: Macmillan.

—— (1979) 'On Latsis' *Method and Appraisal in Economics*: A Review Essay', *Journal of Economic Literature* 17: 996–1004.

Robinson, J. (1974) *History Versus Equilibrium*, Thames Papers in Political Economy. Reprinted in *Collected Economic Papers*, vol. 5 (1979) Oxford: Basil Blackwell.
—— (1977) 'What are the questions?', *Journal of Economic Literature* 15(4): 1318–39. Reprinted in *Collected Economic Papers*, vol. 5 (1979) Oxford: Basil Blackwell.
Rorty, R. (1979) *Philosophy and the Mirror of Nature*, Oxford: Basil Blackwell.
—— (1982) *Consequences of Pragmatism*, Minneapolis: University of Minnesota Press.
—— (1989) *Contingency, Irony and Solidarity*, Cambridge: Cambridge University Press.
Rosenberg, A. (1976) *Microeconomic Laws: A Philosophical Analysis*, Pittsburgh: University of Pittsburgh Press.
—— (1988a) 'Economics is too important to be left to the rhetoricians', *Economics and Philosophy* 4(1): 129–49.
—— (1988b) 'Rhetoric is not important enough for economists to bother about', *Economics and Philosophy* 4(1): 173–5.
—— (1992) *Economics – Mathematical Politics or Science of Diminishing Returns?* Chicago: University of Chicago Press.
Rossetti, J. (1992) 'Deconstruction, Rhetoric and Economics', in N. de Marchi (ed.) *Post-Popperian Methodology of Economics: Recovering Practice*, Boston: Kluwer.
Ruben, D.H. (ed.) (1993) *Explanation*, Oxford: Oxford University Press.
Salanti, A. (1987) 'Falsificationism and fallibilism as epistemic foundations of economics: A critical view', *Kyklos* 40: 368–92.
—— (1989) 'Recent work in economic methodology: Much ado about what? *Ricerche Economiche* 43: 21–39.
Salmon, W.C. (1984) *Scientific Explanation and the Causal Structure of the World*, Princeton: Princeton University Press.
Samuels, W.J. (ed.) (1990) *Economics as Discourse; An Analysis of the Language of Economists*, Boston: Kluwer.
Samuelson, P.A. (1938) 'The empirical implications of utility analysis', *Econometrica* 6: 344–56.
—— (1948a) *Foundations of Economic Analysis*, Cambridge, Mass: Harvard University Press.
—— (1948b) 'Consumption theory in terms of revealed preference' *Economica* 152: 43–53.
—— (1964) 'Theory and Realism: A Reply', *American Economic Review* 54: 736–40.
Schleiermacher, F.D.E. (1959) *Hermeneutik*, Heidelberg: Carl Winter Universitätsverlag.
Schmidt, R.H. (1982) 'Methodology and finance', *Theory and Decision* 14: 391–413.
Schumpeter, J.A. (1954) *History of Economic Analysis*, New York: Oxford University Press.
Searle, J. (1980) 'Metaphor' in A. Ortony (1980) *Metaphor and Thought*, Cambridge: Cambridge University Press, 92–123.
—— (1983) *Intentionality: An Essay in the Philosophy of Mind*, Cambridge: Cambridge University Press.
Sellars, W. (1962) *Science, Perception and Reality*, New York: Humanities Press.
Sims, C.A. (1980) 'Macroeconomics and reality', *Econometrica* 48: 1–48.
Sneed, J. (1971) *The Logical Structure of Mathematical Physics*, Dordrecht: Reidel.
Sober, E. (1985) 'Constructive empiricism and the problem of aboutness', *British Journal for the Philosophy of Science* 36: 11–18.
Sosa, E. and Tooley, M. (eds) (1993) *Causation*, Oxford: Oxford University Press.
Stegmüller, W. (1976) *The Structure and Dynamics of Theories*, New York: Springer-Verlag.

—— (1979) *The Structuralist Views of Theories*, New York: Springer-Verlag.

Suppe, F. (1972) 'What's wrong with the received view on the structure of scientific theory?', *Philosophy of Science* 39: 1–19.

Suppe, F. (ed.) (1977) 2nd edn *The Structure of Scientific Theories*, Urbana: University of Illinois Press.

Thirlwall, A.P. (1987) *Nicholas Kaldor*, Brighton, Sussex: Wheatsheaf Books.

Thompson, J.B. (1981) *Critical Hermeneutics*, Cambridge: Cambridge University Press.

Tooley, M. (1987) *Causation: A Realist Approach*, Oxford: Oxford University Press.

van Fraassen, B. (1980) *The Scientific Image*, Oxford: Clarendon Press.

—— (1989) *Laws and Symmetry*, Oxford: Clarendon Press.

von Mises, L. (1949) *Human Action A Treatise on Economics*, New Haven: Yale University Press.

—— (1978) 2nd edn. *The Ultimate Foundation of Economic Science: An Essay on Method*, Kansas City: Sheed, Andrews and McMeel.

—— (1981) *Epistemological Problems of Economics*, trans. G. Reisman, New York: New York University Press.

Weintraub, E.R. (1985) *General Equilibrium Analysis: Structures in Appraisal*, Cambridge: Cambridge University Press.

—— (1988) 'The Neo-Walrasian program is empirically progressive', in N. de Marchi (ed.) *The Popperian Legacy in Economics*, Cambridge: Cambridge University Press.

—— (1989) 'Methodology doesn't matter but the history of thought might', *Scandinavian Journal of Economics* 91: 477–93.

—— (1991) *Stabilizing Dynamics: Constructing Economic Knowledge*, Cambridge: Cambridge University Press.

—— (1992) 'Roger Backhouse's straw herring', *Methodus* 4(2): 53–7.

Whitley, R. (1984) *The Intellectual and Social Organization of the Sciences*, Oxford: Clarendon Press.

Woo, H. (1990) 'Scientific reduction, reductionism and metaphysical reduction – a broad view of economic methodology', *Methodus* 2(2): 61–8.

INDEX